The
Reference Shelf ®

For Reference

Not to be taken from this room

Prescription Drug Abuse

The Reference Shelf
Volume 89 • Number 5
H.W. Wilson
A Division of EBSCO Information Services, Inc.

Published by
GREY HOUSE PUBLISHING
Amenia, New York
2017

The Reference Shelf

The books in this series contain reprints of articles, excerpts from books, addresses on current issues, and studies of social trends in the United States and other countries. There are six separately bound numbers in each volume, all of which are usually published in the same calendar year. Numbers one through five are each devoted to a single subject, providing background information and discussion from various points of view and concluding with an index and comprehensive bibliography that lists books, pamphlets, and articles on the subject. The final number of each volume is a collection of recent speeches. Books in the series may be purchased individually or on subscription.

Publisher's Cataloging-In-Publication Data
(Prepared by The Donohue Group, Inc.)

Names: H.W. Wilson Company, compiler.
Title: Prescription drug abuse / [compiled by] H. W. Wilson, a division of EBSCO Information Services.
Other Titles: Reference shelf ; v. 89, no. 5.
Description: Amenia, NY : Grey House Publishing, [2017] | Includes bibliographical references and index.
Identifiers: ISBN 978-1-68217-455-5 (v. 89, no. 5) |
  ISBN 978-1-68217-450-0 (volume set)
Subjects: LCSH: Medication abuse--United States. | Opioid abuse--United States. | Americans--Drug use.
Classification: LCC RM146.5 .P74 2017 | DDC 362.29/9--dc23

Printed in Canada

Contents

3

Doctors, Big Pharma and the Gateway to Abuse

4

A Search for Solutions—Treatment

5

A Search for Solutions—Policy

Preface

Prescription Drug Abuse

Long before the development of language or laws, humans foraging on the plains of East Africa found and experimented with many different types of herbs, roots, and other substances. They found that some of these substances, now called drugs, had physiological effects, altering the brain or body and often produced euphoria or intoxication. Scientists have also found that many species of nonhuman animals seek out substances for their euphoric or tranquilizing effects. Elephants in Africa, have been seen purposefully eating fermented fruits to ingest the alcohol contained in the tissues, while some species of lemur in Madagascar bite into the bodies of poisonous centipedes, swallowing small, but nonlethal, quantities of poison to produce an intoxicating effect.

Any discussion of drug abuse and addiction might therefore begin with the realization that the desire to seek out pleasurable sensations (including drug-induced intoxication) is basic to the behavior of animals with the capacity to experience pleasure. Drug use, sexuality, extreme sports, and many other aspects of human culture derive in part from this fundamental human drive to experiment with pleasurable experiences. However, such behaviors, in many cases, can become pathological and this is especially likely to occur when individuals use pleasure- seeking activities as a form of "self-medication," intended to alleviate stress, depression, anxiety, or a variety of other issues related to a person's quality of life.

Over the millennia, cultivating and using intoxicating drugs remained a central facet of human culture to such an extent that prized intoxicants were incorporated into many of humanity's oldest religious and cultural traditions.[1] Some of the most ancient known intoxicants, like opium, cannabis, and alcohol, also gave rise to the earliest medicines as ancient apothecaries (the forerunners of modern physicians and chemists) worked on extracting substances from plants and fungi that could be used to treat a variety of ailments.

In the modern world, physicians prescribe a multitude of medications, most derived from natural substances, to treat various bodily and mental disorders and some of the substances used also have a pleasurable neurological effect, creating a sense of euphoria, a tranquilizing effect, or intensifying alertness and focus. Over time, drug addiction and abuse has become a social justice and public health concern around the world. Governments have responded to addiction and drug abuse epidemics by banning the use of certain substances, but such efforts are not very efficacious and, instead, tend to result in the birth of black markets and criminal underworld industries involved in the production and distribution of illicit substances. When the United States attempted to ban the sale of alcohol in the "prohibition era," for instance, it led to the growth of a criminal underworld selling illegally obtained or manufactured alcohol, while drinkers unable to obtain legal alcohol switched to far more dangerous versions of the substance, with often disastrous effects. Prohibition and criminalization are ineffective because such measures do not eliminate the perceived "need" among those who seek out intoxication.

In the 2010s, the drug crisis du jour in the United States involves the misuse and abuse of prescription drugs, substances developed as medications that have an intoxicating effect and so are also sought and used by individuals for recreation or to self-medicate. Unethical corporate behavior has helped to create this problem as drug manufacturers have downplayed or overtly misrepresented the dangers of certain drugs in an effort to maintain profits (even going so far as to promote false research to support their marketing) and so allowed many patients to become accidentally addicted to drugs taken to combat various disorders. This is only a small part of the problem, however, as the vast majority of prescription drug abusers and addicts obtain drugs through illicit channels that may include stealing medication prescribed for another individual or from a pharmacy or hospital, misleading physicians, or purchasing pharmaceutical grade intoxicants through a variety of black market sources.

The National Institute on Drug Abuse (NIDA) reported in 2016 that an estimated 54 million people in the United States (more than 20 percent) have used prescription drugs for non-medical reasons at least once in their lives.[2] A 2009 study indicated that more Americans use prescription drugs illegally than use cocaine, heroin, hallucinogens, or inhalants combined.[3] In response, in 2012 the Obama administration described prescription drug abuse as the nation's fastest-growing and most serious drug problem.[4] Prescription drugs that are commonly abused fall into three general categories, opioid pain relievers, central nervous system (CNS) depressants, and stimulants. Each of these classes of drugs has a long history in human culture, both as recreational intoxicants and as the basis for medical treatments. The effort to combat prescription drug abuse is complicated by the fact that drugs in all three categories are still legitimately used in medicine. Because the supply of drugs cannot be completely eliminated without placing patients at risk, legislators, public health experts, and others working on the issue must struggle to balance the needs of patients with the effort to stem the tide of abuse.

Opioids: From Poppies to Prescription Pain Relief

Opioids all come from *Papaver somniferum*, the opium poppy, a flowering plant that has been transplanted and cultivated around the world for so long that botanists are uncertain where the plant originally occurred, though it is believed to come from somewhere in the Mediterranean. The Latin species name used for the plant, given by Carus Linneus in 1753, derives from the term *somnus*, which can mean sleep, drowsiness, or even death. The first known reference to the use of opioids comes from at least 3400 BCE in Mesopotamia. Hippocrates (460–357 BCE), sometimes hailed as the father of Western medicine, recommended the juice of the poppy mixed with nettle seed as a sedative and Alexander the Great, who conquered huge swaths of the world in the fourth century BCE, is credited with introducing the substance to India, Rome, and the Arab world.[5]

Inside the body, opioids bind to receptors in the central nervous system (CNS) and the enteric nervous system (nerves surrounding the digestive system). Opioids alleviate the experience of pain, which is the basis for their use in modern medicine, but also produce a euphoric effect, which is the basis of opioid popularity on the illicit market.[6] Opium, in all its forms, is highly addictive, both psychologically and physiologically. With continued use, users develop a resistance that encourages higher doses and withdrawing from the drug can cause a variety of problems, including respiratory depression, pain, mood swings, and anxiety. Opium addiction created a national crisis in 1700s and 1800s China as the East India Trading Company, the world's first multinational corporation and a precursor of the massive pharmaceutical giants of the twenty-first century, shipped huge quantities of opium into China and refused to stop when China banned the substance. The Chinese government fought two wars with Britain and France, through their corporate representatives, in an effort to restrict the supply of opium being shipped into the nation.

A derivative called "morphine" was isolated from opium in 1806 by German chemist Friedrich Setürner, and named after the Greek god of dreams, Morpheus. In 1898, pharmacological giant Bayer Co. created an injectable version called heroin, but it soon became clear that injecting heroin led to a more significant euphoric effect and the new opioid became the drug choice for abusers. The development of opioid drugs has involved pharmaceutical companies searching for a way to retain the pain-relieving properties of the drug while avoiding the potential for addiction and abuse. As of 2017, this effort has not been entirely successful. Pharmaceutical versions like Percocet, Vicodin, OxyContin, and Fentanyl, were marketed as "safer" versions of the drug, but proved to be just as addictive, if not more so, as the heroin and morphine of earlier eras.[7] Promising research suggests that it may be possible, in the near future, to develop opioids that are nonaddictive, but still effective in pain management and such developments could effectively eliminate the abuse of prescription opioids, but may not eliminate the use and abuse of opioids altogether as users unable to get prescription versions often switch to black market versions of the same drugs.

Depressants and the Anxiety Epidemic

Central nervous system depressants are drugs that act on the brain in such a way as to reduce CNS activity by binding to receptors in the brain and have therefore been used to treat disorders related to hyperactivity in the nervous system, such as insomnia, anxiety, and convulsions/seizures. The most widely used drug in the world, alcohol, is a depressant that can be used to produce a tranquilizing effect but, in large doses, damages the brain and body tissues, becoming physiologically addictive and producing a host of potentially deadly side effects. The first CNS depressant used in medicine (outside of alcohol) was potassium bromide, which was isolated in 1826 by French apothecary A.J. Balard, from the ashes of burned seaweed. In the 1850s, bromides were used to treat seizures and convulsions, but it was also

discovered that continued use has toxic effects.[8] The search for a depressant to replace bromides resulted in the invention of barbiturates, like Nembutal, Pentothal,
and Mebaral, which can help control sleeplessness and reduce anxiety, but were
found to be dangerous and highly addictive.[9]

Searching for a safer, less addictive substance to replace barbiturates, in the
1950s scientists discovered a new class of CNS depressants known as benzodiazepines, marketed and sold in the form of pharmaceutical drugs like Xanax, Valium,
Halcion, Klonipin, and Ativan. Benzodiazepines work by helping the molecule gamma-aminobutyric acid (GABA) bind to receptors in the brain, thus decreasing brain
activity, which produces a calming, tranquilizing effect. Though initially hailed as a
safer, risk-free alternative to barbiturates, it was soon discovered that the use of benzodiazepines also carried significant risks, including, notably, risk of addiction and
abuse. Individuals who abuse depressants with high doses can experience seizures,
insomnia, and disorientation and, in serious cases, overdosing on depressants can
lead to death especially when blending benzodiazepines with other depressants, like
alcohol.

Despite these risks, which have been downplayed by drug companies marketing
benzodiazepines, CNS depressants are among the most popular drugs in the United
States. Researchers have found that as many as 1 in 5 Americans suffers from severe anxiety, making anxiety the most common psychiatric ailment, and Americans
are more anxious than people in most other places around the world. For instance,
the World Mental Health Survey of 2002 found that Americans are five time more
likely to suffer from excessive anxiety than Nigerians, despite the fact that Nigerians cope with higher levels of poverty, political violence, and many other environmental stressors than Americans.[10]

The Chemistry of Stimulation

While there are a variety of different types of stimulants, most of them affect the
body in similar ways. Stimulants stimulate the release of neurotransmitters in the
brain, substances that facilitate communication between neurons, thus releasing
adrenaline within the body that increased heard rate, the speed of neural responses
(creating alertness and sharpening focus), and thus creating a sense of increased
energy. Some stimulants, like cocaine and nicotine, overstimulate the nervous system, activating parts of the brain that produce chemicals that cause euphoria and a
sense of well-being.[11]

Naturally derived stimulants, like cocaine and nicotine, which are also intoxicants have been used by humans for hundreds of thousands of years and many
of the most ancient stimulants were also used in medical applications for centu-
ries. Scientists synthesized a type of stimulant known as an amphetamine in the
1880s, and amphetamines were used to treat nasal decongestion, obesity, depression, and hyperactivity in the 1930s. Because amphetamines produce a euphoric
effect, the abuse of amphetamines and other stimulants began to become a problem
in the 1930s as well. Over the years, governments have prohibited some forms of

stimulants (like cocaine and methamphetamine), while other forms have remained legal and are still used in medicine to treat hyperactivity, depression, and sleep disorders.

In 2017, the most widely abused prescription stimulants were medications created and marketed for the treatment of Attention Deficit Hyperactivity Disorder (ADHD). ADHD, a mental illness marked by an inability to concentrate, bouts of manic hyperactivity, depression, and difficulty focusing on tasks, is controversial as some have alleged that physicians have overdiagnosed ADHD in patients and so have overprescribed potentially dangerous medications used to treat the disorder. The most commonly prescribed medication for ADHD is Adderall, which was accidentally discovered by scientists searching for a treatment for asthma in the 1920s and was later repurposed as a treatment for hyperactivity. Adderall, and other ADHD stimulant medications, have become popular with young adults as "study drugs," substances taken to enhance concentration and focus and so used as an aid for stressed students and professionals coping with high workloads. The problem is, Adderall and other stimulants tend to be highly addictive and users can experience lethargy, depression and a host of other symptoms when they attempt to stop using the drugs. In 2004, illegal Adderall use was second only to marijuana as the most common illicit drug in American colleges and universities.[12]

No Easy Solutions

The prescription drug crisis occurs at the nexus of many interrelated factors. Drug companies have irresponsibly marketed potentially dangerous substances and this coupled with unethical and uninformed practices among physicians has led to overreliance on dangerous drugs to treat complex conditions. In many cases, the potentially addictive substances used as treatments, though well intentioned, only treat symptoms and do not provide a cure for underlying dysfunction. This landscape of corporate self-interest and professional misconduct occurs within a society in which millions of individuals, for a variety of reasons including poverty, high levels of stress and anxiety, low levels of life and job satisfaction, and mental illness, are seeking ways to alleviate the perceived problems that exist in their daily lives. When this search for self-medication involves addictive substances, disastrous results too often occur as individuals rapidly progress to higher and higher doses and potentially switch to more dangerous street versions of their favored drugs. In 2017, state governments and federal agencies are trying to recognize the scale of the problem and address it by limiting the supply of prescription drugs, making doctors and pharmaceutical companies more accountable and promoting treatment as a public policy. A lasting solution to the prescription drug abuse crisis must also address the underlying issues like mental health, poverty, homelessness, unemployment, depression, anxiety, and hopelessness that have fostered a population prone to self-medication and abuse.

Micah L. Issitt

Works Used

"A Brief History of Opioids: Pain, Opioids and Medicinal Use." *The Atlantic*. The Atlantic Monthly Group. 2017. Web. 17 Aug 2017.

Ban, Thomas A. "Bromides." *INHN*. International Network for the History of Neurophychopharmacology. Feb 8 2017. Web. 17 Sep 2017.

Cooper-White, Macrina. "Humans Have Been Getting High Since Prehistoric Times, Research Shows." *Huffpost*. Huffington Post. Feb 12 2015. Web. 25 Aug 2017.

"Fact Sheet: Prescription Drug Abuse," *NCADD*. National Council on Alcoholism and Drug Dependence. 2012. Web. 17 Aug 2017.

Ghelardini, C., Mannelli, L., and E. Bianchi. "The Pharmacological Basis of Opioids." *Clinical Cases in Mineral and Bone Metabolism*. Sep-Dec 2015, Vol. 12, No. 3, 219–21.

Hanson, G.R., Venturelli, P.J., and Annette E. Fleckenstein, eds. "CNS Depressants: Sedative-Hypnotics," in *Drugs and Society*. Burlington, MA: Jones & Bartless Learning, 2018.

Kelley, Maura. "An Anxiety Epidemic Is Sweeping the US." *Business Insider*. Jul 17 2012. Web. 26 Aug 2017.

Moghe, Sonia. "Opioid History: From 'Wonder Drug' to Abuse Epidemic." *CNN Health*. Oct 14 2016. Web. 17 Aug 2017.

"Prescription Drug Abuse." Drugabuse.gov. National Institute on Drug Abuse (NIDA). Sep 22 2010. Web. 17 Aug 2017.

Preta, Adrian and Eduardo Dunayevich. "Stimulants." *Medscape*. WebMD, LLC. Dec 15 2015. Web. 26 Aug 2017.

Schwartz, Casey. "Generation Adderall." *The New York Times*. The New York Times Co. Oct 12 2016. Web. 25 Aug 2017.

"What Is the Scope of Prescription Drug Misuse?" *Drugabuse.gov*. National Institute on Drug Abuse (NIDA). Aug 2016. Web. 17 Aug 2017.

Notes

1. Cooper-White, "Humans Have Been Getting High Since Prehistoric Times, Research Shows."
2. "What Is the Scope of Prescription Drug Misuse?," *Drugabuse.gov*.
3. "Prescription Drug Abuse," *Drugabuse.gov*.
4. "Fact Sheet: Prescription Drug Abuse," *NCADD*.
5. "A Brief History of Opioids," *The Atlantic*.
6. Ghelardini, Mannelli, and Bianchi, "The Pharmacological Basis of Opioids."
7. Moghe, "Opioid History: From 'Wonder Drug' to Abuse Epidemic."
8. Ban, "Bromides."
9. Hanson, Venturelli, and Fleckenstein, "CNS Depressants: Sedative-Hypnotics."
10. Kelley, "An Anxiety Epidemic Is Sweeping the US."
11. Preta and Dunayevich, "Stimulants."
12. Schwartz, "Generation Adderall."

1
Pain and Anxiety in America

Credit: Photo by Chip Somodevilla/Getty Images

Holly's Song of Hope founder Tonda DaRe of Carrollton, OH, weeps as she testifies about the moments after she found her daughter, Holly, overdosed on heroin during a hearing of Senate Judiciary Committee about the recent spike in heroin and prescription drug abuse and deaths on Capitol Hill January 27, 2016 in Washington, DC. The committee is working on several pieces of legislation that would assist states with abuse prevention and treatment and prosecution of those responsible for the recent spike in heroin and prescription drug overdose deaths.

National Disorder: Treating Chronic Conditions

Prescription drug abuse is a difficult issue to address because many of the substances most commonly abused are also important pharmacological tools in the treatment of certain conditions. Patients suffering from chronic pain, for instance, are typically offered little recourse other than using opioid pain relievers and so must decide between using a medication that carries a risk of dependency or living with pain that may make it nearly impossible to carry on a normal life. Any debate about how to address prescription drug abuse must therefore begin with an understanding of the relationship between chronic conditions and potentially dangerous medications.

The Age of Anxiety

W.H. Auden's 1947 poem "The Age of Anxiety" describes America at a time in which Americans were, in Auden's view, having difficulty searching for fulfillment and identity in a society rapidly transformed by industrialization. Auden's depiction of America, as a nation increasingly gripped by a state of national anxiety, seems to have been a prescient prediction as, over the course of the ensuing decades, more and more Americans seem to suffer from severe anxiety. In some cases, anxiety is environmental, brought about by factors that occur in a person's life. During the malignant 2016 presidential election, an American Psychological Association (APA) study found that widespread anxiety was increasing, with more than 57 percent describing the nation's political environment as a source of anxiety.[1]

The 2002 World Mental Health Survey found that Americans were the most anxious people out of 14 nations studied, including nations like Nigeria and the Ukraine where long-term political unrest and violence would seem to suggest that the average Nigerian or Ukrainian would be more prone to anxiety than the average American.[2] The reasons for America's excessive anxiety rate are still unclear, but it is likely that the nature of American culture itself is one of the primary causes. American society is and has become intensively stratified along socioeconomic lines and this evolution has occurred amidst a mythos in which the nation is and has long been depicted as a land that rewards merit (intelligence, work ethic, effort). The experience of life in America fails to match the cultural mythos such that the vast majority of Americans might feel excessively disappointed by their inability, despite effort, skill, and imagination, to recreate the fundamental American success story in their own lives. In addition, despite being the most economically powerful nation in the world, American mental health services are insufficient to address the nation's need and social stigmatization creates the perception that such activities are only necessary for the clinically insane or wastefully affluent.[3]

The existential angst described by Auden and the APA depicts anxiety and stress for "average" individuals, but there are also many for whom anxiety and depression are not solely the result of industrialization, economic inequality, or political turpitude, but are signs of serious, and potentially debilitating mental illness. The Anxiety and Depression Association of America (ADAA) reports that anxiety disorders are the most common form of mental illness, affecting 40 million adults, or nearly 18 percent of the population.[4] It is a common misperception that anxiety disorders are a function of a person's environment, but, as a mental *illness*, anxiety can emerge from a combination of factors that include genetics, neurophysiology, AND environmental variables. A study of anxiety in rhesus monkeys, for instance, found that nearly 30 percent of anxiety symptoms appeared to result from innate, genetic factors, rather than environmental stress.[5] According to the *Diagnostic and Statistical Manual (DSM)*—the benchmark for the diagnosis of mental disorders in the United States—a person can only legitimately be diagnosed with an anxiety disorder if the severity of the person's symptoms exceeds that which might be expected in certain conditions.

There are different types of anxiety disorders that manifest in different ways. Generalized Anxiety Disorder (GAD), which affects 6.8 million Americans and is especially prevalent among women, is characterized by excessive and seemingly unprovoked stress and worry about a variety of situations or everyday life issues.[6] Social Anxiety Disorder (SAD), which affects nearly 15 million Americans, is not, as it is sometimes viewed, simply being "shy" or "nervous," but, instead, involves a physiological response to social situations that can, in many cases, make it difficult for a person to lead a normal life.[7] There are a variety of other common anxiety disorders as well, including Obsessive-Compulsive Disorder (OCD), which effects 2.2 million Americans, Posttraumatic Stress Disorder (PTSD), which affects 7.7 million, and many different types of Phobic Disorders in which an individual may suffer from excessive fear or stress surrounding a certain feature of their environment, including things like animals, dental procedures, flying, driving, thunder, heights, or germs.

For those with diagnosable anxiety disorders, the perception of a social stigma surrounding mental illness discourages many individuals from seeking professional help, while the cost of mental health treatments, which are in some cases not covered by medical insurance, is another factor that discourages treatment. Further, because anxiety exists on a spectrum, it can be difficult for an average individual to determine when and if his or her symptoms are proportional to average experiences or signs of a mental illness. In many cases, severe anxiety disorders are treated using central nervous system (CNS) depressants, most notably the family of medications called benzodiazepines that includes Klonopin, Ativan, and Valium. While sometimes helpful in treating the symptoms of an anxiety disorder, CNS depressants are not a cure and lasting treatment typically must include behavioral or social therapy and other interventions in addition to any medication regime.

There are also a number of serious risks involved in using CNS depressants, including addiction and a number of potentially debilitating side effects that can include confusion, paranoia, agitation, dizziness, and impaired concentration. Studies indicate that overprescription of depressants has been common and, though this practice is gradually changing, has led to higher rates of addiction and abuse. In addition, depressants that are legitimately prescribed are often illegally distributed as recreational drugs, thus extending the risk of addiction and damaging side effects beyond the population using depressants to treat legitimate mental health symptoms.

The Chronic Pain Epidemic

Acute pain is considered a normal physiological response to injury or illness, alerting the brain to a physical problem. In most cases, pain subsists as the injury or illness subsides. Chronic pain is different in that it lasts longer—for weeks, months, or even years—and in that the source of pain may be unidentifiable or untreatable. In some cases, chronic pain arises from an injury or illness, while, in other cases chronic pain sufferers experience pain without any evidence of present or past injury.[8] According to the National Institutes of Health (NIH), chronic pain can be defined as any pain lasting more than 12 weeks.

An NIH study in 2015 found that more than 1 in 10 Americans, 11.2 percent of the population or 25 million people, reported daily chronic pain, with 23 million reporting severe pain.[9] While, in some cases, chronic pain may arise without a clear cause, there are also a variety of medical disorders that frequently cause chronic pain. For instance, patients suffering from arthritis, various types of cancer, and certain muscular-skeletal disorders frequently experience long-lasting and sometimes severe pain. In some cases, chronic pain is neuropathic, linked to CNS impulses, which may be caused by disorders like sciatica, diabetes, or carpal tunnel syndrome. In other cases, chronic pain can arise from a malfunction in the nervous system itself, sending out false pain responses without an underlying dysfunction or injury. Diagnosing chronic pain is problematic, as the experience is subjective and there are no direct tests that can precisely locate and measure the intensity of a person's experience.[10]

Individuals suffering from chronic pain, especially severe pain, may have tremendous difficulty living normal lives. In some cases, pain interferes with an individual's ability to work, care for themselves or dependents, or to engage in enjoyable activities. In the United States, chronic pain and related conditions constitute the leading cause of long-term disability and, because chronic pain can impact many other facets of a person's life, sufferers frequently suffer from other emotional and physical problems, like fatigue, mood changes, decreased appetite, depression, and anxiety. A 2016 study in the *Journal of Pain Research* found that chronic pain also tends to have detrimental effects on a person's social or family environment.[11]

Some of the primary medications used to treat the symptoms of chronic pain, opioid pain relievers like Vicodin and Percocet, are highly addictive, lose effectiveness with continued use, and can cause a number of side effects. Because opioid pain relievers lose effectiveness over time, there is also an increased risk of overdose as patients use higher doses to address their symptoms. The Centers for Disease Control and Prevention (CDC) estimates that 44 people in the United States die each day as a result of prescription opioid overdose, which is more than the number of deaths from motor vehicle accidents. The dangers faced by patients using opioids is also only part of the problem, as prescription medications are also frequently sold illegally as recreational drugs and studies now show that more drug abusers use prescription opioids than most other types of illicit drugs combined.[12]

The Nature of the Problem

Prescription drug abuse is difficult to combat because of the legitimate use of addictive drugs in medicine and mental health treatment. Studies have shown that many opioid addicts start using opioids after either receiving a prescription of their own or by taking prescription medication prescribed to a friend or family member. Similarly, addiction to depressants often begins with friends sharing their medication with other friends who are experiencing a bout of anxiety or stress. Those who develop an addiction might use subterfuge and "doctor shopping" to obtain more drugs and, if this fails, might turn to the black market for illegal prescriptions. When this fails, some drug seekers will turn to other substances in the hopes of achieving the same or a similar effect. Thus, opioid addicts who start on a prescription painkiller like OxyCodone might end up using heroin or morphine, while an Adderall addict might turn to methamphetamine or cocaine, and a Valium addict might abuse alcohol. In many cases, it is the activity of switching between a prescription and illicit forms that leads to overdose and death. Thus, many heroin addicts who have switched to the prescription opioid fentanyl, and failed to realize that fentanyl is far more powerful, have unwittingly overdosed in their search for a high.

Anxiety, chronic pain, and chronic stress are familiar factors of American life and these underlying motivations are key to understanding patterns of drug addiction and abuse. Any attempt to fight prescription drug abuse must take into account the legitimate needs of patients struggling with debilitating illness but should also be enacted with the awareness that drug abuse and drug addiction are *also* forms of mental illness and are therefore essentially a disease that must be treated before it can be cured. America's chronic pain, anxiety, and depression problems are part of this disease, underlying socioeconomic and mental health issues that must be addressed before any legitimate end to drug abuse can be achieved.

Micah L. Issitt

Works Used

"AAPM Facts and Figures on Pain." *AAPM*. American Academy of Pain Medicine. 2011. Web. 20 Aug 2017.

"Chronic Pain: Symptoms, Diagnosis, & Treatment." *NIH*. NIH Medline Plus. Spring 2011. Web. 20 Aug 2017.

Dennis, Brady. "NIH: More Than 1 in 10 American Adults Experience Chronic Pain." *The Washington Post*. Nash Holdings. Aug 11, 2015.

Duenas, M., et al. "A Review of Chronic Pain Impact on Patients, Their Social Environment and the Health Care System." *Journal of Pain Research*. 2016. Vol. 9, 457–67.

"Facts & Statistics." *Anxiety and Depression Association of America*. 2017. Web. 20 Aug 2017.

"Generalized Anxiety Disorder (GAD)." *Anxiety and Depression Association of America*. 2017. Web. 20 Aug 2017.

Greenberg, Melanie. "Americans Just Broke a New Record for Stress and Anxiety." *Psychology Today*. Feb 19 2017. Web. 20 Aug 2017.

Kelley, Maura. "An Anxiety Epidemic Is Sweeping the US." *Business Insider*. Business Insider, Inc. Jul 17 2012. Web. 26 Aug 2017.

Luhrmann, T.M. "The Anxious Americans." *The New York Times*. The New York Times Co. Jul 18 2015. Web. 20 Aug 2017.

Pappas, Stephanie. "Anxious Brains Are Inherited, Study Finds." *LiveScience*. Jul 8 2015. Web. 20 Aug 2017.

"Relieving Pain in America: A Blueprint for Transforming Prevention, Care, Education, and Research." *Institute of Medicine*. National Academies. 2011. Pdf. 20 Aug 2017.

Notes

1. Greenberg, "Americans Just Broke a New Record for Stress and Anxiety."
2. Luhrmann, "The Anxious Americans."
3. Kelley, "An Anxiety Epidemic Is Sweeping the US."
4. "Facts & Statistics," *Anxiety and Depression Association of America*.
5. Pappas, "Anxious Brains Are Inherited, Study Finds."
6. "Generalized Anxiety Disorder," *Anxiety and Depression Association of America*.
7. "Social Anxiety Disorder," *Anxiety and Depression Association of America (GAD)*.
8. "AAPM Facts and Figures on Pain," *AAPM*.
9. Dennis, "NIH: More Than 1 in 10 American Adults Experience Chronic Pain."
10. "Chronic Pain: Symptoms, Diagnosis, & Treatment," *NIH*.
11. Duenas, et al., "A Review of Chronic Pain Impact on Patients, Their Social Environment and the Health Care System."
12. Dennis, "NIH: More Than 1 in 10 American Adults Experience Chronic Pain."

Taking On the Scourge of Opioids

By Sally Satel
National Affairs, Summer 2017

On March 1, 2017, Maryland governor Larry Hogan declared a state of emergency. Heroin and fentanyl, a powerful synthetic opioid, had killed 1,468 Maryland residents in the first nine months of 2016, up 62% from the same period in 2015. Speaking at a command center of the Maryland Emergency Management Agency near Baltimore, the governor announced additional funding to strengthen law enforcement, prevention, and treatment services. "The reality is that this threat is rapidly escalating," Hogan said.

And it is escalating across the country. Florida governor Rick Scott followed Hogan's lead in May, declaring a public-health emergency after requests for help from local officials across the state. Arizona governor Doug Ducey did the same in June. In Ohio, some coroners have run out of space for the bodies of overdose victims and have to use a mobile, refrigerated morgue. In West Virginia, state burial funds have been exhausted burying overdose victims. Opioid orphans are lucky if their grandparents can raise them; if not, they are at the mercy of foster-care systems that are now overflowing with the children of addicted parents.

An estimated 2.5 million Americans abuse or are addicted to opioids—a class of highly addictive drugs that includes Percocet, Vicodin, OxyContin, and heroin. Most experts believe this is an undercount, and all agree that the casualty rate is unprecedented. At peak years in an earlier heroin epidemic, from 1973 to 1975, there were 1.5 fatalities per 100,000 Americans. In 2015, the rate was 10.4 per 100,000. In West Virginia, ground zero of the crisis, it was over 36 per 100,000. In raw numbers, more than 33,000 individuals died in 2015—nearly equal to the number of deaths from car crashes and double the number of gun homicides. Meanwhile, the opioid-related fatalities continue to mount, having quadrupled since 1999.

The roots of the crisis can be traced to the early 1990s when physicians began to prescribe opioid painkillers more liberally. In parallel, overdose deaths from painkillers rose until about 2011. Since then, heroin and synthetic opioids have briskly driven opioid-overdose deaths; they now account for over two-thirds of victims. Synthetic opioids, such as fentanyl, are made mainly in China, shipped to Mexico, and trafficked here. Their menace cannot be overstated.

Fentanyl is 50 times as potent as heroin and can kill instantly. People have been found dead with needles dangling from their arms, the syringe barrels still partly full of fentanyl-containing liquid. One fentanyl analog, carfentanil, is a big-game tranquilizer that's a staggering 5,000 times more powerful than heroin. This spring, "Gray Death," a combination of heroin, fentanyl, carfentanil, and other synthetics, has pushed the bounds of lethal chemistry even further. The death rate from synthetics has increased by more than 72% over the space of a single year, from 2014 to 2015. They have transformed an already terrible problem into a true public-health emergency.

The nation has weathered drug epidemics before, but the current affliction—a new plague for a new century, in the words of Nicholas Eberstadt—is different. Today, the addicted are not inner-city minorities, though big cities are increasingly reporting problems. Instead, they are overwhelmingly white and rural, though middle- and upper-class individuals are also affected. The jarring visual of the crisis is not an urban "gang banger" but an overdosed mom slumped in the front seat of her car in a Walmart parking lot, toddler in the back.

It's almost impossible to survey this devastating tableau and not wonder why the nation's response has been so slow in coming. Jonathan Caulkins, a drug-policy expert at Carnegie Mellon, offers two theories. One is geography. The prescription-opioid wave crashed down earliest in fly-over states, particularly small cities and rural areas, such as West Virginia and Kentucky, without nationally important media markets. Earlier opioid (heroin) epidemics raged in urban centers, such as New York, Baltimore, Chicago, and Los Angeles.

The second of Caulkins's plausible explanations is the absence of violence that roiled inner cities in the early 1970s, when President Richard Nixon called drug abuse "public enemy number one." Dealers do not engage in shooting wars or other gang-related activity. As purveyors of heroin established themselves in the U.S., Mexican bosses deliberately avoided inner cities where heroin markets were dominated by violent gangs. Thanks to a "drive-through" business model perfected by traffickers and executed by discreet runners—farm boys from western Mexico looking to make quick money—heroin can be summoned via text message or cell phone and delivered, like pizza, to homes or handed off in car-to-car transactions. Sources of painkillers are low profile as well. Typically pills are obtained (or stolen) from friends or relatives, physicians, or dealers. The "dark web," too, is a conduit for synthetics.

It's hard to miss, too, that this time around, the drug crisis is viewed differently. Heroin users today are widely seen as suffering from an illness. And because that illness has a pale complexion, many have asked, "Where was the compassion for black people?" A racial element cannot be denied, but there are other forces at play, namely that Americans are drug-war weary and law enforcement has incarceration fatigue. It also didn't help that, in the 1970s, officers were only loosely woven into the fabric of the inner-city minority neighborhoods that were hardest hit. Today, in the small towns where so much of the epidemic plays out, the crisis is personal. Police chiefs, officers, and local authorities will likely have at least one relative, friend, or neighbor with an opioid problem.

If there is reason for optimism in the midst of this crisis, it is that national and local politicians and even police are placing emphasis on treatment over punishment. And, without question, the nation needs considerably more funding for treatment; Congress must step up. Yet the much-touted promise of treatment—and particularly of anti-addiction medications—as a panacea has already been proven wrong. Perhaps "we can't arrest our way out of the problem," as officials like to say, but nor are we treating our way out of it. This is because many users reject treatment, and, if they accept it, too many drop out. Engaging drug users in treatment has turned out to be one of the biggest challenges of the epidemic—and one that needs serious attention.

The near-term forecast for this American Carnage, as journalist Christopher Caldwell calls it, is grim. What can be done?

Roots of a Crisis

In the early 1990s, campaigns for improved treatment of pain gained ground. Analgesia for pain associated with cancer and terminal illness was relatively well accepted, but doctors were leery of medicating chronic conditions, such as joint pain, back pain, and neurological conditions, lest patients become addicted. Then in 1995 the American Pain Society recommended that pain be assessed as the "fifth vital sign" along with the standard four (blood pressure, temperature, pulse, and respiratory rate). In 2001 the influential Joint Commission on Accreditation of Healthcare Organizations established standards for pain management. These standards did not mention opioids, per se, but were interpreted by many physicians as encouraging their use.

These developments had a gradual but dramatic effect on the culture of American medicine. Soon, clinicians were giving an entire month's worth of Percocet or Lortab to patients with only minor injuries or post-surgical pain that required only a few days of opioid analgesia. Compounding the matter, pharmaceutical companies engaged in aggressive marketing to physicians.

The culture of medical practice contributed as well. Faced with draconian time pressures, a doctor who suspected that his patient was taking too many painkillers rarely had time to talk with him about it. Other time-consuming pain treatments, such as physical therapy or behavioral strategies, were, and remain, less likely to be covered by insurers. Abbreviated visits meant shortcuts, like a quick refill that may not have been warranted, while the need for addiction treatment was overlooked. In addition, clinicians were, and still are, held hostage to ubiquitous "patient-satisfaction surveys." A poor grade mattered because Medicare and Medicaid rely on these assessments to help determine the amount of reimbursement for care. Clearly, too many incentives pushed toward prescribing painkillers, even when it went against a doctor's better judgment.

The chief risk of liberal prescribing was not so much that the patient would become addicted—though it happens occasionally—but rather that excess medication fed the rivers of pills that were coursing through many neighborhoods. And as more painkillers began circulating, almost all of them prescribed by physicians, more opportunities arose for non-patients to obtain them, abuse them, and die.

OxyContin formed a particularly notorious tributary. Available since 1996, this slow-release form of oxycodone was designed to last up to 12 hours (about six to eight hours longer than immediate-release preparations of oxycodone, such as Percocet). A sustained blood level was meant to be a therapeutic advantage for patients with unremitting pain. To achieve long action, each OxyContin tablet was loaded with a large amount of oxycodone.

Packing a large dose into a single pill presented a major unintended consequence. When it was crushed and snorted or dissolved in water and injected, OxyContin gave a clean, predictable, and enjoyable high. By 2000, reports of abuse of OxyContin began to surface in the Rust Belt—a region rife with injured coal miners who were readily prescribed OxyContin, or, as it came to be called, "hillbilly heroin." Ohio along with Florida became the "pill mill" capitals of the nation. These mills were advertised as "pain clinics," but were really cash-only businesses set up to sell painkillers in high volume. The mills employed shady physicians who were licensed to prescribe but knew they weren't treating authentic patients.

Around 2010 to 2011, law enforcement began cracking down on pill mills. In 2010, OxyContin's maker, Purdue Pharma, reformulated the pill to make it much harder to crush. In parallel, physicians began to re-examine their prescribing practices and to consider non-opioid options for chronic-pain management. More states created prescription registries so that pharmacists and doctors could detect patients who "doctor shopped" for painkillers and even forged prescriptions. (Today, all states except Missouri have such a registry.) Last year, the American Medical Association recommended that pain be removed as a "fifth vital sign" in professional medical standards.

Controlling the sources of prescription pills was completely rational. Sadly, however, it helped set the stage for a new dimension of the opioid epidemic: heroin and synthetic opioids. Heroin—cheaper and more abundant than painkillers—had flowed into the western U.S. since at least the 1990s, but trafficking east of the Mississippi and into the Rust Belt reportedly began to accelerate around the mid-2000s, a transformative episode in the history of domestic drug problems detailed in Sam Quinones's superb book *Dreamland*.

The timing was darkly auspicious. As prescription painkillers became harder to get and more expensive, thanks to alterations of the OxyContin tablet, to law-enforcement efforts, and to growing physician enlightenment, a pool of individuals already primed by their experience with prescription opioids moved on to low-cost, relatively pure, and accessible heroin. Indeed, between 2008 and 2010, about three-fourths of people who had used heroin in the past year reported non-medical use of painkillers—likely obtained outside the health-care system—before initiating heroin use.

The progression from pills to heroin was abetted by the nature of addiction itself. As users became increasingly tolerant to painkillers, they needed larger quantities of opioids or more efficient ways to use them in order to achieve the same effect. Moving from oral consumption to injection allowed this. Once a person is already injecting pills, moving to heroin, despite its stigma, doesn't seem that big a step.

The march to heroin is not inexorable, of course. Yet in economically and socially depleted environments where drug use is normalized, heroin is abundant, and treatment is scarce, widespread addiction seems almost inevitable.

The last five years or so have witnessed a massive influx of powder heroin to major cities such as New York, Detroit, and Chicago. From there, traffickers direct shipments to other urban areas, and these supplies are, in turn, distributed further to rural and suburban areas. It is the powdered form of heroin that is laced with synthetics, such as fentanyl. Most victims of synthetic opioids don't even know they are taking them. Drug traffickers mix the fentanyl with heroin or press it into pill form that they sell as OxyContin.

Yet, there are reports of addicts now knowingly seeking fentanyl as their tolerance to heroin has grown. Whereas heroin requires poppies, which take time to cultivate, synthetics can be made in a lab, so the supply chain can be downsized. And because the synthetics are so strong, small volumes can be trafficked more efficiently and more profitably. What's more, laboratories can easily stay one step ahead of the Drug Enforcement Administration by modifying fentanyl into analogs that are more potent, less detectable, or both. Synthetics are also far more deadly: In some regions of the country, roughly two-thirds of deaths from opioids can now be traced to heroin, including heroin that medical examiners either suspect or are certain was laced with fentanyl.

The Basics

Terminology is important in discussions about drug use. A 2016 Surgeon General report on addiction, *Facing Addiction in America*, defines "misuse" of a substance as consumption that "causes harm to the user and/or to those around them." Elsewhere, however, the term has been used to refer to consumption for a purpose not consistent with medical or legal guidelines. Thus, misuse would apply equally to the person who takes an extra pill now and then from his own prescribed supply of Percocet to reduce stress as well as to the person who buys it from a dealer and gets high several times a week. The term "abuse" refers to a consistent pattern of use causing harm, but "misuse," with its protean definitions, has unhelpfully taken its place in many discussions of the current crisis. In the Surgeon General report, the clinical term "substance use disorder" refers to functionally significant impairment caused by substance use. Finally, "addiction," while not considered a clinical term, denotes a severe form of substance-use disorder—in other words, compulsive use of a substance with difficulty stopping despite negative consequences.

Much of the conventional wisdom surrounding the opioid crisis holds that virtually anyone is at risk for opioid abuse or addiction—say, the average dental patient who receives some Vicodin for a root canal. This is inaccurate, but unsurprising. Exaggerating risk is a common strategy in public-health messaging: The idea is to garner attention and funding by democratizing affliction and universalizing vulnerability. But this kind of glossing is misleading at best, counterproductive at worst. To prevent and ameliorate problems, we need to know who is truly at risk to target resources where they are most needed.

In truth, the vast majority of people prescribed medication for pain do not misuse it, even those given high doses. A new study in the *Annals of Surgery*, for example, found that almost three-fourths of all opioid painkillers prescribed by surgeons for five common outpatient procedures go unused. In 2014, 81 million people received at least one prescription for an opioid pain reliever, according to a study in the *American Journal of Preventive Medicine*; yet during the same year, the National Survey on Drug Use and Health reported that only 1.9 million people, approximately 2%, met the criteria for prescription pain-reliever abuse or dependence (a technical term denoting addiction). Those who abuse their prescription opioids are patients who have been prescribed them for over six months and tend to suffer from concomitant psychiatric conditions, usually a mood or anxiety disorder, or have had prior problems with alcohol or drugs.

Notably, the majority of people who develop problems with painkillers are not individuals for whom they have been legitimately prescribed—nor are opioids the first drug they have misused. Such non-patients procure their pills from friends or family, often helping themselves to the amply stocked medicine chests of unsuspecting relatives suffering from cancer or chronic pain. They may scam doctors, forge prescriptions, or doctor shop. The heaviest users are apt to rely on dealers. Some of these individuals make the transition to heroin, but it is a small fraction. (Still, the death toll is striking given the lethality of synthetic opioids.) One study from the Substance Abuse and Mental Health Services Administration found that less than 5% of pill misusers had moved to heroin within five years of first beginning misuse. These painkiller-to-heroin migrators, according to analyses by the Centers for Disease Control and Prevention, also tend to be frequent users of multiple substances, such as benzodiazepines, alcohol, and cocaine. The transition from these other substances to heroin may represent a natural progression for such individuals.

> **As prescription painkillers became harder to get and more expensive, thanks to alterations of the OxyContin tablet, to law-enforcement efforts, and to growing physician enlightenment, a pool of individuals already primed by their experience with prescription opioids moved on to low-cost, relatively pure, and accessible heroin.**

Thus, factors beyond physical pain are most responsible for making individuals vulnerable to problems with opioids. Princeton economists Anne Case and Angus Deaton paint a dreary portrait of the social determinants of addiction in their work on premature demise across the nation. Beginning in the late 1990s, deaths due to alcoholism-related liver disease, suicide, and opioid overdoses began to climb nationwide. These "deaths of despair," as Case and Deaton call them, strike less-educated whites, both men and women, between the ages of 45 and 54. While the life expectancy of men and women with a college degree continues to grow, it is actually decreasing for their less-educated counterparts. The problems start with poor job opportunities for those without college degrees. Absent employment, people come unmoored. Families unravel, domestic violence escalates, marriages dissolve, parents are alienated from their children, and their children from them.

Opioids are a salve for these communal wounds. Work by Alex Hollingsworth and colleagues found that residents of locales most severely pummeled by the economic downturn were more susceptible to opioids. As county unemployment rates increased by one percentage point, the opioid death rate (per 100,000) rose by almost 4%, and the emergency-room visit rate for opioid overdoses (per 100,000) increased by 7%. It's no coincidence that many of the states won by Donald Trump— West Virginia, Kentucky, and Ohio, for example—had the highest rates of fatal drug overdoses in 2015.

Of all prime-working-age male labor-force dropouts, nearly half—roughly 7 million men—take pain medication on a daily basis. "In our mind's eye," writes Nicholas Eberstadt in a recent issue of *Commentary*, "we can now picture many millions of un-working men in the prime of life, out of work and not looking for jobs, sitting in front of screens—stoned." Medicaid, it turns out, financed many of those stoned hours. Of the entire non-working prime-age white male population in 2013, notes Eberstadt, 57% were reportedly collecting disability benefits from one or more government disability programs. Medicaid enabled them to see a doctor and fill their prescriptions for a fraction of the street value: A single 10-milligram Percocet could go for $5 to $10, the co-pay for an entire bottle.

When it comes to beleaguered communities, one has to wonder how much can be done for people whose reserves of optimism and purposefulness have run so low. The challenge is formidable, to be sure, but breaking the cycle of self-destruction through treatment is a critical first step.

Treatment Options

Perhaps surprisingly, the majority of people who become addicted to any drug, including heroin, quit on their own. But for those who cannot stop using by themselves, treatment is critical, and individuals with multiple overdoses and relapses typically need professional help. Experts recommend at least one year of counseling or anti-addiction medication, and often both. General consensus holds that a standard week of "detoxification" is basically useless, if not dangerous—not only is the person extremely likely to resume use, he is at special risk because he will have lost his tolerance and may easily overdose.

Nor is a standard 28-day stay in a residential facility particularly helpful as a sole intervention. In residential settings many patients acquire a false sense of security about their ability to resist drugs. They are, after all, insulated from the stresses and conditioned cues that routinely provoke drug cravings at home and in other familiar environments. This is why residential care must be followed by supervised transition to treatment in an outpatient setting: Users must continue to learn how to cope without drugs in the social and physical milieus they inhabit every day.

Fortunately, medical professionals are armed with a number of good anti-addiction medications to help patients addicted to opioids. The classic treatment is methadone, first introduced as a maintenance therapy in the 1960s. A newer medication approved by the FDA in 2002 for the treatment of opioid addiction is buprenorphine, or "bupe." It comes, most popularly, as a strip that dissolves under the tongue. The suggested length of treatment with bupe is a minimum of one or two years. Like methadone, bupe is an opioid. Thus, it can prevent withdrawal, blunt cravings, and produce euphoria. Unlike methadone, however, bupe's chemical structure makes it much less dangerous if taken in excess, thereby prompting Congress to enact a law, the Drug Addiction Treatment Act of 2000, which allows physicians to prescribe it from their offices. Methadone, by contrast, can only be administered in clinics tightly regulated by the Drug Enforcement Administration and the Substance Abuse and Mental Health Services Administration. (I work in such a clinic.)

In addition to methadone or buprenorphine, which have abuse potential of their own, there is extended-release naltrexone. Administered as a monthly injection, naltrexone is an opioid blocker. A person who is "blocked" normally experiences no effect upon taking an opioid drug. Because naltrexone has no abuse potential (hence no street value), it is favored by the criminal-justice system. Jails and prisons are increasingly offering inmates an injection of naltrexone; one dose is given at five weeks before release and another during the week of release with plans for ongoing treatment as an outpatient. Such protection is warranted given the increased risk for death, particularly from drug-related causes, in the early post-release period. For example, one study of inmates released from the Washington State Department of Corrections found a 10-fold greater risk of overdose death within the first two weeks after discharge compared with non-incarcerated state residents of the same age, sex, and race.

Any amount of time spent in care has some benefit for the individual and for society as well. This is a truism of treatment and alone justifies enrollment, even if attrition rates are high and even if lasting benefits are negligible. While on methadone, for example, patients almost always fare better. Though a sizeable fraction of patients will continue to use drugs and alcohol, engage in crime, and use emergency-room services, they do harmful things to themselves and others at a mercifully lower rate. Retention in treatment is also associated with substantial reductions in death from overdose and other medical causes. In my methadone clinic, for example, many patients hold very decent jobs; they come to the clinic at 6 A.M. to take their dose—or pick up a month's worth if they have been drug-free for a period of time—and go off to work. Still, as research has repeatedly shown, even patients who have done well on methadone have even odds of falling back to old patterns within a year of leaving the clinic.

The same general pattern of reduced risk applies to people while they are taking buprenorphine and injectable naltrexone: The longer they stay in treatment, the better they do, and anti-addiction medication reliably prolongs the stay. But once the patient is out of treatment, relapse rates are significant—at least half. Of course, the more stable a person is when he leaves treatment—with a settled place to live, a job, and a healthy social network—the better his odds of staying off drugs. But too few get that far. In a recent article in the *American Journal of Psychiatry*, Kathleen Carroll and Roger Weiss present a comprehensive review of buprenorphine studies to date and find that half of all patients drop out within six months.

The mixed performance of bupe has surprised many health authorities. After all, its relatively benign safety profile allows doctors who pass an eight-hour test to prescribe it from their offices. Easier access has made bupe the most popular anti-addiction medication initiated today—often in such demand, in fact, that many opioid users have difficulty finding a doctor to prescribe it. The dearth of prescribers is partly a problem of spotty Medicaid coverage, to be sure, but an arguably larger impediment is actually physician reluctance to prescribe bupe. No matter how well intentioned, few doctors have the time or training to work with these patients, who can be exceptionally challenging and who often require counseling and monitoring in the form of observed urine toxicology screens.

Though the National Institute on Drug Abuse, the former Surgeon General, and many public officials insist (rather naïvely) that addiction is a "disease like any other," or a "brain disease" easily treated out of an office with the right medication (that is, bupe), it hasn't turned out that way. Medication can do only so much when patients' lives need fixing, and hard-won personal transformations are not readily fostered in rushed primary-care offices, even by the most devoted clinician.

Another problem is the abuse of bupe itself. The medication is now the third most diverted prescription opioid after oxycodone and hydrocodone. Some patients sell part of their monthly supply, and cash-only bupe mills are springing up. Smuggling into jail is easy, too, as the strips are so easily concealed (about half an inch by a quarter-inch and clear, they can be applied over a child's drawing or text in a book). Finally, bupe is also extremely potent in people who do not consume opioids regularly. A mere two milligrams are enough to kill. In fact, bupe poisonings of children have increased as unintentional exposure of young children to prescription opioids has been declining since 2009 (after the CDC established an initiative to prevent pediatric exposures in the home).

Drug-abuse treatment is not a straightforward enterprise. Patients are a heterogeneous crowd. Some merely require the stabilizing effect of replacement medication, while others need a full existential makeover; most fall in between. In addition, not every patient wants or needs anti-addiction medication. No matter the form of treatment, one of the biggest challenges, it turns out, is getting individuals to enter treatment and stay in it.

Tools of Engagement

When a person overdoses and personnel rush to the scene, they administer naloxone, or Narcan, a short-acting antidote that is generally delivered as a nasal spray. One might think that upon regaining consciousness the victim would pledge to relinquish drugs. All too often, though, the just-revived individual simply walks away. "A lot of times, [the users] get upset with you when you bring them back," Timmy Hall, a former Baltimore police officer, told *PBS NewsHour*, "because they feel like you wasted the money they spent. You know, that's the feeling that they wanted. They wanted that feeling, and you took it away from them."

The paradox of naloxone is that it saves people who can then overdose again. "We've had people who have been 'Narcanned' in excess of five to 10 times," one New Jersey police chief told a reporter. If the patient does agree to be taken by ambulance to the emergency room, there's a good chance he'll bolt before a treatment referral is even made. And even if he enters treatment, there is a 40% to 60% chance he will drop out within a few months. Recently, the *Wall Street Journal* reported on two facilities in New Jersey. At one Ocean County hospital run by RWJBarnabas Health, 200 patients who were revived with naloxone were offered treatment. Over two years, only two of them agreed to enter detox programs, which precede actual treatment and rehabilitation, and both dropped out within a couple of days. In nearby Camden County, a program offered revived patients $15,000 vouchers for detox and intensive outpatient treatment. Only nine of the nearly 50 patients who were offered the vouchers starting in October 2015 entered treatment—and four of them quickly dropped out.

No one sets out to become an addict. People just want to get relief in the short term. This is why many addicts are so ambivalent about quitting. Years of use have conditioned them to desire drugs, to crave them powerfully, at the first feeling of distress. Opioids have helped them cope with anxiety, despair, loneliness, emptiness, boredom, and hopelessness. And after years of neglecting themselves, their families, and their futures, a new layer of misery has settled itself upon their bedrock of discontent. Relief, not nodded-out oblivion, is what most users seek. What's more, addicts are not particularly good at delaying gratification. So when craving hits, they often act.

Thus, forging a bridge between overdose victims and treatment requires new ideas. In Pittsburgh, for example, a group of specially trained emergency medical technicians conduct 90-minute interviews with overdose victims who have been revived so they can connect them to existing social-support programs and do follow-up visits. Chillicothe, Ohio, has instituted a similar program; police visit the home of each person in the county who overdosed during the prior week and try to connect him to treatment.

Maryland now offers the Overdose Survivors Outreach Program where "recovery coaches," who are specially trained former addicts, are paired with overdose survivors after they arrive in the emergency room. Coaches encourage treatment: perhaps a starter dose of buprenorphine in the emergency room to curb the urge to use within the next day or so. If ongoing treatment is refused, coaches supply naloxone and stay in close touch after the patient goes home, encouraging formal treatment and helping with outstanding court obligations, social services, and job searches. The National Governors Association has endorsed the approach. Evaluations of its impact are underway.

Opioid addicts in Boston can walk into Faster Paths, where they are quickly given access to an addiction urgent-care center at Boston Medical Center. The idea is to engage the person when he feels receptive and move him into treatment. There is access to a primary-care doctor for medical problems, plus follow-up from a licensed drug counselor. Doctors at Zuckerberg San Francisco General offer a similar program with special emphasis on attending to opioid users who are already in the hospital for a medical problem like endocarditis, infections, or Hepatitis C.

Departing from their traditional roles, police officers are becoming "counselors, doctors, and social workers," as a headline in the *Washington Post* described it. For example, in Gloucester, Massachusetts, drug users can walk into the police station, hand over their heroin, and enter treatment within hour—without arrest or charges. It's called the "Angel Program." Many men of the Gloucester fishing fleets who took opioids for their battered bodies are among the participants. A community nonprofit called PAARI—or Police Assisted Addiction and Recovery Initiative—was developed to support the Gloucester addiction initiative and to aid other police departments in implementing similar programs.

Enhanced Retention

More intensive contact with patients should help to keep more of them in care, but dropout will still happen. Less time in treatment means less exposure to vital recovery strategies, such as identifying the highly specific circumstances in which they are most vulnerable to craving, and thus to relapse, and developing and practicing strategies for subduing urges to use. This is why leverage to keep patients in treatment is so vital to success. Most of the time, that leverage comes from the addict's own life, as many if not most patients come to treatment because someone—a spouse, boss, child, or parent—mightily twisted their arms.

But sometimes this is not enough to keep them there. Researchers have discovered several strategies for prolonging treatment. One involves incentives. A vast literature exists, for example, on the use of redeemable vouchers to extend retention and reduce drug use. Such vouchers have monetary value that patients can exchange for food items, movie passes, or other goods or services that are consistent with a drug-free lifestyle. In one incentive model, a research team out of Johns Hopkins offered $10 an hour to addicts to work in a "therapeutic workplace," but only if they submitted clean urine. Workplace participants provided significantly more opiate-negative urine samples than controls; they also reported more days employed, higher employment income, and less money spent on drugs.

To enhance retention, all treatment programs should put serious effort into combining incentives with quality counseling and anti-addiction medication if necessary. But this will be a challenge, as cash-strapped clinics cannot afford to provide material encouragement to patients, let alone devote precious personnel time to supervising an incentive program. One domain stands out as having leverage built into its way of doing business: the criminal-justice system. With its emphasis on monitoring and accountability, the criminal-justice system is home to some of the most promising treatment and rehabilitation models. In fact, we should revise the oft-repeated "we can't arrest our way out of this epidemic," to say, more accurately, that we can't *incarcerate* our way out of it.

Drug courts are a prime example. Many of the nation's roughly 3,000 drug courts offer offenders dismissal of charges for completion of a 12- to 18-month treatment program. Critically, the courts impose swift, certain, and fair consequences when participants fail drug tests or commit other infractions, such as missing meetings with probation officers or skipping work-training classes. The sanctions can escalate depending on the number of infractions committed, ranging from mild, such as a warning from the judge, to community service and more intensive probation supervision, to flash incarceration (temporary sentences of one to 10 days).

These courts are more effective than conventional corrections options, such as mandatory jail time or traditional probation. According to the National Association of Drug Court Professionals, offenders whose cases are handled by drug courts are about one-half to one-third less likely to return to crime or drug use than those who are monitored under typical probationary conditions. On average, two-thirds of drug-court participants graduate drug-free at 18 months. The relatively recent use of anti-addiction medications is already showing great potential to make such mandated treatment even more effective.

What's more, if carrot-and-stick approaches are scrupulously applied, and perhaps combined with anti-addiction medication, it is very possible that not every opioid addict will even need rehabilitation. A program called HOPE (Hawaii's Opportunity Probation with Enforcement) that treats methamphetamine addiction, for which there is no medication, shows how sanctions such as flash incarceration and incentives alone can work, while reserving treatment for the most refractory participants. A randomized study found that after one year participants were 55% less likely to be arrested for a new crime compared with those on traditional probation, and 72% less likely to use drugs. They were also 61% less likely to skip appointments with their supervisory officer, and 53% less likely to have their probation revoked. Programs modeled on Hawaii's "swift, certain and fair" approach are having success in Washington state, Alaska, Texas, South Dakota, and other places. Manchester, New Hampshire, and Worcester, Massachusetts, have programs specifically tailored to opioid addicts (including anti-addiction medication) that are in the process of being evaluated.

With many drug users involved in addiction-related crime, such as shoplifting, prescription forgery, and burglary, there comes a point when shielding them from the criminal-justice system is not in society's best interests—or their own. Criminal-justice authority combined with contingencies can impart order to lives in disarray. The addition of anti-addiction medications—methadone, buprenorphine, or naltrexone—will almost surely make that synergy even stronger.

The most dramatic form of leverage is involuntary civil commitment. Most states have some form of involuntary substance-abuse treatment, though it is rarely used. That may be changing, however. In Kentucky, for example, Casey's Law allows parents, relatives, or friends to petition the court for treatment of two to 12 months on behalf of an addicted person who "presents a danger or threat of danger to self, family, or others." New Hampshire is considering a bill that would impose involuntary care on individuals who lack "the capacity to care for [their] own welfare."

The governor of Indiana recently signed a similar bill into law. A proposed Washington state measure would allow a person to be committed if, within a 12-month period, he had three or more arrests connected to substance abuse, had one or more hospitalizations related to drug abuse, or displays three or more visible track marks indicating intravenous heroin use.

> **But in the midst of an entrenched crisis, localities are turning to once-inconceivable strategies under the banner of harm reduction, a strategy geared first toward reducing opioid-related death and disease, and second toward reducing drug use—if, and only if, the user wants to.**

Harm Reduction

The health-care and law-enforcement systems are the traditional portals through which addicts pass. But in the midst of an entrenched crisis, localities are turning to once-inconceivable strategies under the banner of harm reduction, a strategy geared first toward reducing opioid-related death and disease, and second toward reducing drug use—if, and only if, the user wants to. A classic example is needle exchange, first implemented in the U.S. in the late 1980s to halt the spread of HIV among intravenous drug users. Today, as a way to reduce harm, users are also instructed in "smart use" rules, such as buying only from dealers they know and trust; using with a buddy, making sure one's buddy doesn't pass out before injecting oneself; and taking a small amount before the full shot.

Spurred by the rapid rise of fentanyl-related deaths, harm-reduction strategies are gaining momentum. In spring 2016, for example, Boston opened the Supportive Place for Observation and Treatment, or the SPOT, on Albany Street near Boston University's medical campus. Individuals who have already injected drugs can go to SPOT to ride out the high, be treated by nurses should complications develop, and, ideally, be persuaded to embark on a path to recovery. According to its website, "The SPOT will offer engagement, support, medical monitoring, and serve as an entryway to primary care and treatment *on demand* for 8-10 individuals at a time who are over-sedated from the use of substances and who would otherwise be outside on a street corner, alleyway, or alone in a public bathroom, at high risk of overdose."

The idea of "Safe Consumption Sites," or SCSs, is also gaining traction. As the name implies, people bring their own drugs to inject in hygienic booths in the presence of nurses who can administer oxygen and naloxone if needed. A Vancouver facility called Insite is considered a model for North America. Insite staff members urge patrons to go into treatment, but also distribute clean needles to help prevent the spread of viruses such as HIV and Hepatitis C, and naloxone kits just in case. Data show fewer incidences of public injection in neighborhood venues (such as public bathrooms where someone can overdose undiscovered and die), fewer overdose deaths, and, in some evaluations, greater cost effectiveness due to averted health-care costs.

Early this year, the Ontario government agreed to help fund three supervised sites in Toronto and one in Ottawa. There are no SCSs in the U.S., but in January local officials endorsed the creation of two supervised sites in the Seattle area. A bill introduced in the California Assembly would allow localities to establish SCSs. In San Francisco, Burlington, New York City, Philadelphia, Ithaca, and Baltimore, they are under serious consideration by local health officials.

It is imperative that these initiatives be studied closely and in real time by independent researchers. Safe Consumption Sites are intended for areas already marred by high levels of public drug use. Still, it's hard to imagine communities greeting them with uniform enthusiasm; grudging tolerance may be the best such facilities can expect. Presumably, programs that are good at ushering clients into treatment would be more attractive to a skeptical public. Likewise with programs that require clients to pay a nominal fee to use the services or expect them to make an in-kind contribution, such as helping to maintain the facility or tending to the urban environs. This kind of reciprocity, while unfortunately considered by some harm-reduction advocates to be an imposition on the patrons of the sites, would be therapeutic, as people need to feel useful, and to see that others are grateful for their efforts.

Consumption sites enable drug use, critics charge; they represent a form of surrender. Perhaps, as they allege, some clients would have eventually quit had the facility not been there to make it safer to use drugs. Then again, other users might well have overdosed and died but for the existence of those sites; better yet, perhaps staff managed to usher into treatment some users who would not otherwise have enrolled. It's a fraught tradeoff—keeping some people using who might have stopped, while trying to make the population and the neighborhood safer overall. But when so many users avoid or drop out of treatment, one can see the virtue of such a tradeoff. It is imperative, then, that the costs and benefits of injection sites be elucidated by researchers who are scrupulously independent and conduct their studies prospectively, not after the fact. Up to now, most analyses of such facilities have been conducted by the programs' own developers, a methodology that undermines the credibility of their findings.

An even more drastic concept is actual distribution of pharmaceutical-grade heroin to individuals who have failed methadone treatment. A number of such clinics exist in some European countries, and one opened a couple of years ago in Vancouver. It is difficult to foresee serious interest developing in this country, and even harder to imagine a campaign for flat-out legalization. After all, we essentially just tried it, starting in the 1990s, with the liberalized prescribing of a legal substance (opioid painkillers) dispensed by legal entities (physicians and pharmacists) and effectively provided on request. The results are tragically familiar.

Looking Forward

Through the pall, creative energy and good will are bursting forth all over the country, from fishing communities in Massachusetts to coal towns in Kentucky to

Seattle's edgy experiment. Amid anxieties about the implications of health-care reform for treatment coverage and possible cuts to the Drug Czar's office, there are some positive signs from the nation's capital: President Trump has placed the opioid crisis fairly high on his agenda. In February, he told a gathering of police chiefs and sheriffs that "Prisons should not be a substitute for treatment." And in March, he established the President's Commission on Combating Drug Addiction and the Opioid Crisis. In April, Secretary of Health and Human Services Tom Price rolled out a five-point agenda and released the first half of the $1 billion appropriated by Congress.

The federal government can provide much-needed additional funding for treatment. This will be imperative if the Medicaid expansion is rolled back, as it has brought coverage to about 1.3 million substance abusers who were too poor for private insurance but not poor enough for Medicaid. But it is at the state and county levels that the real progress will be made. Locales are developing inventive modes of engagement; treatment programs are beginning to test novel kinds of incentives; and justice programs are starting to combine enforced structure with medication. As we have seen, the worst of the crisis is in small communities where everyone knows someone who has been affected by an opioid addiction. It makes sense that the effort to find inspired solutions would be most concentrated there; we should invest in those solutions and learn from them. There won't be a master blueprint that works everywhere—this is not a problem that will ever lend itself to such a scalable solution, especially in small towns.

At least at this point, if not for the duration of this crisis, we need to allow medical professionals, law-enforcement officials, community organizations, and the loved ones of those affected to attempt different, even radical, solutions and evaluate their effectiveness. Policymakers should support such experimentation, and fund it, but must resist the urge to pretend that better funding alone will end the scourge of opioids.

Indeed, the lingering lesson of the opioid crisis is that nothing ever changes. This time around, the casualties are largely white drug users with little education dying young in communities that are "hemorrhaging jobs and hope," in the words of J. D. Vance. But this bleak fact is an instance of a larger truth. No matter where people live or how much money they have, those in great pain will seek solace and oblivion through intoxicants, as they have done forever.

Print Citations

CMS: Satel, Sally. "Taking On the Scourge of Opioids." In *The Reference Shelf: Prescription Drug Abuse*, edited by Betsy Maury, 9-24. Ipswich, MA: H.W. Wilson, 2017.

MLA: Satel, Sally. "Taking On the Scourge of Opioids." *The Reference Shelf: Prescription Drug Abuse*. Ed. Betsy Maury. Ipswich: H.W. Wilson, 2017. 9-24. Print.

APA: Satel, S. (2017). Taking on the scourge of opioids. In Betsy Maury (Ed.), *The reference shelf: Prescription drug abuse* (pp. 9-24). Ipswich, MA: H.W. Wilson. (Original work published 2017)

How Prescription-Drug Abuse Unleashed a Heroin Epidemic

By Kevin D. Williamson

The National Review, **February 29, 2016**

Birmingham, Ala.—"Dogfood—yeah, *dogfood*—because it looks like ground-up dogfood." He is embarrassed to be talking about this. "Or sand, because it's brown. Or diesel. Or killa or 911. That's the influence of rap culture down here." Young, clean-cut, Eagle Scout–ish white kid, hesitant about using the words "rap culture." But he goes on, matter-of-factly. He's been off heroin for only a few months, so the details are fresh in his mind, even if he remains a little hazy on some of his autobiographical timeline. "The 911, they call it that because they want you to know it's potent, that you'll have to go to the emergency room."

That's a weird and perverse and nasty kind of advertising, but then dope-buying psychology isn't very much like Volvo-buying psychology: Crashing is just another part of the ride. One spiteful dealer boasts about spiking his product with excessive amounts of fentanyl, an all-business pharmaceutical analgesic used for burn victims and cancer patients, that particular entrepreneur's plan being to intentionally send overdosed users to the hospital or the morgue . . . for marketing purposes. Once the word got out about the hideous strength of his product, that killa went right out the door ricky-tick.

The young man explaining the current vocabulary of opiate addiction in Birmingham is barely old enough to buy a beer, and his face and voice are soft. He describes the past several years of his life: "dope-sick and stealing," going from job to job—eight jobs in six months—and robbing his employers blind, alienating his family, descending. He was an addict on a mission: "You're always chasing that first shot of dope, that first high—and the first one for me almost killed me. I was 17 or 18 years old, and I met a guy who had just got out of prison, doing a 13-year sentence for heroin possession and distribution. He was staying at the Oak Mountain Lodge, which is a nice little classic place." (In 2013, four police officers and a drug dog had to be treated for exposure to dangerous chemicals after raiding a suspected meth lab in that hotel; the customer reviews online are decidedly mixed.) "I was snorting heroin when I met up with him, and set him up with my connect. He offered to shoot me up, and I wanted to do it. And I remember him looking me in the eyes and telling me, 'If you do this, you'll never stop, and you'll never go back.' And I said, 'Let's do it.'"

He doesn't know what happened for the next several hours. When he regained consciousness, his junkie buddy's girlfriend was worriedly ministering to him. "That was first thing in the morning," he says. "That night, I did another one." Same results. "I'd nodded out from snorting it, but there's nothing like shooting it." He was, for a time, a "pretty good junkie."

This particular opiate odyssey starts off in a Walgreens, which turns out to be absolutely appropriate. I'm headed up the south coast and then inland on the heroin highway up to Atlanta, starting from the Port of Houston, which connects that city with 1,053 ports in nearly 200 countries and which in December alone welcomed the equivalent of 63,658 20-foot cargo containers of goods into the United States. There was, the feds are pretty sure, some dope squirreled away in there, and in fact all sorts of interesting stuff comes in and out: In May, U.S. Customs seized a Fast Attack Vehicle with gun mounts, headed to the Netherlands. I've got a long drive ahead and I'm going to be out of pocket for a bit, and I have a prescription to fill: a Schedule II Controlled Substance, in the official nomenclature, which covers some pretty interesting stuff, including the oxycodone and fentanyl I'll be hearing so much about in the next few days. Some of us are going to heaven, some of us are going to hell, but all of us have to stop at Walgreens first.

The clerk is on the phone with a doctor's office: "What's your DEA number?"

For working-class white guys who haven't found their way into those good jobs in the energy economy or the related manufacturing and construction booms that have reverberated throughout the oil patch, who aren't college-bound or in possession of the skills to pay the bills, things aren't looking so great: While much of the rest of the world gets healthier and longer-lived, the average life expectancy for white American men without college educations is declining. Angus Deaton, the Princeton economist who recently won the Nobel prize, ran the numbers and found (in a study coauthored by his Princeton colleague Anne Case) that what's killing what used to be the white working class isn't diabetes or heart disease or the consumption of fatty foods and Big Gulps that so terrifies Michael Bloomberg, but alcohol-induced liver failure, along with overdoses of opioid prescription painkillers and heroin: Wild Turkey and hillbilly heroin and regular-old heroin, too, the use of which has increased dramatically in recent years as medical and law-enforcement authorities crack down on the wanton overprescription of oxy and related painkillers.

Which is to say: While we were ignoring criminally negligent painkiller prescriptions, we helped create a gigantic population of opioid addicts, and then, when we started paying attention, first thing we did was take away the legal (and quasi-legal) stuff produced to exacting clinical standards by Purdue Pharma (maker of OxyContin) et al. So: lots of opiate addicts, fewer prescription opiates.

What was left was diesel, sand—dogfood.

The clerks at this Walgreens are super friendly, but the place is set up security-wise like a bank, and that's to be expected. This particular location was knocked over by a young white man with a gun the summer before last, an addict who had been seen earlier lurking around the CVS down the road. This is how you know you're a pretty good junkie: The robber walked in and pointed his automatic at the clerk and demanded oxy first, then a bottle of Tusinex cough syrup, and then, almost as an afterthought, the $90 in the till. Walgreens gets robbed a lot: In January, armed men stormed the Walgreens in Edina, Minn., and made off with $8,000 worth of drugs, mainly oxy. In October, a sneaky young white kid in an Iowa State shirt made off with more than $100,000 worth of drugs, again, mainly oxy and related opioid painkillers, from a Walgreens in St. Petersburg, Fla. Other Walgreens locations—Liberty, Kan., Virginia Beach, Va., East Bradford, Pa., Elk Grove, Calif., Kaysville, Utah, New Orleans—all have been hit by armed robbers or sneak thieves over the past year or so, and there have been many more oxy thefts.

It won't make the terrified clerks feel any better, but there's a little bit of poetic justice in that: In 2013, Walgreens paid the second-largest fine ever imposed under the Controlled Substances Act for being so loosey-goosey in handling oxy at its distribution center in Jupiter, Fla., that it enabled untold quantities of the stuff to reach the black market. The typical pharmacy sells 73,000 oxycodone pills a year; six Walgreens in Florida were going through more than 1 million pills a year—each. A few years before that, Purdue was fined $634.5 million for misleading the public about the addictiveness of oxycodone. Kentucky, which has been absolutely ravaged by opiate addiction, is still pursuing litigation against Purdue, and it has threatened to take its case all the way to the Supreme Court, if it comes to that.

Ground Zero in the opiate epidemic isn't in some exotic Taliban-managed poppy field or some cartel boss's fortified compound: It's right there at Walgreens, in the middle of every city and town in the country. I pick up my prescription and get on my way.

The next afternoon, having driven past billboards advertising boudin and strip joints with early-bird lunch specials and casino after casino after sad little casino, help wanted signs for drilling-fluid businesses and the Tiger Truck Stop (which has a 24-hour Cajun café and an actual no-kidding live tiger in a cage out front), past Whiskey Bay and Contraband Bayou, where the pirate Jean Lafitte once stashed his booty, around the Port of New Orleans, another York entrepôt for heroin and cocaine—it is almost as close to Cartagena as it is to New —I arrive at a reasonably infamous New Orleans drug corner, where I inquire as discreetly as I can about the availability of prescription painkillers, which are getting harder and harder to find on the street.

This particular area was until recently under the control of an energetic fellow called "Dumplin," who, judging from his police photos, isn't nearly so cute and approachable as that nickname would suggest. Dumplin ran a gang called 3NG, which presumably stands for "Third and Galvez," the nearby intersection that constituted the center of his business empire. In March, Dumplin went away on three manslaughter charges and a raft of drug-conspiracy complaints. No Dumplin, but the opiate trade doesn't seem to have noticed. Little teams of two or three loiter in residential doorways, and business gets done. Who is running the show now? Somebody knows. Everybody has heroin, but asking about oxy is greeted as a breach of protocol by my not especially friendly neighborhood drug dealer, who doesn't strike me as the kind of guy who suffers breaches of protocol lightly. He looks at me with exactly the sort of contempt one would expect from a captain of an industry that uses lethal overdoses as a marketing gimmick.

"This ain't Walgreens, motherf***er."

"We partner with Walgreens."

If Dr. Peter DeBlieux sometimes sounds as if he's seen it all, it's possible that he has. As his name suggests, he's a New Orleans local, and he's been practicing medicine in the city long enough to have seen earlier heroin epidemics. Now the chief medical officer and medical-staff president at University Medical Center, he speaks with some authority on how changes in global heroin logistics affect conditions in his emergency rooms, which have just seen a 250 percent spike in opiate-overdose cases in one month. "The first time we'd seen these numbers is when the heroin supply chain moved from the Orient to South America. Before that, New Orleans's supply traditionally came with everybody else's supply, from the Far East through New York, and then down to us. By the time it got to New Orleans, it was adul-

> **Ground Zero in the opiate epidemic is right there at Walgreens, in the middle of every city and town in the country.**

terated, much less pure. But then competitors from South America began bringing heroin along the same routes used to import cocaine. They brought a purer product, which meant more overdoses requiring rescue." That was in the late 1980s and early 1990s, right around the time when our self-appointed media scolds were bewailing the "heroin chic" in Calvin Klein fashion shoots and celebrity junkie Kurt Cobain was nodding off during publicity events.

The current spike in overdoses is related to a couple of things. One proximate cause is the increased use of fentanyl to spike heroin. Heroin, like Johnnie Walker, is a blend: The raw stuff is cut with fillers to increase the volume, and then that diluted product is spiked with other drugs to mask the effects of dilution. Enter the fentanyl. Somebody, somewhere, has got his hands on a large supply of the stuff, either hijacked from legitimate pharmaceutical manufacturers or produced in some narco black site in Latin America for the express purpose of turbocharging heroin. (Where did it come from? Somebody knows.) Fentanyl, on its own, isn't worth very much on the street: It might get you numb, but it really doesn't get you high, and such pleasures as are to be derived from its recreational use are powerfully offset by its tendency to kill you dead. But if the blend is artfully done, then fentanyl can make stepped-on heroin feel more potent than it is. If the blend isn't right . . . medical personnel are known to refer to that as a "clean kill."

New Orleans has taken some steps to try to get ahead of this mess. One of the things that the city's health providers had been experimenting with was giving addicts and their families prescriptions for naloxone, sold under the brand name Narcan, which is the anti-intoxicant used to reverse the effects of opiates in people who have overdosed. Put another way: The best clinical thinking at the moment—the top idea among our best and brightest white-coated elite—is to help junkies pre-plan their overdoses. If that's shocking and depressing, what's more shocking and depressing is that it really is needful. Essential, even. A few other cities have experimented with it, too, and not long after my conversation with Dr. DeBlieux, New Orleans's top health officials handed down an emergency order to make Narcan available over the counter. Jeffrey Elder, the city's director of emergency medical services, said that with the New Orleans emergency rooms seeing as many as ten opiate overdoses a day, the step was necessary. Dr. DeBlieux's emergency rooms saw seven overdose deaths in January alone. In high places, there are stirrings of awareness about heroin's most recent ferocious comeback, but it has taken a while. Congress held hearings, and Senator Kelly Ayotte, the charismatic young New Hampshire Republican, introduced the Heroin and Prescription Opioid Abuse Prevention, Education, and Enforcement Act of 2015, currently on ice in the Judiciary Committee. That bill would . . . convene a task force.

Dr. DeBlieux compares the public perception of heroin to the public perception of AIDS (the issues are not entirely unrelated) a generation ago: It is seen as a problem for deviants. AIDS was for perverts who liked to have anonymous sex with men at highway rest stops, and heroin is a problem for toothless pillbillies who turn to the needle after running out of oxy and for whores and convicts and menacing black men in New Orleans ghettos. Heroin, this line of thinking goes, is a problem for people who deserve it. "Nobody cares, because of who is affected," Dr. DeBlieux says, or at least the perception of who is affected. "There are two problems with that. One, it's unethical. Two, it isn't true." It isn't just the born-to-lose crowd and career criminals and deviants and undesirables. It's working-class white men and college-bound suburban kids, too. Dr. DeBlieux and his colleagues are doing what they can to minimize the damage. University Medical Center distributes that Narcan through a private embedded pharmacy in the hospital, operated by—you won't be surprised—Walgreens.

Odyssey House is not a happy place. It's a necessary place.

I arrive too early for my appointment, so I have a look around the neighborhood. It is downscale, and there definitely is a little bit of unlicensed pharmaceutical trade being transacted nearby, but it's far from the worst I've seen in New Orleans. I decide to go pick up some extra notebooks, and I end up—inevitably—at Walgreens. There are 8,173 Walgreens locations filling 894 million prescriptions a year, and that big ol' record-book fine doesn't look too big up against $77 billion in sales a year. CVS does $140 billion a year, filling one-third of all U.S. pharmaceutical prescriptions. In a country of 319 million, there were 259 million opiate-painkiller prescriptions written last year. There were 47,000 lethal overdoses in the U.S. in 2014, almost 30,000 of which were prescription painkillers and heroin. Some 94 percent of heroin users told researchers that they got into heroin because the pills they started on became too expensive or too difficult to find, whereas heroin is cheap and plentiful. How do we keep up with all those pills? Where do they go? Somebody knows. It's been only two weeks since there was an armed robbery of a Walgreens in New Orleans, but it wasn't this one. That one is about 20 minutes away.

I park my car on the street across from Odyssey House, down the block from a sign advertising free HIV screening, and an older white man comes out of his home to stand on the porch, staring at me. He's still there, still staring, when I go inside the building across the street. Odyssey House is the largest addiction-treatment facility in Louisiana, treating about 700 people a month, about half of them from greater New Orleans. It was founded in response to New Orleans's first major heroin epidemic, some 45 years ago. Its clients are about half white in a city that isn't, and predominantly male. About half of its clients are there on court orders, and the other half have simply decided that they want to live. Its CEO, Ed Carlson, has a master's in clinical psychology and not much in the way of kind words for Louisiana's former governor, conservative health-policy wonk Bobby Jindal. It's partly a familiar complaint—Jindal's rejection of the Medicaid expansion under the Affordable Care Act means that about 90 percent of Odyssey House's patients have to be covered by general state funds, which are scarce. But it's also an illustration of one of the hidden costs of privatizing public-health services: the transfer of administrative costs from state agencies onto third parties, including nonprofits such as Odyssey House.

"Under the privatization of the Bayou Health plans," Carlson says, "it's like this: I have a guy who shows up, who's a heroin addict, who's been in and out of the criminal-justice system, maybe a 20-year heroin addict, maybe semi-homeless, and he wants to get off heroin in our detox. And I have to spend an hour explaining to [insurance bureaucrats] why this guy needs treatment, usually with someone who doesn't understand treatment at all." That meant hiring more administrative help. "What it did was, it shot up our costs. Now we have people who all they do all day long is sit down and try to convince somebody that this person needs treatment. And they'll say, 'Has he tried outpatient?' He's a heroin addict. He's homeless. He's here at our door. I don't have a problem justifying to them that a person needs services, but, once we've justified it, then let's go with the level of services that a medical professional recommends." Outpatient treatment? Heroin addicts as a class don't have a real good record for keeping appointments

Odyssey's program is intensive: It begins with a medically supported detox program, which isn't all that critical for opiate addicts (the popular image of the effects of heroin withdrawal are theatrically exaggerated, as Theodore Dalrymple documented in his classic on the subject, Romancing Opiates) but which is absolutely necessary for alcohol withdrawal, which can be fatal. The reality is that most heroin addicts drink their fair share, too. Detox is followed by a 28-day residential program, followed by housing support and an outpatient program. Odyssey has primary-care physicians and psychiatrists on staff, a separate residential program for adolescents, and more. They aren't promiscuous with the money—for example, they don't send methamphetamine addicts to detox, because their withdrawal lasts only a few hours and its main effects are discomfort and a few days of insomnia—but, even so, all this treatment gets expensive, and the city of New Orleans kicks in the princely sum of $0.00 in municipal money for these services, with the exception of some pass-through money from state and federal agencies.

The general consensus is that this sort of treatment provides the best chance for helping some—fewer than you'd think—of the chronically addicted, homeless and semi-homeless, destitute, low-bottom population. There's no cheap way to do it. "There's really only two things we know, from a scientific standpoint, about addiction," Carlson says. "The first thing we know is that when a person has a problem with addiction and they have that moment, that break in the wall of —if they can access treatment at that point, then they're more likely to engage in the treatment process and to be more serious about it. The other thing we know is that the longer we keep people in treatment, the longer they're going to stay clean and sober."

In total, it costs just under $1 million a month to run Odyssey House and provide those services to its 700 or so patients. And what do the funding agencies get for that money? A one-year success rate of a little more than 50 percent—which is significantly better than that of most comparable programs. Beyond that one year? No one really knows. "The fact is that most people who need addiction treatment don't really want it," Carlson says.

It isn't clear that there really is a solution to the opiate epidemic, but if there is, there's one thing you can be sure of: It is going to cost a great deal of money. "We have waiting lists for all our programs," Carlson says with a slight grimace. "We could probably double in size and still have waiting lists."

Homelessness in New Orleans isn't the only model of heroin addiction, or even the most prevalent one. Up in the land of Whole Foods and Starbucks and yoga studios in one of the nicer parts of Birmingham, it looks like a different world. But it isn't. More white people, more Volvos—same junkies.

Danny Malloy doesn't sound like he belongs here. He has a heavy Boston accent, and he still shakes his head at some aspects of life in the South: "We measure snow in feet up there, but it's inches down here," he scoffs. There's a little snow blowing around, and a few streaks of white on the grass. "No plows, no salt trucks, and nobody knows how to drive in it." He ended up in Alabama the way people end up places. His parents were divorced when he was very young, his alcoholic father eventually sent him to live with an aunt, and he later sought out his estranged mother in Birmingham. "I didn't know her," he says. He was already a blackout drunk and had found his way to the pills, which he was both consuming and dealing.

"I never realized I had a problem. I thought I was having a good time. I got into prescription pills. I really liked them—I mean like really liked them. It took probably three years of me dabbling in those before I was fully addicted, and every day I had to have Lortabs. I got into OxyContin and was selling those. I got set up by someone and sold to an undercover police officer. So I was arrested for distribution, and I was facing time. At that point, someone came along and said, 'These pills are expensive, and you can't sell them any more. So why don't

> **In a country of 319 million, there were 259 million opiate-painkiller prescriptions written last year. There were 47,000 lethal overdoses in the U.S. in 2014, almost 30,000 of which were prescription painkillers and heroin.**

you do heroin?' I said I would never do that. I don't want to use a needle. But, eventually, like a good drug addict, I was like, 'Let me try that.' The rest was history. I've been to 15 or 20 rehabs, including psychiatric hospitals, arrests, detoxes, methadone rehabs. I couldn't get rid of it. I did that for about seven years. Things got . . . really bad." He'd been a college student, majoring in "whatever started at noon," but he ended up being kicked out. "The first time I ever thought maybe I had a problem was when I got arrested and my face was down in a puddle with a cop on my back. That's what it took." Eventually, he put himself on a Greyhound and checked into the Foundry, a Christian rehab facility. "I never looked back. I turned my life over to God, and He took away the desire to use." He pauses as if reconsidering what he's said. "It isn't magic."

Alabama doctors write more opiate prescriptions per capita than those of any other state. And where there is oxy, there will be dogfood. "The pills lead to heroin," Malloy says. "You see these doctors getting arrested for running a pill mill. Well, they have hundreds of people they're prescribing to, and when they tighten down on that, the next thing is the heroin."

Far from being an inner-city problem and a poor-white problem, heroin is if anything more prevalent in some of the wealthier areas around Birmingham, says Drew Callner, another recovering addict and a volunteer at the Addiction Prevention Coalition in Birmingham, a faith-based organization aimed at realistic preventative measures and connecting addicts with recovery resources. "Heroin is easier to get, and it's cheaper." His father was a child psychologist, he was planning on becoming one himself, and he was a trust-funder—twice. "Yeah, I blew through two trusts," he says, snorting. He'd been a Marine and wanted to become a firefighter, but the only thing he could commit to for the long term—15 years—was oxy and heroin. Beyond the depleted trust funds, the deficit that seems to weigh on him most heavily is that of time. He is 32 years old and has spent nearly half of his life as an active drug user. "Going back to school is interesting," he says. "I'm in some English 101 class at 8:30 in the morning, that I've taken four or five times"—there were five or six colleges, and five rehabs in four years—"and I'm in there with a bunch of 18- and 19-year-olds. It's humbling. Humiliating. But when you get sober, you need something to ground you." He'd derailed his life before it had really gotten under way, but his roommates in his last residential program—which he got out of just last week, with seven months' sobriety—were a personal-injury attorney, a senior banker, and an accountant. "And then there was me."

They call it the "red flag." Some heroin addicts fall in love with the ritual of shooting up. Some of them have been known to shoot up when they don't have any heroin, just to feel the calming presence of the needle in the arm. The ritual is familiar enough to anybody who has spent any time in that world: You put the chunk of tar or bit of powder in the spoon, squirt a little water in with the syringe, heat it up to get it to dissolve, drop a little pinch of cotton into the spoon for a filter, pull the heroin solution up through the cotton into the syringe, find a —this isn't always easy, and it gets harder—work the needle in, pull the plunger back . . . And then, you see it: the red flag, a little flash of blood that gets pulled into the syringe and lets you know that you have found a vein, that you aren't about to waste your junk on an intramuscular injection that isn't going to do anything except burn and waste your money and disappoint you and leave you with a heroin blister. Certain addicts become, for whatever reason, almost as addicted to the needle—and addicted to the red flag, to the sight of their own blood being extracted—as to the heroin itself.

"When I couldn't get heroin, I would just shoot anything," Malloy says. "I would load up hot water and shoot it, just to feel the needle. I had to load it up and shoot it—it was a routine. So I started shooting Xanax, Klonopin, trying to shoot Vicodin, but that never works."

"I was the opposite," Callner says. "Every time I shot up, I would hear my mom's voice, telling me I'm a piece of sh**. Plus, I'm not very vascular, so I had to shoot up on the outside of my arm, which meant looking at myself in the mirror. There was just something about that, five or six times a day, looking yourself in the eye and seeing the deterioration. And hating it." "I remember using dull, dull needles, and having to stab myself until I found a vein," recovering addict Dalton Smith says. "But I was obsessed with when you got the needle in, and pulling it back and seeing the blood. The red flag." Smith sometimes shot up imaginary heroin, convinced that bits of carpet lint were heroin. "The fuzz—I remember seeing the fuzz from the carpet in my rug." None of these guys comes from Heartbreak Hill. Some of them came from some money, came from good schools, went to college, had successful, high-income parents. But there was also divorce, and addiction in the family—one young recovering addict is in the precarious situation of having to live with his alcoholic father—and a general sense of directionlessness. They are from that great vast America whose people simultaneously have too much and too little.

One or two breaks in a different direction and Dalton Smith might have been the youth minister at your church. (He still might be.) He's got that heartbreakingly distinctive shamefacedness that you see whenever you're around young addicts or young prisoners (there's some substantial overlap on that Venn diagram) or other young people with woeful self-inflicted injuries, a shadow across the face that says that while he may be trying to have faith in whatever Higher Power sets His almighty hand on recovering junkies in Alabama, that everything happens for a reason and that he's right where he's supposed to be, he'd really give anything to be able to go back and change one thing on that chain of decisions that led to his messing his life up nearly irreparably before he was old enough to rent a car from Avis. He's 22 years old. There's a long chain of bad decisions that goes back to the beginning of his self-destructive career as a drug addict, and at its beginning is a twelve-year-old child. And now he knows a lot of words for heroin.

"Down here, they sometimes call it 'boy.'"

Print Citations

CMS: Williamson, Kevin D. "How Prescription-Drug Abuse Unleashed a Heroin Epidemic." In *The Reference Shelf: Prescription Drug Abuse*, edited by Betsy Maury, 25-34. Ipswich, MA: H.W. Wilson, 2017.

MLA: Williamson, Kevin D. "How Prescription-Drug Abuse Unleashed a Heroin Epidemic." *The Reference Shelf: Prescription Drug Abuse*. Ed. Betsy Maury. Ipswich: H.W. Wilson, 2017. 25-34. Print.

APA: Williamson, K. D. (2017). How prescription-drug abuse unleashed a heroin epidemic. In Betsy Maury (Ed.), *The reference shelf: Prescription drug abuse* (pp. 25-34). Ipswich, MA: H.W. Wilson. (Original work published 2016)

The Truth about Prescription Pills: One Writer's Story of Anxiety and Addiction

By Kelley McMillan
Vogue, April 25, 2014

Almost four years to the day after I quit drinking, I visited my gynecologist for a routine annual exam. It was July 2012; I was 33 and exactly where I wanted to be: in love, writing for national magazines, and living the kind of adventurous life I'd always dreamed of. Two years earlier, I'd moved from New York City to Denver. My health was excellent (I was even training for a half Ironman), so I hadn't bothered to find a general practitioner in my new city. I relied on my gynecologist for my few medical needs: blood work, breast exams, birth control, and my psychiatric prescriptions.

After the standard poking and prodding, my doctor and I chitchatted for a bit; then she looked at me and said, "I'm worried you have a dependency on Klonopin. You've been on way too much of it for way too long."

Klonopin is a benzodiazepine, one of a family of antianxiety medications that includes Xanax, Valium, and Ativan. The National Alliance on Mental Illness warns that physical dependency may result after only two weeks of use, but some psychiatrists, like the one I used to see on the Upper West Side, dispense it as a long-term treatment for anxiety. I'd been taking 1.5 milligrams of Klonopin a day, a moderate dose, since I'd stopped drinking, though I'd been on and off it throughout my 20s to help assuage the disquietude I'd long battled. And it worked marvelously. Any self-defeating thoughts and stress about work, family, relationships—the tightness in my chest where my worry takes hold—were almost instantly dissipated once I popped one of those little yellow tablets.

With my anxiety and drinking under control, my life bloomed. I traveled the world as a freelance writer—in a 24-hour span that spring, I'd heli-skied in Alaska, then jumped on a plane to go on safari in Uganda. After many years single, I was dating a handsome captain of a Special Forces team. I was happier and more grounded than I'd ever been. But my doctor was concerned that during the previous six months, I'd refilled my Klonopin prescription early a few times, something she had to approve at each instance. Those early refills, she said, had caught her attention for possible abuse. I was stunned. Sure, I'd refilled my scrip early on occasion, but only by a couple of days, ten days, tops. This was due in part to my hectic travel schedule, but also to the fact that I sometimes took a few more pills than prescribed, on nights when I couldn't sleep or days when I felt particularly anxious. I never took Klonopin to get high; I took it "as needed," as the label said to.

My doctor said that she no longer felt comfortable prescribing Klonopin to me, and she handed me the business cards of a psychiatrist, an addiction specialist, and a general practitioner. To my dismay, after I'd successfully kicked one habit, my doctor was telling me I had to kick another.

Alarming numbers of Americans are taking—and becoming hooked on—prescription pills, according to the Substance Abuse and Mental Health Services Administration (SAMHSA). With more than 47 million prescriptions in 2011, Xanax is the eleventh most prescribed drug overall and the most popular psychiatric medication in the country. That's a 20 percent jump since 2007. Women are more likely than men to take antianxiety medications: 7.3 percent of women between the ages of 20 and 44 and 11 percent of women 45 to 64 are on them, twice the number of men, according to a 2011 study by Express Scripts, a health-care company that tracks data from more than one billion prescriptions a year. The fallout from our affinity for anxiety meds is startling: In 2012, nearly seven million people abused psychotherapeutic drugs, and rehab visits involving benzodiazepines tripled between 1998 and 2008, according to SAMHSA.

Part of the problem stems from the fact that we are the most anxious country in the world, or at least the country fastest to cling to medical diagnoses, with clinical anxiety affecting about 40 million American adults in a given year, according to the most recent figures from the National Institutes of Health. Anxiety is the most common psychiatric diagnosis in the United States, and one in three women will experience such a disorder in her lifetime. "If you wanted to design a culture that is anxiety-producing, stress-producing, mood disorder–producing, and stressful to the self-image of girls and women, you'd draw it up to look a lot like the United States," says Colorado-based psychiatrist Scott Shannon, M.D., who founded the Wholeness Center, the country's largest and most comprehensive integrative mental-health clinic.

That's where the pills come in. Benzodiazepines were first introduced in the 1950s; today more than 94 million benzo prescriptions are dispensed annually, according to a 2012 report by IMS Health, a leading health care–research company. The drug works by enhancing the effect of gamma-aminobutyric acid (GABA), a neurotransmitter that helps calm the mind and body. GABA roams the brain looking for the right receptor to latch onto. When it does, its soothing effects are unleashed. Benzos attach to GABA receptors, amplifying the neurotransmitter's effects and creating an inflated sense of peace.

"Benzos are cheap, easy, and don't require any effort on the part of the patient," says Franklin Schneier, M.D., a research psychiatrist in the Anxiety Disorders Clinic at New York State Psychiatric Institute. "They work rapidly, and they are effective. But they have several disadvantages, too."

For starters, there is little evidence that long-term benzo use cures anxiety. In fact, several small studies suggest that taking benzos on an ongoing basis can cause structural changes in the brain that may result in cognitive damage, according to psychiatrist Peter Breggin, M.D., author of more than 40 articles on the subject and an outspoken critic of psychiatric drugs. One meta-analysis examining patients who had gotten off benzos found deterioration in every area of intellectual and cognitive testing it studied and suggested that the damage may be irreparable. And benzos may actually make your condition worse than before you started taking the drugs because they compromise your ability to deal with it, Breggin says.

While benzo manufacturers and some doctors believe that the drugs are beneficial if they're used properly, they're often prescribed for the wrong reasons; after all, we are a quick-fix culture that seeks immediate alleviation of symptoms. On top of that, general practitioners prescribe 65 percent of all antianxiety medications, and they're often unable to provide sufficient monitoring and may be unfamiliar with medication protocols. Even therapeutic use can lead to addiction, abuse, and physical dependence, which happens when the body adapts in such a way that it needs the drug to function properly.

Withdrawal symptoms can range from panic attacks and nausea to the more extreme—seizures and suicidal thoughts. Studies show that between 15 and 44 percent of long-term benzo users will develop a physical dependency on the drug. According to Breggin, getting off benzos is harder than quitting heroin.

I was 29 and living in New York City when I gave up drinking. Mine wasn't a rock-bottom falling-out but a gradual awakening to the realization that alcohol was getting in the way of the person I wanted to be. There were times when things could have gone terribly wrong and didn't, but the most crippling part of my drinking was the massive anxiety hangovers I'd suffer after big nights out. The morning after, I would have a tightness in my chest that crept up my neck and into my head, where an electric sense of shame overwhelmed me to the point where being in my body was almost unbearable.

There was something else that had been scratching at the raw spots in me for a couple of years. My drinking was starting to remind me of my mother, who had her own complicated relationship with alcohol, mental illness, and psychiatric medications. Like me, she wasn't a vodka-in-the-morning drinker, but when she drank—usually California Chardonnays—she couldn't stop. She'd get high and silly and then, at the drop of a dime, she'd turn mean, lashing out at those closest to her. It was so contrary to her fundamental nature—kind, compassionate, sensitive—and she hated herself for the times she hurt our family. But ultimately, no pill or drink, no amount of love, could soothe her sadness. When I was 22, she took her life. I worried that her suffering was a warning, a glimpse of what my future might be if I didn't change things.

After a fight with my boyfriend in July 2008, I woke up with a guilt-shame-worry hangover that was becoming all too familiar, and I decided to stop drinking. There was no AA or rehab—my drinking never got out of control to the point where friends and family were concerned—just my own steely desire for a better life and the memory of my mother driving me toward it. I committed myself to giving my psych meds, which I'd taken off and on since my teens, a shot to work (alcohol can counteract antidepressants' effects and worsen depression and anxiety). I wanted to tease apart how much of my unhappiness was a re-sult of my lifestyle—late nights and alcohol aren't a recipe for achieving balance—and how much of it was me.

> **With more than 47 million prescriptions in 2011, Xanax is the eleventh most prescribed drug overall and the most popular psychiatric medication in the country.**

Given my mother's mental-health history, I believed that I was genetically predisposed to depression and that psychiatric medications would right my chemically unbalanced brain. My issues, I was told by several doctors throughout my life, were like diabetes. You take medication to balance your brain as a diabetic would take insulin to manage blood glucose levels. (This notion, in fact, has never been proven, nor has the chemical-imbalance theory of depression and anxiety, says Breggin.) My mother gave me my first benzo, Valium, when I was sixteen and came to her one night, unable to sleep. In the world I grew up in, psychiatric drugs promised healing, salvation, a cure—and I bought into all of it. So I didn't hesitate when my psychiatrist prescribed me 100 milligrams of Zoloft and 1.5 milligrams of Klonopin. I was ready to do anything—give up drinking, recommit to my psych meds, run a marathon—to silence the voice of criticism and doubt that lived in my head; anything to be happy.

Fast-forward four years, and I left my gynecologist's office frightened by the word dependency and immediately, rashly, cut my dose in half. I also made an appointment with Mary Braud, M.D., a psychiatrist well known in Denver for her holistic approach toward mental wellness.

On a hot day in late July, Braud explained to me that my story of inadvertently becoming dependent on benzos was all too common. "I've seen a lot of people who are shocked and surprised that a medicine that they were given that they thought was OK is now creating a big problem for them."

In her view, one that is gaining popularity among progressive psychiatrists and supported by new research, anxiety is a complex problem caused by an array of factors including genetic predispositions, digestive health, diet, and trauma. It's not something you're just born with, and it's not something that benzos can truly fix. "The benzo is never going to heal anything or give the body what it truly needs to function better. And, in fact, it may actually stand in the way of that happening for people," Braud said.

Together, we started to unravel the roots of my angst, and I came to better understand how my mother's instability had planted the seeds of my condition. The question of whether she would be there the next day was often very real, and it helps explain the irrational uncertainty I feel about my future and relationships.

I also started to realize there were incidents along the way that, in hindsight, should have been alarming. In 2012, two days into a ski trip in Telluride, Colorado, I ran out of Klonopin. That night, my brain felt like a bundle of frayed electric wires shooting sparks across my skull, I was overwhelmed by self-loathing, and I couldn't sleep, despite the fact that I was exhausted after a day on the slopes and that I'd dosed myself with Tylenol PM. The next morning, I cut my trip short and drove home. What I didn't understand then was that I was in benzo withdrawal.

Some studies suggest that long-term benzo use may impair the body's natural ability to produce and access GABA. When benzos are discontinued or the dose is lowered, the central nervous system may go into overdrive, causing withdrawal, which can even occur between pills if your body has developed a tolerance to your dose.

More than a year after my gynecologist refused to renew my prescription, I've started to slowly taper my dose, with Braud's guidance, and I'm down to .62 milligrams a day. I've revamped my diet, cutting back on refined sugar and caffeine, which really rev up my anxiety, as well as gluten and dairy, which recent studies indicate may cause inflammation in the gut that triggers mood disorders. I've started taking supplements like Pharma GABA (amazing), magnesium, and fish oil, which studies suggest help the brain make the good chemicals that moderate mood and anxiety. I try to get at least eight hours of sleep a night. I ski, bike, run, climb mountains, and spend time in nature every chance I can.

Here I am nearly six years alcohol-free and staring down a different beast, benzodiazepines. For the most part, giving up alcohol was easy and the results were almost immediate. But whenever I lower my Klonopin dose too rapidly, my world starts to teeter out of control. If I had known back in 2008 what I know now about benzos, I don't think I would have filled all those prescriptions. Yet amid the fear of quitting, there's a familiar feeling: that same desire for a better life and my mother's whisper urging me toward it.

Print Citations

CMS: McMillan, Kelley. "The Truth about Prescription Pills: One Writer's Story of Anxiety and Addictions." In *The Reference Shelf: Prescription Drug Abuse*, edited by Betsy Maury, 35-39. Ipswich, MA: H.W. Wilson, 2017.

MLA: McMillan, Kelley. "The Truth about Prescription Pills: One Writer's Story of Anxiety and Addictions." *The Reference Shelf: Prescription Drug Abuse*. Ed. Betsy Maury. Ipswich: H.W. Wilson, 2017. 35-39. Print.

APA: McMillan, K. (2017). The truth about prescription pills: One writer's story of anxiety and addictions. In Betsy Maury (Ed.), *The reference shelf: Prescription drug abuse* (pp. 35-39). Ipswich, MA: H.W. Wilson. (Original work published 2014)

Almost Half of All Opioid Misuse Starts with a Friend or Family Member's Prescription

By Roni Dengler

PBS NewsHour, July 31, 2017

More than half of adults who misused opioids did not have a prescription, and many obtained drugs for free from friends or relatives, according to a national survey of more than 50,000 adults.

Although many people need medical narcotics for legitimate reasons, the National Survey on Drug Use and Health reported Monday that regular access to prescription opioids can facilitate misuse. The results, outlined in the *Annals of Internal Medicine*, indicate when the medical community overprescribes opioids, unused drugs are then available for abuse.

"We need to improve our approaches to evaluating, treating and providing services to people who suffer from pain," Wilson Compton, deputy director at the National Institute on Drug Abuse and the study's lead author, told *NewsHour*.

To get a handle on the nation's drug problem, the Substance Abuse and Mental Health Services Administration surveyed 51,200 individuals from 50 states and the District of Columbia. Each participant completed computer-based surveys at home, was a non-institutionalized civilian over age 12, provided informed consent and received $30 on completion.

Researchers conduct the survey annually, but 2015 was the first time the survey included information about the overall use of prescription opioids. Previously, the survey only asked respondents about rates of misuse or addiction to various substances. This change revealed the proportion of opioid misuse among the general population was tied to doctor's prescriptions.

The researchers expected opioid prescribing to be commonplace. But, the numbers—38 percent of U.S. adults used opioid medication in 2015—were still shocking. "In any one group, every third person or more is using at some point," Compton said.

The major culprit behind the misuse is excessive prescriptions, the survey found, with doctors providing patients with too many pills for too long. After delivering a baby, for example, women typically use half of what they're given, said Stephen Patrick, a Vanderbilt University neonatologist who was not involved in the study.

Physicians worry the road to overprescribing has been paved with good intentions. Concern about undertreating patient pain among physicians was roughly on-par with attention to a patient's heart rate, said Karen Lasser, a general internist at Boston Medical Center who was not involved in the study.

Patrick agreed, saying, "It started in the '80s, thinking about how we take care of untreated pain. We had some science that was wrong about the risk of addiction potential when you treat [people with pain]."

But, medical professionals aren't the only factor driving the epidemic. Hopelessness and despair also likely fuel this problem, she said. Studies have shown people often self-medicate their anxiety and depression with opioids. Lasser has seen this pattern in the clinic.

"When [my patients] come in complaining of physical pain, I can tell it's more than just physical pain," Lasser said. "It's almost like it's suffering or psychosocial issues going on that are manifesting as pain."

Nearly two-thirds of respondents who used opioids inappropriately said they misused them to relieve physical pain. They used the drugs for their own treatment or to cope with pain. Yet, more and more research shows these narcotics are not effective for chronic pain, Patrick said.

The results of the survey agree that the nation's pain problem extends beyond the physical body. People with opioid use disorder were more likely to have a psychiatric diagnosis and poor health. Misuse was more prevalent among those with major depressive episodes or suicidal ideation than those without.

Out of adults who reported misusing opioids, 60 percent did not have a prescription.

Limited access to treatment may compound drug abuse pervasiveness. More people who reported misusing prescription opioids were uninsured, unemployed, had low income or had behavioral health problems.

It may be easier for the uninsured to treat their pain, whether truly physical or not, by skipping the doctor and getting it from other sources instead, Lasser said.

Out of adults who reported misusing opioids, 60 percent did not have a prescription. Nearly half of these individuals—41 percent—obtained non-prescribed drugs for free from friends or relatives.

This information changes physicians' roles. They're not just caring for the person directly in front of them, but also the patient's social network—their family members, friends and neighbors among others. "That's a really big shift in the role for medical professionals," Compton said.

On the national level, the Department of Health and Human Services brought together experts from the National Institutes of Health, NIDA and other agencies to create the National Pain Strategy to develop new approaches to treating pain. The strategy includes measures to standardize pain assessments, which could help physicians determine underlying causes of chronic pain and when opioid prescriptions are appropriate. It also calls for more comprehensive approaches to pain evaluation that include physical, psychological, emotional and social aspects.

One quick and fast solution is to write fewer, smaller prescriptions for opioids because "there are way too many leftover medications that end up being diverted or misused," Compton said.

Along with that, pharmacies now have authority to dispense partial prescriptions. Prescription drug monitoring programs can identify over prescribing doctors and patients who are doctor shopping, Patrick said.

Print Citations

CMS: Dengler, Roni. "Almost Half of All Opioid Misuse Starts with a Friend or Family Member's Prescription." In *The Reference Shelf: Prescription Drug Abuse*, edited by Betsy Maury, 40-42. Ipswich, MA: H.W. Wilson, 2017.

MLA: Dengler, Roni. "Almost Half of All Opioid Misuse Starts with a Friend or Family Member's Prescription." *The Reference Shelf: Prescription Drug Abuse*. Ed. Betsy Maury. Ipswich: H.W. Wilson, 2017. 40-42. Print.

APA: Dengler, R. (2017). Almost half of all opioid misuse starts with a friend or family member's prescription. In Betsy Maury (Ed.), *The reference shelf: Prescription drug abuse* (pp. 40-42). Ipswich, MA: H.W. Wilson. (Original work published 2017)

Yes, Benzos Are Bad for You

By Allen Frances
The Huffington Post, July 1, 2016

Most new wonder drugs turn out to be not so wonderful once we get to know them better. The family of drugs known as benzodiazepines (commonly called "benzos" for short) were wonder drugs of the 1960s. I and many others welcomed their introduction and began prescribing Valium or Librium not just for anxiety, but also for all sorts of other clinical problems beyond this primary indication—for instance, to soothe psychotic patients' symptoms, to help people with alcohol use disorders quit drinking, to take the edge off agitation in depression and dementia, and to aid sleep. Benzos were reputed to be safe, and initially we were pretty oblivious to the risk of addiction. Before long, benzos became among the most frequently prescribed medications in America.

A second benzo craze began in the 1980s when Xanax became the new wonder drug. Its maker, Upjohn (then run by a former head of the NIH), fashioned a brilliant marketing strategy—hiding the company's wolfish greed for profit under the sheep's clothing of research sponsorship. Upjohn was able to co-opt the top academic psychiatrists from all around the world by organizing the first large-scale international clinical trial of any psychiatric drug. The results were disturbing to me as an outside observer. By then I had wised up to the great risk of benzos and was not surprised to discover that the dose of Xanax needed to treat panic disorder was dangerously close to the dose needed to result in addiction. This should have scared off everyone from using Xanax, but it didn't. Xanax quickly became, and remains, a best seller.

The real wonder of the benzos is that sales continue to boom, despite their having so little utility and no push from pharma marketeering (because patents have run out—thereby decreasing costs and profits.) Between 1996 and 2013, the percentage of people in the U.S. using benzos jumped more than one-third from an already remarkable 4.1 to 5.6 percent. Especially troubling is that benzo use is ridiculously high (nearly one out of ten) in the elderly, the group most likely to be harmed by them. And women are twice as likely as men to be given a prescription.

You would expect such a ubiquitous drug to have many clinical uses but you would be wrong—the psychiatric indications for benzos can be counted on the fingers of one hand. While benzos do wonders for patients with catatonia, this disorder is rarely encountered. Benzos are also useful short-term for severe agitation in psychosis, mania, and depression. And they are sometimes helpful for patients with severe panic disorder who need instant relief in the several weeks before selective serotonin reuptake inhibitor (SSRIs) kick in. Benzos would be fine for occasional "as needed" use in times of special stress or insomnia. But since you can't predict who will get hooked, it is wise not to try them at all for this purpose. In my opinion, all of the legitimate indications for benzos are very short term. However, in real life most people take them long term, in doses high enough to be addicting, and for the wrong reasons.

Benzo popularity derives from their ability to quickly relieve anxiety, reduce worry, help people relax, and lubricate social anxiety—kind of like drinking alcohol but in a convenient pill form. Doctors love prescribing benzos because it's the most efficient way to get a complaining patient out of the office in the shortest possible time. The patient is very satisfied at the moment, but may go on to develop a devastating addiction. People love taking them but once hooked can't stop. In short, benzos are very easy to get on, almost impossible to get off. Benzos harm in three ways— most dramatic dangers are deadly overdoses. Between 1996 and 2013, the death rate from benzo overdoses exploded by more than 500 percent, from 0.58 per 100,000 people to 3 per 100,000. Benzos are now involved in more than 30 per cent of all overdose deaths, usually in combination with opioids or alcohol.

> Benzo popularity derives from their ability to quickly relieve anxiety, reduce worry, help people relax, and lubricate social anxiety—kind of like drinking alcohol but in a convenient pill form.

Second on the list of harms come the painful and dangerous withdrawal symptoms that foster addiction. Benzo withdrawal is a beast—often terrifying, sometimes dangerous, and almost always drawn out over a very long period of time. The anxiety and panic experienced by people stopping benzos is usually much worse than the anxiety and panic that initially led to their use. Other common symptoms are irritability, insomnia, tremors, distractibility, sweating, and confusion. At the extreme, if doses were high and discontinuation is quick, the symptoms resemble alcoholic delirium tremens with hallucinations, psychosis, seizures, and the risk of death. Withdrawal is made even more difficult if, as is common, benzo dependence is complicated by concomitant abuse of alcohol and/or opioids or other drugs. Most people fail in their first attempts at withdrawal. Success rates increase if the withdrawal is done very gradually over a period of many months. Careful medical supervision is always a must.

Third and most insidious, but still very damaging, are the day-to-day impacts on brain functioning. On-going benzo use can be devastating, especially in the elderly, who (bizarrely) are the group most likely to receive a benzo prescription. If you meet an elderly patient who seems dopey, confused, has memory loss, slurred speech, and poor balance, your first thought should be benzo side effects—not Alzheimer's disease or dementia. Many elders begin their downward spiral to disability and death after a benzo-induced fall that results in broken hips, concussions, or subdural hematomas (a collection of blood outside the brain.) Benzos are also a major risk factor for car and machine accidents.

Easier said than done. Along with opioids and methamphetamine, benzos are the most seductive of drugs. The combination of benzos and opioids is especially seductive and especially deadly. In my book, no one with any history of substance abuse should ever be prescribed a benzo. It will most likely just get added to the mix.

Benzos should never be used as they are most typically used. While safe and effective in low doses for just a few days, they are ineffective and unsafe when taken, as they usually are, in increasing doses over a long period of time. If prescribed at all in someone who has never used them before, it should be cautiously and with warnings. The time period should be short, the dose low, and quantity very limited at any one time. Real world practice flagrantly violates all these concerns—90 percent of benzo prescriptions are written, often carelessly, by primary care doctors, who can spend only seven minutes with the patient without giving serious thought to the considerable risk of addiction.

The bottom line is that there is only one way to confidently avoid addiction to benzodiazepines: never start taking them. Since we can't predict who will eventually get hooked, the short term gains are rarely worth the long term risks.

It has been more than 30 years since I last prescribed a benzo for anxiety. In my view, the only legitimate uses in psychiatry now are very short-term relief of catatonia, for severe agitation, and for detox from benzos. For everyone else, risk of addiction outweighs the potential benefit of use.

The tough question is what to recommend for those many unfortunates already suffering the tyranny of benzo addiction. Should they stay the course to avoid the rigors and risks of withdrawal or should they make the great effort to detox? This is an individual decision that can't be forced on someone. But the longer you are on them, the harder it gets to stop, and the cognitive side effects of benzos create more and more dysfunction as your brain ages. The best bet is to stick with a determined effort to detox, however long and difficult, under close medical supervision. On a hopeful note, some of the happiest people I have known are those who have overcome their dependence on benzos.

Print Citations

CMS: Frances, Allen. "Yes, Benzos Are Bad for You." In *The Reference Shelf: Prescription Drug Abuse*, edited by Betsy Maury, 43-46. Ipswich, MA: H.W. Wilson, 2017.

MLA: Frances, Allen. "Yes, Benzos Are Bad for You." *The Reference Shelf: Prescription Drug Abuse*. Ed. Betsy Maury. Ipswich: H.W. Wilson, 2017. 43-46. Print.

APA: Frances, A. (2017). Yes, benzos are bad for you. In Betsy Maury (Ed.), *The reference shelf: Prescription drug abuse* (pp. 43-46). Ipswich, MA: H.W. Wilson. (Original work published 2016)

Casualties of the VA

By David French
The National Review, July 11, 2016

I drove home from the doctor's office as sad and depressed as I'd ever been in my life. Sitting on the seat beside me were two bags. One contained a small bottle of Ambien, to help me sleep. The other contained sample boxes of Lexapro, an anti-depressant.

For the last three months—the three months since I'd come home from Iraq—I'd been unable to sleep. Every night at ten o'clock, no matter how tired I was, I'd come alive. I'd feel that familiar tension. In Iraq, night was when bad things happened. Night was when friends died. Night was when we had to make our tough choices. When I was outside the wire, it was often at night. Night was when the detainees rolled in. At night I had to be alert.

But not at home. At home I needed sleep. The kids would be up at 7:00 a.m. I had to be at work around 8:00. I supervised a dozen lawyers and practiced law against attorneys from some of America's best law firms. I had to be sharp. I was anything but.

And so I went to the doctor—like so many other American vets. I wanted to sleep again. I wanted to feel normal again. I didn't go to the VA (who needs that kind of wait?), so I went to a local doctor, who told me that I didn't exactly have post-traumatic stress disorder, I mainly just had post-traumatic stress. My brain chemistry had changed while I was downrange, he explained, and now I was wired to wake up at night and catch sleep when I could. He said I needed help. The pills were the help.

I've thought about that day many times as I've met more and more vets who have struggled after coming home. As a JAG officer, you get to know soldiers better than many other staff officers do. They'll drop by to ask about a family issue, or to discuss their finances, or to ask for career and educational advice. When you're a reserve officer, they know you also work in the "real world," and I've helped dozens of men and women work on their résumés—trying to write about their military experience in ways that civilian employers would understand.

When I was with men (and it was mostly men) who'd had rough deployments—or who'd been deployed multiple times—I'd always ask, "How are you doing? Everything okay?" Most of the time the answer was a quick, "I'm cool." Often enough,

---

however, it was something else—some variation of "Sir, I don't know. I just don't feel like myself."

Then they'd open up. They couldn't sleep, so they had to take Ambien. They were depressed, so they were taking Lexapro. They had chronic neck and back pain after hanging 90 pounds of gear on their frame day after day, month after month, so they took Lortab. They were anxious, so they took Xanax. But it wasn't helping, they said. They felt sluggish. They had trouble staying motivated. They just didn't feel *right*.

But how could they? It was as if their VA doctor had simply listened to a list of symptoms, located a pill to address each complaint, loaded up the patient with prescriptions, and called it "treating" a soldier for PTSD. But the treatment left young men in the prime of their lives with hollowed eyes and slurred speech. They didn't want to live like that—and they hated what they'd become—but they had PTSD, right? What choice did they have?

And so it goes, the cycle for "treating" American veterans. Under pressure for failing to take care of them, the VA and civilian doctors dramatically over-diagnose PTSD, over-prescribe often-addictive pills, and then wonder why their patients often report profound dissatisfaction with their lives.

The numbers are staggering. In 2014, the VA reported that it had treated almost 375,000 returning Afghanistan and Iraq vets for PTSD, and it estimated that roughly one in five post-9/11 veterans suffered from the disorder. The contrast with the British army is striking. While the U.S. dealt with a PTSD epidemic, the Brits—whose soldiers also fought hard in Iraq and Afghanistan—reported that only 7 percent of their returning combat soldiers suffered from PTSD. The proportion of noncombat soldiers suffering from PTSD was only between 2 and 5 percent.

Are the Brits more stoic than Americans? Can they better handle the trauma of war? Perhaps at the margins, but certainly not enough to account for the dramatic difference in the percentages.

So what is the explanation? The VA publishes a list of PTSD symptoms, and these lists are repeated endlessly during post-deployment briefings. Having trouble sleeping? You might have PTSD. Are you startled by loud noises? You might have PTSD. Do you keep busy to avoid thinking about a traumatic event? You might have PTSD. As I surveyed the list, I could check off approximately half the symptoms.

It's a recipe for over-diagnosis. People who come back from war—especially if they were either in combat arms or deployed with a combat-arms unit—are going to experience dramatic psychological changes. It's inevitable. Young men will find themselves grieving death perhaps for the first time in their lives. They'll face stress that civilians can't possibly imagine, and they'll feel fear at a level they could never have anticipated. What does "normal" life look like after an experience like that? Is it even possible to be "normal" again? Yet rather than prepare soldiers for a new normal, we try vainly to "fix" what's allegedly broken. And we do it with pills.

In 2014, an inspector-general report found that the VA was systematically over-medicating its patients—even to the point of death. The findings were horrifying. A stunning 93 percent of long-term narcotics patients in VA hospitals were also

> **Under pressure for failing to take care of them, the VA and civilian doctors dramatically over-diagnose PTSD, over-prescribe often-addictive pills, and then wonder why their patients often report profound dissatisfaction with their lives.**

prescribed benzodiazepines, a combination that increases the risk of a fatal overdose. Fewer than half of narcotics patients on multiple drugs "had their medications reviewed by VA staff," according to *CBS News*. One vet told *CBS News* that he'd lost more friends at home to narcotics than he'd lost overseas to enemy action.

Wisconsin's Senate race is being roiled by a report on the VA facility at Tomah, a place so notorious for freely writing narcotics prescriptions that it gained the nickname "Candyland." Senator Ron Johnson and his Democratic challenger, former senator Russ Feingold, are locked in a war of words over the scandal, with a familiar question hovering over the controversy: Who knew? The facility has been linked to multiple fatal overdoses.

It is difficult for veterans to reverse course once they become dependent on their prescriptions. Many of the over-prescribed drugs are extraordinarily addictive, and young soldiers are now facing rehab and long-term care not just for PTSD but also for drug dependence. They came to the VA for help getting through a difficult life experience, many were diagnosed with a malady they did not have, and now they're addicted to drugs they never truly needed.

I've often reflected on the vast and yawning gap between my expectations and reality. I went to war as one of the oldest members of my unit—a 38-year-old captain who'd joined later in life. I thought that the extra years would give me the maturity I needed to absorb the shock of war. I thought I could go to war and return more or less the same person.

I was wrong—profoundly wrong. When I came home, grief clung to me. My personality had changed. I was far more aggressive and far less tolerant of others than I'd ever been before. And I just couldn't sleep. No matter how exhausted I was.

And so there I was, in my car, staring at medications I never thought I'd take. Medication was how other people handled their problems. But now I was "other people." I didn't know what else to do.

That first night, I took the Ambien, and I didn't remember anything from 11:00 p.m. until my alarm rang the next morning. I felt terrible. I hated that I couldn't remember part of the night before, I didn't feel rested, and I felt mildly hung over. But I took it again and again, and I just felt worse. I felt boxed in. I could sleep only with Ambien, but when I slept, I didn't truly rest. I was becoming the exact person I'd seen others become.

So I stopped. I didn't take another Ambien, and I didn't take a single Lexapro. Instead, I prayed and I talked. I prayed that God would grant me rest, and I opened up more to friends and family—describing the men they'd never known but who'd become closer than brothers to me, and describing what it was like to stand at attention saluting them one last time as their bodies were carried away.

Gradually, things got better. I slept a little more each night as my body retrained itself, remembering that here at home the night is not full of stress and fury. As I got more sleep, I got less aggressive, less irritable.

But I never became normal again. Or, more precisely, I had a new normal. My wife says I'm dramatically different from the man she married, and she says that it's mostly for the better. My experience was nothing like that of some of the heroes I served with, but war changes us all. There is not a pill made that can change us back.

There are veterans who truly suffer from PTSD—complete with symptoms that are the stuff of nightmares. But there are many other veterans who don't suffer from PTSD but are treated for it. There are many veterans who can learn to manage their pain, but they're drugged to the point of near-death.

I still have the Lexapro boxes. They sit in my medicine cabinet—right next to a small bottle of now-expired Ambien pills. They remind me of where I was, they remind me of God's grace, and they remind me of the men and women who are trapped by their own prescriptions.

Here is the sad reality: Your husband or son can come home from war but get lost in a pill bottle—a pill bottle pushed into his hands by the instruments of America's most dysfunctional medical bureaucracy. That's not treatment, it's abuse. And it's abuse that is increasing the casualties of America's longest war. The VA is killing men the Taliban couldn't touch.

Print Citations

CMS: French, David. "Casualties of the VA." In *The Reference Shelf: Prescription Drug Abuse*, edited by Betsy Maury, 47-50. Ipswich, MA: H.W. Wilson, 2017.

MLA: French, David. "Casualties of the VA."   *The Reference Shelf: Prescription Drug Abuse*. Ed. Betsy Maury. Ipswich: H.W. Wilson, 2017. 47-50. Print.

APA: French, D. (2017). Casualties of the VA. In Betsy Maury (Ed.), *The reference shelf: Prescription drug abuse* (pp. 47-50). Ipswich, MA: H.W. Wilson. (Original work published 2016)

War on Prescription Drugs: What If You Depend on Opioids to Live a Decent Life?

By S.E. Smith
The Guardian, July 12, 2016

The US is facing what many are describing as an opioid crisis, with growing numbers of deaths associated both with opioid medications and overdoses on heroin—19,000 in 2014 linked to opioids alone. But in the swirl of debate over the subject, there's one group of Americans we aren't hearing from: chronic pain patients, many of whom need to use opioids on a long-term basis to control their pain effectively.

Unlike patients with acute, short-term pain or pain associated with terminal illnesses such as cancer, they're looking at a lifetime of living with conditions such as Ehlers-Danlos syndrome, fibromyalgia and endometriosis, along with many other disorders associated with chronic pain. Others are dealing with persistent pain from injuries.

Many have conflicted relationships with the medications they need to enjoy a good quality of life, and they fight a tough battle against negative public perception and cultural attitudes. They're struggling with issues that aren't being accounted for in conversations about dependence, addiction and the safe use of opioids for long-term pain management.

Heather Ace Ratcliff, who has Type 3 Ehlers-Danlos, a connective tissue disorder characterized by hypermobility which allows her joints to dislocate and subluxate easily, says uninformed views can stigmatize chronic pain patients who are struggling to access relief. "I am regularly treated as if I am overreacting, a hypochondriac, or a drug addict for wanting an increase in pain management," she says, illustrating the consequences of misinformation about opioids and pain.

But those attitudes are internalized as well. Even though many patients recognize that opioids help them manage pain effectively, some still fear them, worrying that their relationship with their medication may be sliding into addiction. At the same time, they're dealing with side effects like fatigue, "brain fog" and gastrointestinal stress. In an environment where physicians who aren't extensively familiar with pain management and opioids can leap to conclusions, it can be difficult for patients to have honest conversations with their doctors about their concerns, as they may fear being chastised or cut off.

Shayla Maas, another patient with Type 3 Ehlers-Danlos who also has an auto-immune disorder, says that the conversation surrounding opioids sometimes makes her paranoid about her medications. "Maybe I'm just blowing it out of proportion," she says, "looking for attention, looking for meds." She can hardly be blamed for her self-doubt, as that's precisely the kind of messaging she receives as a chronic pain patient, and it's easy to internalise the fear, she says, that you might become a "dope fiend."

Anna H, a patient with fibromyalgia, shares these worries. "I've been taking relatively small doses of pain meds every day for about six years, but I'm still afraid that taking a certain amount of pills—even if I'm in a lot of pain—will send me down the path of addiction."

Their fears are to some extent grounded in reality: opioid medications can have an addicting effect. But the real story is more complicated.

"Opioids are the cornerstone of the treatment of pain," explains doctor Anita Gupta, a board-certified anesthesiologist, pain specialist, pharmacist and vice-chair of Drexel College of Medicine's division of pain medicine in Philadelphia. Among her many roles, she also serves as vice-chair of the American Society of Anesthesiologist's ad hoc committee on prescription opioid abuse and has a vested interest in addressing the misuse of opioids. But she also has concerns about inadequate information that harms both patients and providers.

Gupta makes an important distinction between dependence and addiction, cutting to the heart of one of the greatest misunderstandings in the conversation about pain management. "If you're on opioid medication for a long period of time, you become dependent," she explains. "When a need becomes a want, that is really an example of when someone can become addicted. When you want it and you can't live without it, can't survive without it, it interrupts your day to day life, that's addiction."

> **A motto designed to humanize the experience of addiction has been turned into a weapon that targets people who rely on opioids for pain management, and that translates to real-world stigma.**

Though organizations like the American Academy of Chronic Pain Management, US Pain Foundation and the American Chronic Pain Association engage in patient advocacy work, it can be a struggle. Even with the weight of patients, family, and medical providers behind these groups, they aren't always treated as stakeholders in processes like developing new guidelines for opioid prescription and use.

"There's a saying that goes something like: 'We are all one drink or pill away from addiction,' and I know this is meant to destigmatize what addicts go through, but I feel like I've been seeing variations on this 'common knowledge' more and more lately being used (on social media) as a cudgel to remind patients to not overdo it," Anna says, speaking to the dual-edged sword of awareness. A motto designed to humanize the experience of addiction has been turned into a weapon that targets people who rely on opioids for pain management, and that translates to real-world stigma.

"When other people find out that I'm on opioids," Maas explains, "depending on how close they are and how well they know me, I might get an 'it sucks that your pain is so bad' to a slightly narrowed side eye." The judgmental comments she receives make her feel like people think she's taking opioids for the fun of it.

"Believe me," she says, "this is not for fun."

"I haven't really experienced the stigma personally other than some ill-informed comments from acquaintances," says Anna. "But the media coverage of the 'opiate epidemic' as driven by pill pushing-doctors and by pain patients worries me a lot, and I think it is already being used to forward the idea that people in chronic pain should not have access to relief from their pain."

Both Maas and Anna articulate worries that chronic pain patients are being "thrown under the bus." Doctor Jerrold Winter, professor of pharmacology and toxicology at the University at Buffalo, tends to agree, and is concerned that new CDC guidelines and other efforts to address opioid use could actually make the situation worse.

"I think [the CDC guidelines] go much too far and (a) will leave many in pain and (b) will drive some seeking pain relief into the illicit market with all its hazards," he says. "Indeed, two NIDA officials recently pointed out that the rate of deaths from prescription opiates between 2011 and 2013 were stable while heroin-related death rates rose dramatically. I fear that this trend will only worsen under the CDC guidelines."

Gupta points out that the most important tool for addressing addiction is a simple conversation: patients need to be open with their care providers, working with them on an effective pain management plan and addressing warning signs of addiction promptly. Patients experiencing cravings for their medication along with symptoms like mood changes, difficulty sleeping, oversensitivity to stimuli and increased blood pressure may be exhibiting signs of dependence that has transitioned into abuse.

The ability to be open about these symptoms along with concerns about degree of dependence on opioid medication will help patients make sound decisions about their care.

That requires both clinician and patient education, as well as listening to the fears of chronic pain patients like Maas and Ratcliff as they attempt to balance chronic pain, fears about forming addictive habits and frustration with public perception. Both doctors and patients need to be playing a more prominent role in the unfolding conversation about how to deal with a very real American public health crisis.

Print Citations

CMS: Smith, S.E. "War on Prescription Drugs: What If You Depend on Opioids to Live a Decent Life?" In *The Reference Shelf: Prescription Drug Abuse*, edited by Betsy Maury, 51-54. Ipswich, MA: H.W. Wilson, 2017.

MLA: Smith, S.E. "War on Prescription Drugs: What If You Depend on Opioids to Live a Decent Life?" *The Reference Shelf: Prescription Drug Abuse*. Ed. Betsy Maury. Ipswich: H.W. Wilson, 2017. 51-54. Print.

APA: Smith, S.E. War on prescription drugs: What if you depend on opioids to live a decent life? In Betsy Maury (Ed.), *The reference shelf: Prescription drug abuse* (pp. 51-54). Ipswich, MA: H.W. Wilson. (Original work published 2016)

2
Drugs for Young and Old

Credit: Photo by Linda Davidson / The Washington Post via Getty Images

A man walks his dog along the road to Mackworth Island in Falmouth, ME on July 2, 2015. The middle to upper-class suburb of Portland is not immune to heroin addiction which was once thought to be a drug for the lower class. Heroin use among Americans nationwide is skyrocketing as the price of the drug dropped to as low as $10 a hit. The availability is widespread and users could range anywhere from the upper middle-class professional to soccer moms to college students. Many started on prescription pills like oxycodone and found themselves addicted. Once that was cut off, they found themselves in need of a black market opiate.

Spectrum of Risk

While prescription drug abuse affects individuals of every age and background, there are certain groups for whom the risk of abuse and dependence is especially high. Researchers studying the problem have found patterns of risk related to an individual's gender, ethnicity, age, socioeconomic status, and mental health status, in addition to other factors. In attempting to combat the problem, it is important for researchers to understand why some groups are at higher risk and, when possible, to create treatment and prevention strategies tailored to each at-risk group.

Teens and Young Adults

According to the National Institute on Drug Abuse (NIDA), prescription drug abuse is highest among teens (ages 12 to 17) and young adults (ages 18 to 25), with 5.9 percent of the young adult population and 3 percent of the teen population reporting nonmedical use of prescription drugs in a 2010 survey. Teens and young adults are also more likely to mix prescription drugs with other intoxicants and so are more likely to have problems with drug interactions that can increase the likelihood of an overdose.[1]

There are many reasons why teens and young adults gravitate towards drug use, and numerous studies have found a correlation between drug abuse and self-esteem or self-image and individuals who suffer from self-esteem issues are more likely to abuse both illicit and prescription drugs. According to a 2012 article in *LiveScience*, studies indicate that many children and teenagers begin using drugs to cope with the social and emotional turbulence of adolescence and that many view prescription drugs as a safer alternative to illicit substances because the drugs are used in legitimate therapy and because teens and young adults can identify with many of the issues treated with prescription drugs, like depression and anxiety.[2]

In addition, teens and young adults in different social groups or youth cultures display a marked tendency towards certain types of drugs. A 2008 study found that stimulants were the most popular prescription drug abused by college students, who typically reported using stimulants to enhance their ability to work and study.[3] A 2013 report in *Drug Alcohol Review* found that prescription drug abuse was highest in the electronic dance music and alt rock/indie rock music subcultures, with more than half of all participants in these subcultures reporting some degree of prescription drug use. By contrast, prescription drugs are far less popular within the hip hop subculture, where 25 percent reported abuse. The authors found that the prevalence of prescription drugs within the various subcultures also reflected ethnic, racial, and age preferences within each subculture.[4] Youth subculture overlaps with other cultural divisions in drug use and studies have found, for instance, that

African Americans are far less likely to use prescription drugs than individuals in any other racial group.[5]

A recent trend in the prescription drug crisis involves the use of social media and web markets. In some cases, investigations have found teens and young adults advertising their need for depressants, stimulants, or pain medication to friends on Facebook or other social media channels and these avenues of communication have thus fostered a dangerous exchange of drugs in some social circles. In addition, there are websites, some forming part of what criminal justice specialists call the "dark web," on which users can seek out and purchase a wide variety of illegal goods, from firearms, to pirated media, to prescription drugs. While any individual might be able to access online drug markets, younger individuals are typically more aware of, familiar with, and better able to use emerging digital resources and so are more likely to use online markets to locate and purchase prescription drugs. Online markets pose an additional danger because the buyer cannot be certain if the substances purchased are legitimate and because it is difficult to determine the strength and/or purity of pills purchased from anonymous users.

According to NIDA, in 2014 more than 1,700 young adults, ages 18 to 24, died from a prescription drug overdose, equaling nearly 5 overdoses per day. Reviewing annual statistics, the Centers for Disease Control and Prevention (CDC) found that four times as many young people overdosed on prescription drugs in 2014 than in 1999. Furthermore, for every one of the 1700 young adults who died from an overdose in 2014, 119 young adults were admitted to an emergency room for prescription drug complications and 22 young adults were admitted into a treatment program for drug abuse.[6]

Drug Abuse among the Elderly

Older adults are also at increased risk of abusing and misusing prescription drugs, though often for different reasons than children, teens, and young adults. One of the primary reasons that older adults are at increased risk, is because older individuals more often suffer from physical disabilities that warrant the medical use of prescription pain relievers, stimulants, and depressants. Chronic pain, sleeplessness, insomnia, depression, and anxiety are more common among older individuals and this increases the likelihood of physicians prescribing potentially dangerous medication that can lead to dependency and abuse.

In the United States, individuals age 65 or older account for around 13 percent of the population, but receive more than 33 percent of all prescriptions written by physicians. Moreover, the percentage of older adults taking medication over long periods has increased and overreliance on prescription medication, especially when physicians are working with older patients, is a significant problem that contributes to the high levels of prescription drug misuse among the elderly. A study in 2000, for instance, indicated that approximately half of US older adults were taking three or more medications per day, an increase from only about one-third in 1988.[7] Studies also indicate that elderly individuals are misusing prescription drugs more frequently than in the past. A 2012 study by the Office of Applied Studies found that

442,000 adults over 65 reported using prescription drugs in a way other than was recommended by their physicians.[8]

Surveys of the elderly indicate that intentional misuse and abuse of drugs is relatively rare, compared to other subsets of the population. However, unintentional misuse is especially high among the elderly and this is partially due to cognitive difficulties leading to poor medical management. In addition, because elderly individuals are more likely to be taking two or more medications simultaneously, older individuals are at an increased risk for unintentional side effects due to drug interactions. The risk of interactions is also higher due to the fact that a person's metabolism slows with age, making it more difficult to process and eliminate drugs and alcohol from the body. Elderly individuals who consume alcohol, therefore, run a higher risk of experiencing side effects due to alcohol and drug interactions due to the fact that older bodies process both substances more slowly. Alcohol intensifies the effects of opioids and central nervous system (CNS) depressants, depressing cognitive abilities and causing drowsiness and a loss of coordination. This can be especially dangerous in older individuals, leading to accidental injury, while the depression of the nervous system caused by both alcohol and some prescription drugs can prove fatal when substances are mixed. Research indicates that the combination of alcohol and medication misuse is a problem affecting as many as 19 percent of older Americans.[9]

The Narrowing Gender Gap

The hit Rolling Stones song, "Mother's Little Helper," pays homage to the popularity of the depressant Valium among women, especially mothers, in the 1960s and '70s, to cope with the challenges of motherhood. Despite this pop-culture association, until the 2010s, studies regularly found that women were far less likely to suffer from drug abuse and addiction than men. However, recent research suggests that prescription drug abuse among women is increasing. While men are still more likely to die from overdose or other complications of prescription drug abuse, the gap has begun to close and researchers from the CDC found that the rate of fatal overdoses (of opioids) among women quintupled in the first decade of the twenty-first century, with 6,600 women dying from painkiller overdoses in 2010, compared to 1,300 in 1999.[10]

In some ways, drug addiction and abuse are more dangerous for women than men. For instance, in a 2010 review of research published in the *Psychiatric Clinical North American Journal*, the authors cite a variety of research suggesting that while women abuse drugs less often than men, a variety of psychosocial and hormonal factors suggest that women are more likely to develop addiction once they begin abusing drugs.[11]

In addition, studies indicate that drug abuse affects women more rapidly than men such that a short time abusing alcohol or drugs might have the same negative effects on a woman's body as a much longer period of abuse for a male. This is partially due to the fact that women, on average, have slower metabolisms and so process drugs and alcohol more slowly. In addition, the ratio of fat/water in a woman's body, compared to a man's, means that women tend to retain alcohol and drugs in their tissues for longer and so run a higher risk of drug interactions and other complications.

Furthermore, research has shown that women are more likely than men to suffer from conditions that involve chronic pain and so are more likely to be exposed to opioid pain relievers through a prescription.[12] For instance, due to hormonal differences, women are much more likely to develop the muscular-skeletal disorder fibromyalgia, with women accounting for as much as 90 percent of diagnosed cases, which causes debilitating, long-term pain and is often treated with powerful opioid pain relievers. Studies also indicate that women are more than twice as likely than men to suffer from serious anxiety, thus making women more likely to seek out prescription depressants, like Valium and Xanax. Researchers are investigating the possibility that differences in the production of neurotransmitters, like serotonin, may be the causal factor behind the increased tendency towards anxiety and depression in women. Some studies have also suggested that women are more likely than men to *admit* having pain, anxiety, or depression to their physician and so more likely to receive pharmacological treatment. The most dangerous situations occur when CNS depressants are mixed with alcohol or with opioid painkillers, producing a potentially fatal effect on the nervous system.[13]

Risks and Strategies

While prescription drug abuse affects individuals in many different groups and subsets of society, there are commonalities between at-risk groups that might help explain why some individuals are more prone to abuse than others. Overall, women, the elderly, and younger individuals are more likely to suffer from depression and anxiety, and studies have shown that mental health plays a major role in the potential for drug abuse and addiction. Those at risk are therefore also those with the most pressing need for help coping with mental and physical difficulties that limit quality of life and motivate the desire to alleviate suffering through substance use.

In many cases, individuals who become dependent on prescription drugs deepen their use of drugs in part because they trust that medications prescribed by physicians are less dangerous or carry less stigma than illegal drugs. Therefore, individuals who might not use heroin, because of the social cultural stigma surrounding the drug or the impression that heroin use is dangerous and potentially life-threatening, might be comfortable taking prescription opioids that contain the same chemical ingredients. Drug industry manipulation and misinformation is partially to blame for this mistaken impression of prescription drugs and education is therefore one of the most important keys to the problem. Moving forward, individuals in at-risk groups must be made aware of the dangers of prescription drug abuse and, when such medications are needed, should be provided with ways to mitigate risk and avoid dangerous complications.

Micah L. Issitt

Works Used

"Abuse of Prescription (Rx) Drugs Affects Young Adults Most." *NIDA*. National Institute on Drug Abuse. Aug 2016. Web. 21 Aug 2017.

"Addiction in Women." *Harvard Health Publications*. Harvard Medical School. Jan 2010. Web. 22 Aug 2017.

"Adolescents and Young Adults." *NIDA*. National Institute on Drug Abuse. National Institute of Health. Aug 2016. Web. 20 Aug 2017.

Basca, Belinda. "The Elderly and Prescription Drug Misuse and Abuse." *Center for Applied Research Solutions*. California Department of Alcohol and Drug Programs. 2008. Pdf. 21 Aug 2017.

Broman, Clifford L., Miller, Paula K., and Emmanue Jackson. "Race-ethnicity and Prescription Drug Misuse: Does Self-esteem Matter?" *Journal of Child and Adolescent Behavior*. Sep 3 2015. Vol. 3, No. 239. Web. 21 Aug 2017.

Greenfield, Shelly F., et al. "Substance Abuse in Women." *Psychiatric Clinical North American Journal*. Jun 2010. Vol. 33, No. 2, 339–55.

Kelly, Brian C., et al. "Prescription Drug Misuse among Young Adults: Looking across Youth Cultures." *Drug Alcohol Review*. May 1 2014. Vol. 32, No. 3, 288–94. Web. 21 Aug 2017.

"Painkiller Overdoses in Women." *The New York Times*. The New York Times Co. Jul 7 2013. Web. 22 Aug 2017.

"Prescription Drug Misuse among Older Adults: Understanding the Problem." *SAMHSA*. Substance Abuse and Mental Health Services Administration. 2012. Web. 21 Aug 2017.

Rabiner, David L., et al. "Motives and Perceived Consequences of Nonmedical ADHD Medication Use by College Students." *Journal of Attention Disorders*. Jul 29 2008. Web. 20 Aug 2017.

Salamon, Maureen. "Why Prescription Drug Addiction Is Growing among Teens." *LiveScience*. Feb 16 2012. Web. 21 Aug 2017.

"Specific Populations and Prescription Drug Misuse and Abuse." *SAMHSA*. Substance Abuse and Mental Health Services Administration. Oct 27 2015. Web. 22 Aug 2017.

"Women." *ADAA*. Anxiety and Depression Association of America. 2017. Web. 22 Aug 2017.

Notes

1. "Adolescents and Young Adults," *NIDA*.
2. Salamon, "Why Prescription Drug Addiction Is Growing among Teens."
3. Rabiner, et al., "Motives and Perceived Consequences of Nonmedical ADHD Medication Use by College Students."
4. Kelly, et al., "Prescription Drug Misuse among Young Adults: Looking across Youth Cultures."
5. Broman, Miller, and Jackson, "Race-Ethnicity and Prescription Drug Misuse: Does Self-Esteem Matter?"
6. "Abuse of Prescription (Rx) Drugs Affects Young Adults Most," *NIDA*.

7. Basca, "The Elderly and Prescription Drug Misuse and Abuse."

8. "Prescription Drug Misuse among Older Adults," *SAMHSA*.

9. "Specific Population and Prescription Drug Misuse and Abuse," *SAMHSA*.

10. "Painkiller Overdoses in Women," *The New York Times*.

11. Greenfield, et al., "Substance Abuse in Women."

12. "Addiction in Women," *Harvard Health Publications*.

13. "Women," *ADAA*.

Prescription Drug Abuse among Older Adults Is Harder to Detect

By Constance Gustke

The New York Times, June 10, 2016

Drug addiction is not restricted to the young. Donna Weber, now 53, turned to painkillers after undergoing simple surgery. Then a long, tortured path to divorce made her anxious and depressed. Soon, she found herself on a candy-colored pill roller coaster.

Unlike street drugs, the pharmaceutical pills were easy to obtain legally. She got them from emergency rooms, dentists, psychiatrists, even plastic surgeons. "I went to doctors with exaggerated truths," explained Ms. Weber, who once had four doctors. "I said I hurt more and more."

But constant pill popping took a huge toll. A few years ago, she could barely get out of her bedroom. Sometimes she woke up and felt like she couldn't breathe. Last year, she began contemplating suicide.

She finally called an addiction hotline and ended up taking a plane from her home in Colorado to a treatment center in Southern California.

"I didn't think I was addicted," said Ms. Weber, who is now drug-free and living in Los Angeles. "But sometimes the pain pills are causing the pain, not the injuries. So you take more. I was naïve."

The death of Prince in April from an accidental overdose of pain pills has brought new attention to opioid addiction. It has also highlighted the extent of prescription drug abuse among older adults, particularly those with plenty of money to spend. Access to multiple doctors, many helping hands and lots of financial wherewithal can help cloak the warning signs of addiction, experts say.

"They've built a fortress around themselves," said Joseph Garbely, medical director of Caron Treatment Centers. "Their resources allow them to advance in their addiction without detection. So the addiction progresses."

More older adults are becoming addicted to powerful pain pills like OxyContin and Percocet to drown out the aches and pains of aging. Women may end up becoming dependent on pain relievers more quickly than men, according to the Centers for Disease Control and Prevention, and their overdoses have been rising rapidly.

As prosperous baby boomers age, their prescription drug use is increasing, too, said Indra Cidambi, medical director at the Center for Network Therapy, an outpatient detox facility in Middlesex, N.J. It is mostly pain pills, Xanax and Valium, she said. But though wealth provides many boomers with financial freedom, she explained, retirement often gives them anxiety, too.

Addiction can begin with a simple request for something to stop back pain, she said. But even starting on low doses of opioids can quickly turn into abuse. Why? There are two factors for aging adults: drug tolerance that builds with time, and the body's slowing metabolism, which gives drugs a bigger effect.

"By 10 days of usage, you can be addicted," Dr. Cidambi said. "You don't think of affluent, well-put-together women as addicts. But I see this happening constantly. It's out of the box."

Caregivers and doctors rarely notice the problem at its early stages. "Few doctors screen for addiction," said R. Corey Waller, an addiction, pain and emergency medicine specialist and senior medical director for education and policy at the Camden Coalition of Healthcare Providers in New Jersey. "It's not built into treatment yet, and adding that step takes lots of time. Also, patients are usually offended when asked."

So an addiction is often discovered only after a bad fall, confusion or even an accidental overdose, Dr. Garbely said. And even then it can sometimes be difficult to detect since signs of addiction can often be dismissed as symptoms of aging, such as confusion, shaky hands and mood swings.

Dr. Garbely remembers one wealthy woman whose addiction was masked. She lived on a huge estate and had many staff members who cared for her. They continued buying alcohol and prescription drugs for her even though her memory was fading.

"Her helpers were bathing her, changing her clothes and enabling her," he said. "Substances take their toll."

Finally, her son, who discovered her in horrible condition, broke through her human fortress. And the woman was checked into a Caron center's senior unit for three months. "Her cognition was fully restored," Dr. Garbely said. "It brought tears to my eyes."

Affluent people often don't seek treatment, said Richard Taite, chief executive of the luxury drug rehab center Cliffside Malibu in California and one of the authors of *Ending Addiction for Good*. They are used to getting what they want, he said, and may even go to multiple pharmacies and doctors. And they don't understand their addiction.

The loss of self-worth that sometimes comes with retirement, especially after a lifetime of achievement and accolades, can be the spark. Moreover, addiction thrives on a lack of structure and accountability, explained Brenda J. Iliff, executive director of Hazelden Betty Ford Foundation in Naples, Fla.

A lot of baby boomers are now retired, anxious and have trouble sleeping. Add in arthritis, multiple prescription drugs and more drinks, and that can be the beginning of addiction. "It's the perfect storm," she said.

One wealthy woman, said Ms. Iliff, even jumped on her private jet and went from town to town to pick up her pain pills and other medications. "You can have a fresh prescription record in some states," she said, "or hire a doctor who will accommodate you."

Carol Waldman, 64, became addicted to Xanax, which was prescribed by a psychiatrist, and pain pills for chronic back and knee problems. "An aspirin never

> **There are two factors for aging adults: drug tolerance that builds with time, and the body's slowing metabolism, which gives drugs a bigger effect.**

helped me because my resistance is high," she said. "But I knew a Percocet would." She didn't think the pain pills were addictive and even took some of her husband's.

Then last August, she ended up in bed a lot and endured a series of blackouts. "I was in a fog," she remembered, and her husband was doing all the chores. After she dislocated her knee, an emergency room doctor told her family there was something wrong with her medications.

Soon after that, the intervention began. Her family came over for dinner; then the family rabbi rang the doorbell. "Everyone wanted me to get my life back," she said. She ended up at a Caron center in the senior unit for 10 weeks.

Her detox took 20 days, and more than six months passed until her system was clear.

Detoxing older adults from prescription drugs is tricky. "They have to be monitored and slowly withdrawn," Dr. Garbely said. "Opioid withdrawal won't kill you, but you'll wish you were dead." For seniors, he added, treatment is also slower because there may be physical and cognitive issues, too.

"I'm a nice Jewish girl," said Ms. Waldman, who lives in Atlanta. "And I had no idea about detox."

Caron centers offer a chronic pain program, where seniors are taught nonnarcotic ways to treat pain. "Oftentimes, they need new doctors, too," Dr. Garbely said. "If they prescribe dangerous medications, we'll find someone else."

As for Ms. Weber in Los Angeles, she said she is now building healthier relationships and her self-esteem. "It took work and creativity to get my prescription drugs," she said. "Now I put work into being clean and sober."

Print Citations

CMS: Gustke, Constance. "Prescription Drug Abuse among Older Adults Is Harder to Detect." In *The Reference Shelf: Prescription Drug Abuse*, edited by Betsy Maury, 63-65. Ipswich, MA: H.W. Wilson, 2017.

MLA: Gustke, Constance. "Prescription Drug Abuse among Older Adults Is Harder to Detect." *The Reference Shelf: Prescription Drug Abuse*. Ed. Betsy Maury. Ipswich: H.W. Wilson, 2017. 63-65. Print.

APA: Gustke, C. (2017). Prescription drug abuse among older adults is harder to detect. In Betsy Maury (Ed.), *The reference shelf: Prescription drug abuse* (pp. 63-65). Ipswich, MA: H.W. Wilson. (Original work published 2016)

Old and Overmedicated: The Real Drug Problem in Nursing Homes

By Ina Jaffe and Robert Benincasa
NPR, December 8, 2014

It's one of the worst fears we have for our parents or for ourselves: that we, or they, will end up in a nursing home, drugged into a stupor. And that fear is not entirely unreasonable. Almost 300,000 nursing home residents are currently receiving antipsychotic drugs, usually to suppress the anxiety or aggression that can go with Alzheimer's disease and other dementia.

Antipsychotics, however, are approved mainly to treat serious mental illnesses like schizophrenia and bipolar disorder. When it comes to dementia patients, the drugs have a black box warning, saying that they can increase the risk for heart failure, infections and death.

None of this was on Marie Sherman's mind when her family decided that her mother, 73-year-old Beatrice DeLeon, would be better off in a nursing facility near her home in Sonora, Calif. It wasn't because of her Alzheimer's disease, explains Sherman—it was because her mother had had some falls.

"We didn't want my dad to try to lift her, and we wanted to make sure she was safe," says Sherman. It wasn't long before the nursing home staff told Manuel DeLeon, Beatrice's husband, that his wife was agitated and they wanted to give her some medication for that. So he said OK.

"They kept saying she was making too much noise, and that they give her this medicine to quiet her down," he says.

Federal law prohibits the use of antipsychotics and other psychoactive drugs for the convenience of staff. It's called a "chemical restraint." There has to be a documented medical need for the drugs. "But they just kept giving her more and more," says DeLeon, "and I noticed when I used to go see her, she'd just kind of mumble, like she was lost."

The DeLeon's daughter, Marie Sherman, says that when her mother wasn't "lost" she was "out of her skin."

"I mean, she was calling for help," Sherman says. "She was praying, 'Our Father, who art in heaven, please, please help me. Please, take me, please, get me out!' "

It turned out Beatrice DeLeon was given Risperdal and Seroquel, which are approved to treat bipolar disorder and schizophrenia. But professor Bradley Williams, who teaches pharmacy and gerontology at the University of Southern California, says antipsychotics should only be used as a last resort, and just for a month or so, before gradually being eliminated.

Antipsychotic drugs change behaviors, Williams says. "They blunt behaviors. They can cause sedation. It increases their risk for falls." And in the

---

Federal law prohibits the use of antipsychotics and other psychoactive drugs for the convenience of staff. It's called a "chemical restraint." There has to be a documented medical need for the drugs.

---

vast majority of cases, the drugs aren't necessary. "If you want to get to the very basic bottom line," he says, "why should someone pay for something that's not needed?"

But residents or their guardians may not know that the drug is not needed. And they're rarely told about the serious risks, says attorney Jody Moore, who specializes in elder law. She has sued nursing homes in California for failing to get informed consent when they use antipsychotic drugs, as required by law.

"We learned that the families really weren't told anything other than, 'The doctor has ordered this medication for you; please come sign a form,' "says Moore. "And families did."

One of her clients is Kathi Levine, whose mother, Patricia Thomas, had Alzheimer's. Despite her dementia, Thomas had been doing fine in 2010: living in a memory care facility near Santa Barbara, walking and talking, dressing and feeding herself. Levine remembers visiting her mother at the facility one day when there was a party going on, with a Hawaiian theme.

My mom was standing up with a lot of the other ladies, doing the hula," recalls Levine. "And she pulled me up off the chair and said, 'Hula with me. It's fun.' And I think that was the last time I remember her having that 'I love my life' kind of look on her face."

Not long after that, Patricia Thomas fell and fractured her pelvis. After a brief hospital stay, she went to a nursing home for rehab.

"But within a week," says Levine, "she was in a wheelchair, slumped over, sucking on her hand, mumbling to herself, completely out of it, not even aware that I was there."

Her mother was so "out of it," she couldn't do the rehabilitation work that was the reason she went to the nursing home in the first place. So they discharged her. That's when Levine first saw a list of her mother's medications.

"I literally freaked out," says Levine. "I couldn't believe all of these drugs on a list for my mother."

Among them were Risperdal and Haldol, both powerful antipsychotics. Levine tried to slowly wean her mother from the drugs, but Patricia Thomas remained in her wheelchair. She never had another conversation. She was dead in two months.

"When you are your parent's caretaker and their guardian, and things like this happen, you feel terribly guilty," says Levine. "I know the medications they gave her weren't my fault. But the guilt's still there. It's always going to be there."

So Levine and her attorney, Jody Moore, brought a class-action lawsuit—the first of its kind—against the nursing home, charging wholesale violation of informed consent. Moore is a seasoned attorney but says she was amazed at a deposition she took from one of the doctors, who said "not only do I not get informed consent, but I don't know of any doctor who does, and you're crazy to think that that's my job."

The nursing home settled. It's now required to change its practices. An independent monitor will make sure it follows through.

But this facility was not out of the ordinary when it came to dispensing unnecessary antipsychotic drugs. In 2011, a government study found that 88 percent of Medicare claims for antipsychotics prescribed in nursing homes were for treating symptoms of dementia, even though the drugs aren't approved for that. So the next year, the federal government started a campaign to get nursing homes to reduce their use of antipsychotics by 15 percent.

That 15 percent reduction was supposed to take less than a year. It took almost two. And it still left almost 300,000 nursing home residents on risky antipsychotic drugs. But Beatrice DeLeon is no longer one of them.

She's home again with her husband. The family found a state program that sends health aides to the house. And now she can have the kinds of conversations that mean something to her and to her family.

"Can you kiss me?" she asks, apropos of nothing.

"Of course I can, Mama," says her daughter.

"I love you guys."

"We love you too."

Beatrice DeLeon says "thank you." She says that a lot. Currently, she's not taking anything but her Alzheimer's medication. But that seems to be enough, for a life filled with love and gratitude.

Print Citations

CMS: Jaffe, Ina, and Robert Benincasa. "Old and Overmedicated: The Real Drug Problem in Nursing Homes." In *The Reference Shelf: Prescription Drug Abuse*, edited by Betsy Maury, 66-68. Ipswich, MA: H.W. Wilson, 2017.

MLA: Jaffe, Ina, and Robert Benincasa. "Old and Overmedicated: The Real Drug Problem in Nursing Homes." *The Reference Shelf: Prescription Drug Abuse*. Ed. Betsy Maury. Ipswich: H.W. Wilson, 2017. 66-68. Print.

APA: Jaffe, I., & R. Benincasa. (2017). Old and overmedicated: The real drug problem in nursing homes. In Betsy Maury (Ed.), *The reference shelf: Prescription drug abuse* (pp. 66-68). Ipswich, MA: H.W. Wilson. (Original work published 2014)

Fatal Friendships: What Happens When Women Share Drugs on Facebook

By Jill DiDonato
September 1, 2017

In a bungalow apartment overlooking the ocean in Venice Beach, California, a woman sits on her bed counting bars of Xanax.

How had my prescription dwindled without realizing it?

Her stomach gnarled, face flushed, and beginning to lose her breath, she posts to a Facebook group, "Need Xanax. Klonopin also fine. Who can help me out? PM please." Within days, she receives a package from a woman she's never met, nor even talked to on the phone. She's a woman from Brooklyn, who, in the same Facebook group, had on many occasions been desperate for benzos herself. *Got to pay it forward.*

These types of messages, transmitted on secret Facebook groups, reminiscent of early AOL chat rooms, exist in nearly every sector imaginable. Such groups are an effective way to rally and organize, to foster community and help connect people who feel marginalized in some way. Social media helps you find your people.

"Can't afford to see my shrink to refill my prescription and he won't renew without an office visit. Who has benzo$? Will pay."—post from Secret Facebook Group.[*]

Sharing prescription medication, a term those in the medical profession call *diversion*, is a not only a rising phenomenon, it's a felony. So, essentially, by sharing pills, you become a drug dealer. And though benzo diversion is not likely to turn you into a hardened criminal, addictions worsen and women turn on each other after these exchanges. Anxiety professional women encounter in staggering numbers throughout the country has left many dependent on white bars and round blue dolls that offer instant relief. And in a ménage of millennial feminism, surveillance culture, and addiction, what happens when women share drugs over social media is not good.

Five years ago, the White House's Office of National Drug Policy reported that over 54 percent of people who use pain meds obtained them from for free a friend, not a doctor. Today, people in the United States consume 75 percent of the world's prescription drugs.

Abuse of benzodiazepines is largely overshadowed by the opioid epidemic, which according to the Centers for Disease Control and Prevention, resulted in 28,648 deaths in the United States in 2014. Yet, Dr. Karen Miotto, a psychiatrist

---

Reprinted by permission of Jill DiDonato.

[*] *Secret Facebook group remains anonymous throughout this essay to protect the identity of those involved.*

and professor at UCLA who specializes in addiction psychiatry notes, "The epidemic of opioid overdose deaths is in large part due to the combination of opioids, like Vicodin, and benzodiazepines." The CDC reported that benzodiazepines like Xanax, Klonopin, and Valium—a class of medications commonly prescribed for anxiety, insomnia, and other conditions—were involved in 31 percent in those deaths. A 2014 report from the National Institute of Drug Abuse reports a five-fold increase in deaths from benzodiazepine overdose over the previous 13 years.

Further, the CDC's data has severe limitations, meaning that there's a pretty big chance that deaths resulting from benzo abuse are being underreported. Or so says, Marcus Bachhuber, an assistant professor of medicine at Albert Einstein College of Medicine, whose concerns over casual benzodiazepine diversion prompted him to conduct a 2015 study indicating how deadly sharing benzos can be. He counts over-prescription of benzodiazepines the culprit. "It's unclear why doctors are still prescribing benzodiazepines at such a high rate," he says. "We have more effective options, like new SSRI antidepressants with no risk of overdose to treat anxiety, and yet use of benzos is going up," he says.

"I sent this woman something like 20 or 30 2 milligram Klonopins. For years I'd been following her on Facebook and Instagram and we have several mutual friends; we run in the same circle. But I've never met her," says a thirty-four-year-old graphic animator who prefers to remain anonymous. "I have a fixation with her—I can't explain it fully. Part of it is admiration and part of it is envy. I find myself going to her page in a way that strikes me as unhealthy, but I keep doing it. It's a compulsion. I definitely feel competitive with her, but I can't explain that either since we're so different. When I saw she posted about needing anxiety medication, I helped her out. I suppose that fed my ego, to help her. She posted about me being her guardian angel."

Women using each other as yardsticks of self-worth isn't a new phenomenon. Patriarchy benefits from pitting women against each other; this is old news. And having "cyber" relations with people you will never meet in real life also is no longer considered taboo. Why, then is the aforementioned encounter such a chilling indication of anxiety, addiction, and unhealthy bonds women are forging with each other?

Yamalis Diaz, clinical assistant professor in the department of child and adolescent psychiatry at NYU Langone Medical Center, notes, "There are some trends going on that set the stage to make anxiety worse for millennial women." The historical shifts she's referencing include the highest number of women enrolled in college, ever, outnumbering men currently enrolled in college. This is the first time in the history of the United States when this has been the case. "Masters is the new bachelors," she says, pointing out that with more and more highly educated women comes more competition for jobs where systemic inequalities against women are the norm. At the same time, "Women want to establish romantic relationships, and this is another arena millennial women might experience anxiety." Studies show that on average, women are delaying marriage and motherhood. "We're seeing women wait 10 years longer than previous generations to marry and have kids. By the time they're ready, they have a number of anxieties. They're competing with younger women for men." In other words, there's a general panic about finding a man with whom to raise a family. Diaz calls the pressure to find a romantic partner and

> **"Can't afford to see my shrink to refill my prescription and he won't renew without an office visit. Who has benzo$? Will pay."**
> **—post from Secret Facebook Group.***

have kids before their most fertile years have passed is "tremendous."

But, Diaz notes, the greatest anxiety millennial women face stems from the place they turn to alleviate their worries: the internet community. "The way millennial women understand the self and their inner identity has completely shifted," explains Diaz, who blames the ever-present surveillance of social media. "Today's women have a sense of self that is being built by the outside in versus the inside out. This is the prevalent message. There's constant access to what people think about them." The minute you put up your selfie, you're soliciting external validation to feel good. "There's inherent anxiety in waiting for likes."

Stephanie Hartselle, an assistant professor of clinical psychiatry at Brown University adds that the prevalence of social media adds to a feeling that "we're never off. Women of all ages are attached to their phones. We don't take breaks."

When social media becomes a forum for pill sharing, a whole new set of female relationships emerges. "These Facebook groups you're talking about sets up the dynamic where female friendships are being determined by caring from afar," explains Hartselle. "This can easily turn personal relationships into policing relationships."

And it's quite plausible that women are sharing benzos to justify their own use of them, and using digital media to do so only highlights the ways people can internalize social media, and rely on it for a lifeline.

Further, the seduction of benzos has much in common with the instant gratification granted by social media. "Women often believe benzos are innocuous because of their ease of availability and abundance—prompting them to share with others because the medical community, who is to blame, has made them very accessible with no apparent stigma attached to asking for them." says Harold Jonas, a practicing psychotherapist and the president and founder of Sober.com.

However, with benzos to blame for almost a third of the deaths in an American opioid epidemic, the dangers of this addiction cannot be ignored. Sharing pills over social media has become a breeding ground for toxic female relationships and this toxicity has fatal consequences.

Print Citations

CMS: DiDonato, Jill. "Fatal Friendships: What Happens When Women Share Drugs on Facebook." In *The Reference Shelf: Prescription Drug Abuse*, edited by Betsy Maury, 69-72. Ipswich, MA: H.W. Wilson, 2017.

MLA: DiDonato, Jill. "Fatal Friendships: What Happens When Women Share Drugs on Facebook." *The Reference Shelf: Prescription Drug Abuse*. Ed. Betsy Maury. Ipswich: H.W. Wilson, 2017. 69-72. Print.

APA: DiDonato, J. (2017). Fatal friendships: What happens when women share drugs on Facebook. In Betsy Maury (Ed.), *The reference shelf: Prescription drug abuse* (pp. 69-72). Ipswich, MA: H.W. Wilson. (Original work published 2017)

College Students Aren't the Only Ones Abusing Adderall

By Emma Pierson
fivethirtyeight, November 5, 2015

I can easily understand the appeal of Adderall, a drug that treats ADHD by increasing focus and attention span. It has taken me three months to finish this article, several weeks of which was due to Facebook; I wrote the last draft in a caffeine-fueled mania, listening to "Reptilia" on repeat as a deadline loomed. Who wouldn't be tempted by a drug that might make it easier to keep up in a world that runs at overwhelming speed?

Evidently, many people agree. The proportion of Americans using Adderall, and other "study drugs" like Ritalin and Vyvanse, is increasing rapidly. Between 2008 and 2012, the use of ADHD medications increased by 36 percent, according to an analysis of pharmacy prescriptions.

This is partially because ADHD diagnosis rates have increased: by 16 percent among adolescents from 2007 to 2011, a Centers for Disease Control and Prevention analysis found. But many people also use Adderall and similar drugs nonmedically, that is, without a prescription or in ways not recommended by a doctor (for example, by snorting or in very high doses).

This behavior is risky. The Drug Enforcement Administration classifies Adderall as a Schedule II drug, the same category as cocaine, because of its potential for abuse. When used as prescribed to treat ADHD, Adderall and similar medications are both effective and unlikely to be addictive; when used improperly, however, they can be highly addictive, and the evidence that they significantly improve cognition is mixed.

So who is willing to take the risk of nonmedical use? If you believe the media coverage, it's college students: CNN has discussed the "rise of study drugs in college," and last year the Clinton Foundation described misuse of ADHD drugs as an "epidemic."

But it isn't only college students who use study drugs nonmedically—it's young adults more broadly, regardless of whether they're in college. And among college students who use study drugs, there are interesting and almost paradoxical patterns: Study drugs are used more by students at competitive schools, but also more by students with low GPAs. Study drugs may not be used by high-achievers to push themselves even harder; they may be used by those who are falling behind.

The emphasis on nonmedical study drug use in college students stems in part from a government report using data from 2006 and 2007, which said that college students ages 18 to 22 were twice as likely as people of the same age who weren't in college to have used Adderall nonmedically. But when I looked at more recent data from the 2013 National Survey on Drug Use and Health (NSDUH), an annual government survey that includes more than 55,000 Americans, the difference turned out to be closer to 1.3 times, not two times.

This is far smaller than the difference between white 18- to 22-year-olds and black 18- to 22-year-olds, whether they were in college or not (six times, or 18 percent vs. 3 percent), or the difference between 18- to 22-year-olds whose families do not receive food stamps and those whose do (1.6 times, or 14 percent vs. 9 percent). When I looked at Ritalin (an-

> **My research shows that when it comes to nonprescription study drug use, being a young adult matters more than being a college student.**

other common study drug), non-college-students in that age range were slightly more likely than college students to engage in nonprescription use. My research shows that when it comes to nonprescription study drug use, being a young adult matters more than being a college student.

Still, college students are 30 percent more likely than their nonstudent counterparts to use Adderall nonmedically. What drives this trend? Amanda Divin, a professor at Western Illinois University who studies nonmedical prescription drug use and behavior in college students, said that it can be easier to obtain study drugs on college campuses and more socially acceptable to use them. She cited a study in which 55 percent of fraternity members reported using nonmedical ADHD stimulants as evidence that social environment can dramatically affect usage rates.

Are nonmedical study drugs more popular at certain types of colleges? I sought to answer this question with data from Niche.com, which provides information to help people choose neighborhoods and schools. Niche gave me college-by-college surveys in which a total of more than 50,000 college students named the most popular drugs on campus. I connected this data with other data about each college, such as location and selectivity, and found, for example, that study drugs like Adderall and Ritalin were most popular at schools in New England. Only 25 percent of college students in Rocky Mountain schools reported that study drugs were among the most popular on campus versus 40 percent of students in New England, for example.

The differences among regions imply that surveys that look only at a single school may miss important trends in study drug use on campus.

Niche data also showed that study drugs were more popular at colleges that were more selective or had higher test scores. The positive correlation between ACT score and study drug use is highly statistically significant (and previous research has found this pattern as well).

If Adderall is more popular at colleges with competitive admissions standards, you might also expect it to be used more by high-achievers. But multiple studies find that students who use nonprescription study drugs have a lower college GPA—even when controlling for factors such as high school GPA, frequency of skipping classes and hours spent studying.

"These students tend to be lower-achieving students who procrastinate and do not study in advance, attempting to cram studying into one night with the assistance of Adderall to both stay awake as well as stay focused," Divin said.

These students are more likely to struggle in other ways as well. Previous research has found that students who use nonprescription Adderall or Ritalin are more likely to be depressed. The NSDUH data backs this up: College students who had used Adderall nonmedically reported higher levels of depression and were more likely to have considered suicide.

Importantly, these correlations, though significant, do not mean that Adderall causes low GPAs or depression. Causality might run the other way: Students who are already depressed or struggling in school could be using Adderall in order to feel better. Or a third factor may be to blame: Students who use Adderall nonmedically are also more likely to abuse alcohol and marijuana, for example.

So students at high-achieving schools and students with low GPAs are more likely to take Adderall. This could be because students are more likely to take Adderall when they are more stressed about their academic performance. Many studies make it clear that students use study drugs in part because of academic stress. A recent analysis of NSDUH data found that students were more likely to use stimulants for the first time during exam months. Other less conventional data sources support this latter finding: For example, I found that Google searches for "Adderall" in college towns spiked during exam months and dropped during summer months, and a 2013 study of 200,000 tweets mentioning Adderall found that they peaked during exam periods.

Adults older than 25 who use Adderall nonmedically may also struggle. I initially thought that adults working long hours at high-income jobs would be most likely to use Adderall nonmedically. I was wrong. The NSDUH data showed that adults whose family incomes were below $10,000 had the highest rates of nonmedical Adderall use, and those whose family incomes were greater than $75,000 had the lowest. Adults who used Adderall nonmedically also reported higher levels of depression and were more likely to consider suicide.

To a student confronting an exam, or an employee confronting a deadline, Adderall must seem as tempting as steroids to an athlete—particularly if everyone else seems to be using it. But Divin was clear: "There isn't data to suggest or support [the idea] that non-ADHD individuals who use prescription stimulants actually experience any benefits from their use."

Print Citations

CMS: Pierson, Emma. "College Students Aren't the Only Ones Abusing Adderall." In *The Reference Shelf: Prescription Drug Abuse*, edited by Betsy Maury, 73-76. Ipswich, MA: H.W. Wilson, 2017.

MLA: Pierson, Emma. "College Students Aren't the Only Ones Abusing Adderall." *The Reference Shelf: Prescription Drug Abuse*. Ed. Betsy Maury. Ipswich: H.W. Wilson, 2017. 73-76. Print.

APA: Pierson, E. (2017). College students aren't the only ones abusing adderall. In Betsy Maury (Ed.), *The reference shelf: Prescription drug abuse* (pp. 73-76). Ipswich, MA: H.W. Wilson. (Original work published 2015)

Smack Epidemic

By L. Jon Wertheim
Sports Illustrated, June 22, 2015

Roman Montano had barely learned cursive when he was asked to sign his first baseball. Parents of teammates had watched him dominate game after game in Albuquerque's Little League during the summer of 2000, mowing down batters and belting home runs. The autograph requests were mostly facetious, but what they signified was clear: The kid was going somewhere.

The next few years only confirmed that notion. Roman grew to 6'6" and 250 pounds. He made a mockery of the weight room at Eldorado High and ran the 40-yard dash in 4.9. As a sophomore defensive lineman he was honorable mention all-state in Class 5A. He also joined the basketball team his senior year, giving in to the pleadings of the coach, and was instantly the Eagles' best player. And after high school, when he trained with the legion of MMA fighters based in Albuquerque, they encouraged him to compete as a heavyweight.

Baseball, though, was always his favorite sport—"the most funnest," as he had put it to the *Albuquerque Tribune* when he was 12. He once struck out all 18 batters in a Thunderbird League game. The towering righty was Eldorado High's ace, his fastball reaching the 90s. The second starter? Ken Giles, now a flame-throwing Phillies reliever. "You're talking about a guy with a ton of potential: size, natural ability, attitude," Giles says. "Everyone wanted to be him, but everyone wanted to be around him, too. The first word I would use to describe Roman is lovable."

A foot injury his junior year didn't derail Roman. He needed minor surgery on a small bone, but he popped some OxyContin and after a few weeks was back on the mound. His senior year Roman planned to lead Eldorado to a state title and then declare for the 2008 major league draft (the Braves had expressed the most interest in him), spurning about 20 Division I scholarship offers. Before the season, though, Roman committed one of those judgment-deprived acts for which teenagers are known. He and some friends used a stolen credit card at a mall. They got caught. The school found out. Though it was Roman's first offense, he was kicked off the team.

Humiliated, angry and depressed, Roman thought back to the numbing effect of the OxyContin. His prescription had run out, but that wasn't much of an impediment. In the upscale Northeast Heights—more *High School Musical* Albuquerque than *Breaking Bad* Albuquerque—painkillers were competing with marijuana and alcohol as the party drug of choice. "There are pill parties," says Roman's younger brother, Beau. "[Pills are] so easy to get. They're everywhere."

Roman was soon in the grip of Oxy. He lost interest in baseball. He showed up high for graduation. JoAnn Montano and her husband, Bo, who owns a wheel-alignment and body-shop business, figured their son was just floundering—until JoAnn caught him using. She took him to an addiction center, and he was prescribed Suboxone to treat his opioid dependency.

Roman, though, couldn't fully kick his habit. Before graduation he had switched to a cheaper substance that offered the same high at a lower price: heroin.

At first Roman smoked "black" (black-tar heroin), a relatively crude version of the drug that was easy to obtain. Then he began using intravenously. But he hid his addiction well. He stayed on Suboxone, took up competitive bodybuilding and started training at an MMA gym. He had a job selling phones for Verizon. "He looked so healthy, a big, strapping guy, not like a junkie," says Bo. "He was back doing his athletics. We thought the addiction was behind us. We didn't know how cunning and how manipulative this drug is."

On May 2, 2012, Roman was supposed to lift weights with his father in the morning. Roman didn't show up, and texts to him went unanswered. His fiancée, Mikaila Lovato, couldn't find him either.

In the the evening two chaplains went to the Montanos' house, asking for Roman's next of kin. They said that Roman had been found slumped in the driver's seat of his car behind a FedEx store, a syringe in his arm, the motor running. He was 22 and dead from a heroin overdose.

It is, by any measure, an epidemic. Heroin is not new or chic, but its use and abuse are spiking. According to data from the U.S. Centers for Disease Control and Prevention and the National Center for Health Statistics, heroin-overdose deaths rose gradually from 2000 to '10 but then almost tripled in the following three years to 2.7 deaths per 100,000 people. Heroin use cuts across demographics. Young, old. Male, female. Wealthy, indigent. Urban, rural and, most of all, suburban. But public authorities devoted to prevention and law enforcement, from the Drug Enforcement Agency (DEA) to the Centers for Disease Control (CDC), have been struck by a growing concentration in an unlikely subset of users: young athletes.

About a decade ago Jack Riley, the DEA's chief of operations, recognized that high school athletes were becoming "unwitting customers of the cartels," which target people susceptible to prescription-drug abuse. The number of addicts and overdose victims has grown substantially since then. "In the athletic arena, if anything can be likened to a weapon of mass destruction, it's heroin," Riley says. "It is that pervasive now."

While hard data for heroin use among young athletes are difficult to come by, the anecdotal evidence is abundant and alarming. A seven-month *SI* investigation found overdose victims in baseball, basketball, football, golf, gymnastics, hockey, lacrosse, soccer, softball, swimming, tennis, volleyball and wrestling—from coast to coast. Riley saw this as a volunteer in a youth basketball league in St. Louis. He coached a player who, years after suffering an injury, succumbed to a heroin overdose. The cartels, Riley says, "have developed a strategy, with the help of street gangs, to put heroin in every walk of life. They recognize how vulnerable young athletes are."

To understand the increasingly busy intersection of heroin and sports, it's essential first to understand the general path to the drug. According to the U.S. Substance Abuse and Mental Health Services Administration, a full 80% of all users arrive at heroin after abusing opioid painkillers such as OxyContin, Percocet and Vicodin. And according to the National Institute of Drug Abuse, one in 15 people who take nonmedical prescription painkillers will try heroin within the next 10 years. While opioid painkillers can cost up to $30 per pill on the black market, heroin, which is molecularly similar, can be purchased for $5 a bag and provides a more potent high. "It's an easy jump," says Harris Stratyner, a New York City addiction specialist.

Studies have shown that while cumulative pain levels remained constant among Americans, prescriptions for pain medications more than quadrupled between 1999 and 2010. As the sports industry expands each year—and the stakes on rinks, fields and courts grow higher—young athletes face enormous pressure to manage their pain and play through injuries.

A University of Michigan researcher uncovered a startling number in a 2013 national study: By the time high school athletes become seniors, approximately 11% will have used a narcotic pain reliever such as OxyContin or Vicodin—for nonmedical purposes. What's more, UM researcher Philip Todd Veliz, who conducted a 2013 longitudinal study of 743 male and 751 female adolescents in southeast Michigan that was published in the *Journal of Adolescent Health*, told SI that "male adolescent athletes who participated in competitive sports across the three-year study period had two times greater odds of being prescribed painkillers during the past year and had four times greater odds of medically misusing painkillers (i.e., using them to get high and using them too much) when compared to males who did not participate in competitive sports."

Moreover, "sports that involve high levels of contact (e.g., football) tend to socialize youth to view pain, violence and risk as normative features," Veliz said, and these "may influence risky behavior both on and off the playing field. In other words, participants in contact sports learn to view their body as an instrument that can be easily gambled with, even if it would involve permanent damage."

Consider Patrick Trevor. In the spring of 2009, Patrick was a sophomore lacrosse goalie at Rumson–Fair Haven, a well-regarded New Jersey high school with many students whose parents take ferries to jobs on Wall Street. A teammate's fluke shot in practice shattered Patrick's right thumb. He had two immediate concerns: easing the pain and getting back on the field. A future college scholarship, after all, was on the line. The doctor who examined Patrick prescribed Roxicodone (Roxy in the vernacular), a cousin of OxyContin.

Patrick quickly became addicted to the medication and even took to crushing and snorting his pills. But he reckoned that playing high was better than playing in pain—which was better than not playing at all. "Us athletes," he says, "we'll do anything in order to keep playing." Within a few years Patrick had made the transition to heroin. His Roxy prescription had lapsed; his fondness for the high had not.

At first he illegally purchased pills from friends; then he ventured into the worst pockets of Newark to get his heroin fix. College lacrosse had become the least of his concerns.

Patrick was arrested and spent a short time in jail. He went to several rehab facilities before finding success at the Dynamite Youth Center in Brooklyn. He proudly says his clean date is Oct. 2, 2012. He was struck by how many athletes he saw at such a small facility. "Hockey, football, lacrosse," he says. "[Heroin is] a big thing in sports."

How big is difficult to say. "This should be on people's research agenda," Veliz says, lamenting the lack of reliable statistics. "Because this is actually happening."

More than a decade ago Amber Masters played soccer for Esperanza High in Anaheim despite a hyperextended right knee. ("I had to," she says. "We had college scouts there.") Colliding with another player, she tore tissue in the same knee. Surgery ended her season, and she became dependent on the opiate-based painkiller Norco.

When the prescription expired, she wanted to keep experiencing the feeling Norco gave her. A friend introduced her to Oxy. As Amber, once a gifted forward, chased a painkiller high, her soccer career imploded. Academic probation kept her off the team as a junior, and by the time she returned as a senior, she was not the same player. College recruiters disappeared. "I didn't really care," she says. "I had the party scene."

She first took heroin the summer before she enrolled at Orange Coast College in Costa Mesa, Calif. "I was addicted from the first hit I took," she says. Within a year she had dropped out of school, become a dealer ("I was my best customer," she says) and introduced her younger brother, Adam, to the drug. Amber became a mother. She eluded the law, but Adam was less fortunate. He went to jail for possession of narcotics. Then, on April 13, 2012, he died from an overdose. "That sent my addiction into a hard-core downward spiral," Amber says.

More trauma followed. Amber says her parents, Jerry and Ginger, sent her to rehab, kicked her out of the house when she relapsed, and refused to let her visit her daughter. (Ginger contends that she and Jerry set ground rules that Amber refused to obey. "She chose to leave," Ginger says.)

The separation was a sobering jolt to Amber. "I had a waking-up moment," she says. "I knew it was only a matter of time before I would die and leave my daughter behind." She entered rehab. Today she works in the billing department of an addiction recovery center in Irvine, Calif. She says she's been clean since Oct. 19, 2012.

It's disturbing enough that athletes such as Masters come to heroin through painkillers prescribed after an injury. But SI's reporting revealed a shocking contributing factor: Families consistently said that they received no warning from physicians about the addictive power of the opioid painkillers they prescribed. Patrick Trevor recalls that the doctor who prescribed Roxy for him jokingly said, "You got the good stuff." Trevor adds, "I didn't really put two and two together until later … when I was a full-blown heroin addict. I knew painkillers were not good, but I didn't know how crazy addictive they were."

In 2014 the CDC issued a report headlined PHYSICIANS ARE FUELING PRESCRIPTION PAINKILLER OVERDOSES. The study found that doctors were engaging in "dangerous" and "inappropriate" prescription practices. "Anyone who is giving a kid an opioid prescription without serious oversight and supervision is out of their mind," says Joe Schrank, a New York City-based drug counselor and former USC offensive lineman. "That stuff is like kryptonite."

If there is an epicenter for the heroin-in-sports crisis, it's Albuquerque (pop. 550,000), a high-altitude city less than 300 miles from the Mexican border. A report by the New Mexico health department found that the drug-overdose death rate in the state jumped by more than 60% between 2001 and '10, and in New Mexico's Youth Risk and Resiliency survey one in 10 youths admitted to using opiate-based prescription drugs to get high. In Albuquerque at least eight athletes have died from heroin or painkiller overdoses since '11. (The very week in April that *Sports Illustrated* visited the city to report this story, a former local baseball star, James Diz, died of an apparent heroin overdose at 23.)

Cameron Weiss was a strapping wrestler and football special-teams player at La Cueva High. In 2010, his sophomore year, he broke his left collarbone making a tackle in practice and required surgery; months later he fractured his right collarbone while wrestling. He went on pain medication (Percocet and hydrocodone) and was soon ditching school and failing the AP classes he had been mastering. He confessed to his mother that he was addicted to heroin. Because of a federal law that prevents doctors from prescribing buprenorphine, a component of Suboxone, to more than 100 patients at a time, Jennifer Weiss-Burke had to call 80 physicians before she could get her son an appointment for a Suboxone prescription. On the drive to the doctor's, Cameron went into severe withdrawal. He was "combative, sweating, in a ton of pain," Jennifer says. "He was throwing up. He looked horrible."

> It's disturbing enough that athletes such as Masters come to heroin through painkillers prescribed after an injury. But SI's reporting revealed a shocking contributing factor: Families consistently said that they received no warning from physicians about the addictive power of the opioid painkillers they prescribed.

Cameron's body had come to need the sustained opioid intake. Once he received the Suboxone, his withdrawal symptoms vanished. "After 15 minutes it was like he was normal again—laughing and happy," says his mother. But then she learned the reality of addiction: Sobriety can be fleeting. Soon her son was using again. "It was a living hell," she says. He died of a heroin overdose at 18.

Lou Duran can relate. She watched her son, Michael, make the varsity baseball team at Sandia Prep as an eighth-grader and, two years later, become addicted to OxyContin after he strained his knee playing soccer. Michael hardly fit the profile of an addict: He spent hours hitting balls in a batting cage with teammates.

He excelled academically. Owing to his blend of intelligence and athleticism, Lou called him her "Einstein jock."

Because of his addiction, though, his baseball career unraveled. He was kicked out of private school, went to public school and then dropped out. After earning his GED, he went to San Diego City College, but he quickly transferred to New Mexico State in Las Cruces. Then he began using heroin. He went to rehab and attended therapy, only to relapse five times. Lou and her husband, Michael Sr., rode waves of terror followed by temporary relief. They witnessed their son's excruciating withdrawals and fleeting stretches of sobriety. Finally, in early 2011, Michael seemed to have broken free of the drug.

On Feb. 1, the evening of a historic winter snowstorm, a white Audi TT pulled up to the Durans' house in subzero temperatures. Michael, 19, gave the driver cash he had stolen from his mother's purse. The driver handed him a bag of heroin. From a distance Michael Sr. recognized trouble. "Get in the house now," he barked to his son. Turning to the driver, he said, "Get out of here while you still can." The Audi sped away.

Michael had been scheduled to deliver an antidrug speech that evening at Eldorado High. He was going to address a seminar for concerned family members and students organized by Healing Addiction in Our Community, telling them about his struggle with painkillers and heroin: how he had been a standout baseball player who took his first drug at 15; how he revived two friends who had overdosed; how he wound up in jail. The winter blast, though, closed roads and postponed the speech. When Michael went inside his house, he gave his parents a persuasive story: The guy in the car was a friend who had stopped by to check up on him. Michael went upstairs to his bedroom.

Lou remembers the silence when she knocked on Michael's door the next afternoon. She remembers kicking it open and scanning the room. Her eyes flashed across an unmade bed, an empty couch, a television turned on, and she was relieved. Then, as she turned to leave, she found Michael's body.

Later Michael Sr. discovered notes from the antidrug speech his son was supposed to have given. One of the bullet points: Lucky to be here today at all because I've cheated death more times than I can count.

When her son became an addict in 2010, Jennifer Weiss-Burke began an awareness and advocacy group for relatives and friends of drug-dependent children. The group—Healing Addiction in Our Community, which Michael Duran was to have addressed the night he died—has grown to 50 members. It includes several families of young athletes who have overdosed on opioids. Weiss-Burke is also cofounder and executive director of Serenity Mesa, a long-term treatment center for young people in recovery from drug and alcohol addiction, which opened on May 26.

Nearby, the Durans continue to grieve. After her son died, Lou went through his text messages, found his dealer's phone number and tracked down his address. She gave the information to the DEA and FBI. "A week later," she says, "he was arrested." Lou now works at Turning Point Recovery Center, a local treatment facility.

On Albuquerque's northeast side, the Montanos' business, the Wheel Align It II body shop, doubles as a shrine to Roman. The office walls are covered with photos of him on the mound, standing next to UFC fighters, alongside Ken Giles. Giles learned of Roman's death while in the minors—"I lost it for a good week," he says—and now has the letters RM written with permanent marker on each of his major league gloves.

Bo Montano, a former wrestler who still carries himself like an athlete, has an elaborate tattoo on his right forearm in which Roman's initials are framed by the words SO OTHERS MAY LIVE. Like the Durans and Jennifer Weiss-Burke, Bo and JoAnn Montano honor their deceased son by involving themselves in drug treatment and prevention. Through churches and schools around Albuquerque, they lead a 12-step recovery program for addicts and alcoholics and introduce them to sponsors. The Montanos also make a point of hiring recovering addicts at the body shop. "It helps us more than it helps them," says Bo. "It gives us some peace."

Sitting on stools inside the shop this spring, the Montanos recounted these successes. But they stopped short of telling a story that's too tidy. Their saga, finally, is a contemporary tragedy. They replayed the final few years of their son's life, wondering what subtle signs or symptoms they missed. "[Roman] was fighting the best he could, but the drug had control," said Bo. "If things are going great, you use [heroin] to celebrate. If things are going bad, you use it to numb."

JoAnn, blinking back tears, said, "You know what really breaks my heart? My son knew he was meant to be an athlete. Sports was his first addiction. He just ran into another addiction that was so much more powerful."

Print Citations

CMS: Wertheim, L. Jon. "Smack Epidemic." In *The Reference Shelf: Prescription Drug Abuse*, edited by Betsy Maury, 77-83. Ipswich, MA: H.W. Wilson, 2017.

MLA: Wertheim, L. Jon. "Smack Epidemic." *The Reference Shelf: Prescription Drug Abuse*. Ed. Betsy Maury. Ipswich: H.W. Wilson, 2017 77-83. Print.

APA: Wertheim, L. J. (2017). Smack Epidemic. In Betsy Maury (Ed.), *The reference shelf: Prescription drug abuse* (pp. 77-83). Ipswich, MA: H.W. Wilson. (Original work published 2015)

US Child Opioid Overdoses Increased over Past Two Decades, Research Finds

By Jessica Glenza
The Guardian, October 31, 2016

The incidence of American children overdosing on opioids increased dramatically between 1997 and 2012, including a two-fold increase among toddlers, a review of more than 13,000 hospital discharge records has found.

Previous such studies have focused on overdose among adults, or overall poisonings of children.

"Not a lot of attention has focused on children, and because these drugs are so ubiquitous I knew children also had to be impacted by the opioid crisis," said Julie Gaither, a researcher and registered nurse at Yale.

However, she said, "We see little about it really in the press, and little research has been done in this area."

America's opioid crisis has taken a top slot as a public health concern, infiltrating the 2016 presidential election a little more than a year after the US Food and Drug Administration (FDA) approved a powerful opioid, Oxycontin, for use among children.

Gaither's research examined records concerning children from ages one to 19 who were hospitalized for opioid poisoning in three-year intervals between 1997 and 2012. During that time, 176 of the hospitalized children died.

The study found that over 15 years, as the popularity and prescribing of opioids increased, the number of children who were accidentally poisoned or adolescents who attempted to kill themselves also increased.

The most dramatic rise in poisonings was among the youngest children. Toddlers between one and four years old had more than twice the rate of poisonings from painkillers in 2012 as they did in 1997. On a population level, researchers estimated that meant 2.6 of every 100,000 toddlers would be poisoned by opioids, from less than one in 1997.

> In that time, the profile of children hospitalized for opioids also changed, growing significantly whiter and more male.

Most poisonings were accidental—probably from toddlers believing the pills were candy.

Among teens, the rise was also dramatic but was more likely to indicate attempts at intentional self-harm. Overdoses among adolescents from 15 to 19 years old rose by an estimated 176%, the population of teens hospitalized from opioid poisoning rising from 3.6 per 100,000 in 1997 to 10.1.

In the same age group, heroin overdoses increased by 161%. Poisoning from opioid abuse treatment soared—methadone overdoses increased by 950%.

In that time, the profile of children hospitalized for opioids also changed, growing significantly whiter and more male.

In 1997, researchers found that 34.7% of hospitalizations were of boys. That grew to 47.4%. The children were predominantly white, 73.5%, and the proportion who were on Medicaid or government health insurance for low-income families increased from 24.1% to 44% in 2012.

The new work, published in the *Journal of the American Medical Association Pediatrics*, adds to research that showed increases in overdose among children. Boston children's hospital researchers found that overdose rates among children younger than 18 rose by 30% between 2001 and 2008. Poison center officials have also reported increases in opioid overdose among children.

Gaither emphasised the need for more tamper-resistant packaging and for greater care when storing such medications.

"You've got the childproof safety caps, but obviously more needs to be done to keep kids from getting into them," she said.

Though Gaither's research is some of the first to address opioid overdose among children, it is not the first to call on the industry to develop new packaging.

A 2015 Johns Hopkins University report recommended researchers develop tamper-resistant packaging and more rigorously test it. Better packaging, the authors reasoned, would not only stop children from accidentally taking the drugs but would also help stop the diversion of prescription drugs to the black market.

A pill bottle that links doses to a phone app and website is being tested by the National Institutes of Health. Johns Hopkins developed a prototype bottle that links a patient's fingerprint to dosing.

One small study showed that patients in opioid addiction treatment felt tamper-proof bottles dissuaded at least some from diverting their buprenorphine pills (better known by the brand name Suboxone) to the black market.

"Across the board, for all age groups, we need to limit exposure," Gaither said. "We need to limit children getting their hands on these drugs—they may think they're candy.

"Opioids are now ubiquitous in the US, and they're in millions of American homes."

Print Citations

CMS: Glenza, Jessica. "US Child Opioid Overdoses Increased over Past Two Decades, Research Finds." In *The Reference Shelf: Prescription Drug Abuse*, edited by Betsy Maury, 84-86. Ipswich, MA: H.W. Wilson, 2017.

MLA: Glenza, Jessica. "US Child Opioid Overdoses Increased over Past Two Decades, Research Finds."   *The Reference Shelf: Prescription Drug Abuse.* Ed. Betsy Maury. Ipswich: H.W. Wilson, 2017. 84-86. Print.

APA: Glenza, J. (2017). US child opioid overdoses increased over past two decades, research finds. In Betsy Maury (Ed.), *The reference shelf: Prescription drug abuse* (pp. 84-86). Ipswich, MA: H.W. Wilson. (Original work published 2016)

The Hefty Price of "Study Drug" Misuse on College Campuses

By Linda Begdache

The Conversation, May 23, 2016

Nonmedical use of Attention Deficit Hyperactivity Disorder (ADHD) drugs on college campuses, such as Adderall, Ritalin, Concerta and Vyvanse, has exploded in the past decade, with a parallel rise in depression disorders and binge drinking among young adults.

These ADHD drugs act as a brain stimulant that are normally prescribed to individuals who display symptoms of ADHD. These stimulants boost the availability of dopamine, a chemical responsible for transmitting signals between the nerve cells (neurons) of the brain.

But now a growing student population has been using them as "study" drugs—that help them stay up all night and concentrate. According to a 2007 National Institutes of Health (NIH) study, abuse of nonmedical prescription drugs among college students, such as ADHD meds, increased from 8.3 percent in 1996 to 14.6 percent in 2006.

Besides helping with concentration, dopamine is also associated with motivation and pleasurable feelings. Individuals who use these ADHD drugs nonmedically experience a surge in dopamine similar to that caused by illicit drugs which induces a great sense of well-being.

My journey with investigating the effect of the stimulant used nonmedically on college campuses started with a question from a student seven years ago. The question was about the long-term effect of misuse on brain and physical health. Having an educational background in cell and molecular biology with a concentration in neuroscience, I started a literature review and soon became an educator on the topic to teach students about the effects of such stimulant misuse on the maturing brain.

College students who take ADHD drugs without medical need could risk developing drug dependence as well as a host of mental ailments.

Substance Abuse in College

College students have been reported to use many stimulants, including but not limited to Adderrall, Ritalin and Dexedrine.

> **Individuals who use these ADHD drugs nonmedically experience a surge in dopamine similar to that caused by illicit drugs which induces a great sense of well-being.**

According to the 2008 *National Survey on Drug Use and Health*, students who used Adderall for nonmedical purposes were three times more likely than those who had not used Adderall nonmedically to use marijuana. They were also eight times more likely to use cocaine. In addition, 90 percent of the students who used Adderall nonmedically were binge alcohol consumers.

Generally, college students who abuse ADHD drugs are white, male and part of a fraternity or a sorority. Often they have a low GPA as well.

ADHD drugs appear harmless to many, as often they are prescribed by physicians, even though these drugs have a "Black Box warning," which appears on a prescription drug's label to call attention to serious or life-threatening risks. Despite such a strict warning from the FDA, many practitioners end up prescribing them based on subjective reporting of symptoms of ADHD. The lack of a gold standard for ADHD diagnosis has, in fact, led to physicians overprescribing the drug.

Furthermore, students who get hold of these prescriptions can easily sell pills on the black market. Students who buy these pills illicitly miss seeing the warning about potential abuse, addiction and other side effects.

What's more, a chewable form of an ADHD drug has been recently introduced in the market. These are fruity-flavored extended-release drugs that dissolve instantly in the mouth. They are targeted for children for a fast medicated response, but present a great potential for abuse.

The Neurobiology of Addiction

What are the consequences of taking these drugs without a medical condition?

The nonmedical use of the ADHD drugs (stimulants) is of great concern because it raises levels of dopamine the same way illicit drugs do. Therefore, abuse of these drugs may cause the same effect on addiction, brain rewiring and behavioral alteration.

While students may be aware of the harmful effects of "doing drugs," the use of the ADHD drugs nonmedically may seem harmless because they are prescription medicine.

There is a limited body of knowledge on the effect of long-term nonmedical ADHD drug abuse on the developing brain. Of concern are potential permanent alterations taking place in the pathways of nerve cells of the maturing brain.

ADHD drugs could be addictive, if used without medical necessity. Since brain development continues into the mid-20s and the young brain is remarkably plastic, this sets up a risk of developing chronic substance abuse, addiction and mental ailments.

Nonmedical ADHD drugs, like any illegal drug, collectively activate a nerve pathway known as the "reward system of the brain." This reward system is responsible for positive feelings such as motivation and pleasure. From an evolutionary point of view, the circuit controls an individual's responses to motivation and pleasure (e.g., food and sex) which promote survival and fitness, respectively.

The response of the brain reward system to natural cues is highly regulated by a homeostatic mechanism—a process by which the body maintains its constant internal environment.

However, a nonmedical ADHD drug, like an illegal drug, overactivates this "reward circuit," thereby disturbing the brain's internal balance. This causes the brain to maladapt (structurally and functionally) and turn the brain into being "substance-dependent." These changes happen at the genetic level.

A consequence of this is that the brain starts to need an increased dosage of the drug to respond to the natural cues for motivation and life pleasures. This sets the stage for more substance abuse. The individual then reaches for higher doses and more potent substances. Eventually, a cycle of further dependence and drug abuse ensues.

Impact of Abuse

The concern with the nonmedical ADHD drug abuse is that it might prime the brain for use of other substances such as alcohol, cocaine and marijuana (something that the national surveys mentioned above revealed).

Major behavioral changes emerge such as compulsive drug seeking, aggression, mood swings, psychosis, abnormal libido and suicidal thoughts.

In fact, there have been documented cases of college students who have taken their lives following an addiction to nonmedical ADHD drugs.

Animal studies show that the changes that lead to rewiring of the brain are due to an alteration in gene function. Some of these changes become permanent and heritable, especially with prolonged abuse, meaning that the altered (newly programmed) genes are passed down to offspring.

In fact, a body of evidence is linking the process of addiction (among many chronic diseases) to altered gene function profile passed down by ancestors. This altered profile could predispose their offspring to certain disorders.

Currently, prescription of ADHD drug is based mostly on subjective self-reported symptoms, and a gold standard for ADHD diagnosis remains to be perfected. As a lyric from the rock band Marilyn Manson says:

Whatever does not kill you, it's gonna leave a scar.

That's the case with nonprescription ADHD drug abuse.

Print Citations

CMS: Begdache, Linda. "The Hefty Price of 'Study Drug' Misuse on College Campuses." In *The Reference Shelf: Prescription Drug Abuse*, edited by Betsy Maury, 87-90. Ipswich, MA: H.W. Wilson, 2017.

MLA: Begdache, Linda. "The Hefty Price of 'Study Drug' Misuse on College Campuses." *The Reference Shelf: Prescription Drug Abuse*. Ed. Betsy Maury. Ipswich: H.W. Wilson, 2017. 87-90. Print.

APA: Begdache, L. (2017). The hefty price of "study drug" misuse on college campuses. In Betsy Maury (Ed.), *The reference shelf: Prescription drug abuse* (pp. 87-90). Ipswich, MA: H.W. Wilson. (Original work published 2016)

Risky Alone, Deadly Together

By Kimberly Kindy and Dan Keating
The Washington Post, August 31, 2016

Karen Franklin leans against the sink in the pink-tiled bathroom of her childhood home, counting out pills. There's a purple morphine tablet for chronic back pain, a blue Xanax for anxiety and a white probiotic for her stomach, which aches from all the other pills.

In all, Franklin, 60, takes more than a dozen different prescription drugs, washing them down with tap water and puffing on a Marlboro while she waits for them to kick in.

"They take the edge off, but that's about it," Franklin says. So she keeps a bottle of vodka handy for added relief, increasing her risk of joining the legions of American women dying from prescription-drug overdoses.

While death rates are falling for blacks and Hispanics in middle age, whites are dying prematurely in growing numbers, particularly white women. One reason: a big increase in overdoses, primarily from opioids, but also from anti-anxiety drugs, which are often prescribed in tandem.

Between 1999 and 2014, the number of middle-aged white women dying annually from opiate overdoses shot up 400 percent, according to a *Washington Post* analysis of data from the Centers for Disease Control and Prevention. Anti-anxiety drugs known as benzodiazepines contributed to a growing share of the 54,000 deaths over that period, reaching a third in the last several years, the *Post* found, though spotty reporting in death records makes it likely that the combination is even more widespread.

Both drugs depress the central nervous system, temporarily easing pain and anxiety while suppressing respiration, heart rate and the gag reflex. Alcohol has the same effect, and combining any of these can be fatal.

"They act like a dimmer switch on the central nervous system," said Rear Admiral Susan Blumenthal, former U.S. assistant surgeon general and an expert on women's health issues. "When taken in combination, a person's breathing and heart will slow down, and can ultimately stop. People can go to sleep and never wake up."

White women are more likely than women of other races to be prescribed opiates, and far more likely to be prescribed both opiates and anti-anxiety drugs, according to a *Post* analysis of middle-aged participants in the latest National Health and Nutrition Examination Survey. White women prescribed opiates are five times as likely as white men to be given that drug combination—helping to explain why white women may be at special risk.

Federal health officials have recognized the danger. This spring, in a guideline that urged doctors to reduce the general use of opioids for chronic pain, the CDC warned against prescribing them together with benzodiazepines, except for patients battling fatal diseases such as cancer. At the very least, the CDC urged doctors to warn patients of the risks, especially when the drugs are mixed with alcohol.

And on Thursday, the U.S. Food and Drug Administration began requiring warning labels on opioids and benzodiazepines—nearly 400 products in total—with information about the potentially fatal consequences of taking these medications at the same time.

"It is nothing short of a public health crisis when you see a substantial increase of avoidable overdose and death related to two widely used drug classes being taken together," FDA Commissioner Robert Califf said in a statement. "We implore health care professionals to heed these new warnings and more carefully and thoroughly evaluate, on a patient-by-patient basis, whether the benefits of using opioids and benzodiazepines—or CNS depressants more generally—together outweigh these serious risks."

Federal officials have no power to mandate a change in doctors' prescribing habits. Even if they did, a mandate would do little for patients like Franklin who get their prescriptions from multiple physicians.

"An opioid might be prescribed by a pain specialist while a general practitioner or a psychologist may prescribe the benzodiazepine. They may not know about one another," said Deborah Dowell, lead author of the CDC's new opioid guidelines.

Franklin's struggle began 17 years ago with a single prescription for Vicodin. At the time, she had her own home and managed a grocery store. But the side effects of long-term opioid use soon set in. Mounting anxiety. Sleeplessness. Depression. With each new problem, doctors sent her home with more pills.

Now she lives with her 88-year-old father and spends her days shuffling between the TV, a refrigerator stocked with chocolate Ensure and the bathroom, which relatives call her sanctuary. Armed with a Bible and a carton of Marlboros, she prays for God's protection, cracking the bathroom window to let the cigarette smoke drift into the back yard.

Lately, Franklin has been blacking out. Her sister found her facedown in a plate of food, and she started using a walker after losing consciousness on her way to the mailbox.

"What is happening right now is a slow suicide," said her friend Ellen Eggert, a supervisor for the Kern County Mental Health Department. But Franklin is resisting Eggert's appeals to seek help for her addictions.

"I know it's not good for me," Franklin said. "But I would rather say my prayers and take my medication."

Bakersfield lies in the heart of Kern County, a vast sprawl of lush cropland in California's Central Valley. Here, accidental overdoses among white women have tripled since 1999, according to federal health data, and suicides have doubled.

The death toll has alarmed health-care workers like Eggert and given rise to a loose network of therapists, nurses, pastors and drug counselors struggling to understand a generation of women overwhelmed by modern life and undone by modern medicine.

Some, like Franklin, begin their descent after an injury. Others seek relief from conditions related to menopause. Middle-aged women also are more likely than men to suffer from a variety of painful conditions, including lupus, migraines and rheumatoid arthritis.

Whatever the complaint, doctors and drug companies have since the late 1990s responded with highly addictive painkillers, many of them central nervous system depressants previously reserved for the terminally ill. The more expansive use of opioids has fed an epidemic of dependency, leading to new prescriptions for anti-anxiety drugs and a rash of fatal overdoses.

These drugs appear to be a factor even among suicides, another major contributor to rising female mortality. According to an analysis of Kern County coroner records obtained by the *Post*, 85 white women aged 35 to 60 died by suicide here over the past seven years. About half overdosed on prescription drugs, the *Post* found, and about half of those—21 women—had some combination of opioids, benzodiazepines and alcohol in their bloodstreams.

Many of the women who chose other means of suicide, such as gunshot or hanging, also died in a haze of prescription drugs, the *Post* found. In nearly half of the 28 cases in which a toxicology test was performed, the women had consumed opioids, benzodiazepines or other central nervous system depressants.

When a woman dies in Kern County, it falls to Coroner Manager Dawn Ratliff to determine what happened. Her investigators explore medicine cabinets, flip through journals, scrutinize text messages and interview friends. Repeatedly, a pattern emerges, Ratliff said: A personal crisis leads to prescriptions to soothe the pain. And then they lose control.

"They are worn down. And they can't rise above it," said Ratliff, who puts the blame in part on the rise of social media, which can create unrealistic expectations about how life should go.

"Before, if you lived in a rural area, all you knew was your community. You just knew what people in your community looked like, what their lives were like. You didn't expect to look like a movie star—or live like one," she said.

Ratliff, 60, works closely with Eggert, 58, who created an outreach team for surviving family members of suicides that has been lauded as a national model. Eggert said she, too, has noticed the weariness and the desire for a quick fix to life's problems.

"Women have had to be strong for so long. Opioids are a good way out. Benzos are a good way out," Eggert said. Women "start depending on them to get through. Then, after a while, it's not getting them through anymore. It's running their life."

The autopsy reports are filled with stories of dependency:

Bonnie Jean Marshall, 54, overdosed in 2012 after drinking alcohol and taking three prescription drugs, including the opioid Vicodin and the benzodiazepine

Xanax. She lived in Wofford Heights, a village in the southern Sierra Nevada, and suffered from hypertension, pain and anxiety. She left a suicide note: "Sick for months—can't get well so sorry nana."

Holi Michele Mitchell, 43, shot herself in 2014 after taking Vicodin and two benzodiazepines—Klonopin and Xanax. She lived in Bodfish, a small town in the Kern River Valley, and struggled with depression after her son died in a car accident. His picture and a broken charm bracelet were found by her body.

Cheryl Moore, 56, left a journal that described two suicide attempts in the weeks before she overdosed on painkillers and alcohol in February 2015. Moore, who lived in Bakersfield, had begun taking opiates 18 months earlier after breaking her ankle. Then her husband, Duane, died of liver cancer, leaving a stockpile of stronger painkillers.

Moore's brother, Eugene Frey, said he understands why women might turn to suicide, even when, like his sister, they have the means to seek treatment.

"There is an expectation for them to keep it together. People think, 'Hey, you are white. You are privileged. So why do you have so many problems? Maybe you are the problem,'" Frey said. "There isn't a lot of space for them to be vulnerable."

Eggert is part of a network of female health professionals working to understand the increase in white female mortality in Kern County. She said that she believes it is rooted in the cultural shift of the 1960s. As taboos were stripped away, women began drinking, smoking and medicating themselves more like men. As they aged, they began to suffer the effects: Since 1999, the death rate from alcohol abuse has more than doubled among white women aged 45 to 54, according to CDC data, though the rate for white men remains twice as high.

"It's become normalized," Eggert said. "Why does alcohol kill more people than all the other drugs combined? Because it's acceptable, available, and there's not a thing wrong with it. Why do women fail to see the danger of taking so many pills? Because it's legitimate. It comes from a doctor."

Joan Knowlden, a psychologist in Kern County, said she saw a sharp rise in middle-aged female patients in the early 2000s. Many had turned to alcohol, anti-anxiety drugs and painkillers to "mellow them out." Many had delayed childbearing, Knowlden said, and were trying to raise children just as they reached their peak professionally. Many were also entering menopause, which typically causes a drop in serotonin, a chemical that naturally soothes the brain.

"With perimenopause and menopause, you already have anxiety, sleep loss, loss of bladder control and loss of sex drive," Knowlden said. "It can just become too much."

Sometimes, Knowlden sends her clients to Sherri Bergamo, a nurse practitioner known as "the Hormone Queen of Bakersfield." Bergamo noted that the rise of opioid painkillers coincided with a shift in treatment for menopausal women: Doctors stopped prescribing hormone-replacement therapy after studies found it increased the risk of stroke, blood clots and breast cancer.

Forced to "white knuckle" their way through menopause, Bergamo said, many women sought other forms of relief for mood swings and depression. She offers them custom-mixed hormones, which she argues are safer.

"There are some risks, but they are calculated, and they are carefully monitored," said Bergamo, 74, who has undergone hormone therapy for 26 years. "I believe it saves lives."

Medicine is coming back around to Bergamo's point of view. This year, a panel of experts assembled by the North American Menopause Society concluded that hormone replacement is largely safe, especially for women under 60. In October, the society plans to recommend a return to hormone therapy for most healthy women, according to executive director JoAnn Pinkerton, division director of the Midlife Health Center at the University of Virginia Health System.

One thing menopausal women should probably avoid is long-term opioid use, which can further lower hormone levels, said Stanford University professor Beth Darnall, who specializes in pain psychology research.

"When women go through menopause, there are big changes with pain, anxiety and depression. There is a hard body of research on this," Darnall said. "Opioids, taken long term, reduce the level of hormones in the body. This can lead to a greater sensitivity to pain. And it can feed into this dose-escalation cycle."

> "It's become normalized," Eggert said. "Why does alcohol kill more people than all the other drugs combined? Because it's acceptable, available, and there's not a thing wrong with it. Why do women fail to see the danger of taking so many pills? Because it's legitimate. It comes from a doctor."

The turning point in Franklin's life came in the late 1990s, when she said her tailbone was fractured during an episode of domestic violence. The pain led her to Vicodin, starting with the lowest dose: tablets containing five milligrams of the opioid hydrocodone.

"It might as well have been baby aspirin," she says now. "All it did was make me a little sleepy."

At the time, Franklin was managing a grocery store, a physically demanding job that had her lifting Halloween pumpkins, boxes of Easter candy and endless cases of soda. Within a few months, she persuaded her doctor to double the dose. Then she begged for stronger opiates, cycling through prescriptions for codeine, oxycodone and OxyContin.

Periodically, her doctors cut her off. "They would say, 'You kind of like this too much,'" Franklin recalled. So she would call 911 and take a trip to the emergency room, where doctors typically offered a shot of Demerol, another powerful opioid.

In the early 2000s, Franklin's mother died, her second marriage began to unravel, and she decided to quit working. Doctors added antidepressants, sleeping pills and anti-anxiety medications to her list of prescriptions.

Her world began to narrow. She saw fewer people. Franklin said she became "a hermit."

Her friend Eggert suggested a psychologist, group therapy, long walks, church, yoga. Franklin rejected each idea. She came to believe she needed surgery. So in 2004, a surgeon implanted metal rods at the base of her spine.

The surgery failed to provide relief, and Franklin filed for disability.

"I was told it would be 80 percent better," she said, "but instead it was 80 percent worse."

Franklin keeps an X-ray of her back clipped to her refrigerator. If anyone questions her pain, she points to the X-ray: "They see those plates and they know it's bad."

In recent months, her chronic drug use has generated a host of new health problems, including pancreatitis and irritable bowel syndrome. Those conditions led to more doctor visits, which produced more prescriptions, and more pills to shake out of more bottles in her pink-tiled bathroom.

Her bottle of vodka, once stowed under the bathroom sink, now stays out on the floor, within easy reach.

Print Citations

CMS: Kindy, Kimberly, and Dan Keating. "Risky Alone, Deadly Together." In *The Reference Shelf: Prescription Drug Abuse*, edited by Betsy Maury, 91-96. Ipswich, MA: H.W. Wilson, 2017.

MLA: Kindy, Kimberly, and Dan Keating. "Risky Alone, Deadly Together." *The Reference Shelf: Prescription Drug Abuse*. Ed. Betsy Maury. Ipswich: H.W. Wilson, 2017. 91-96. Print.

APA: Kindy, K., & D. Keating. (2017). Risky alone, dead together. In Betsy Maury (Ed.), *The reference shelf: Prescription drug abuse* (pp. 91-96). Ipswich, MA: H.W. Wilson. (Original work published 2016)

3

Doctors, Big Pharma and the Gateway to Abuse

Credit: Photo by John Moore/Getty Images

Jackson, 27, who said he is addicted to prescription medication, lies passed out in a public library on March 14, 2016 in New London, CT. Police say an increasing number of suburban addicts are coming into the city to buy heroin, which is much cheaper than opioid painkillers. On March 15, the U.S. Centers for Disease Control (CDC), announced guidelines for doctors to reduce the amount of opioid painkillers prescribed nationwide. The CDC estimates that most new heroin addicts first became hooked on prescription pain medication before graduating to heroin, which is stronger and cheaper.

The Prescription Drug Business

The prescription drug crisis is the result of many coinciding factors and fault can be spread among many different players, including the pharmaceutical companies that manufacture prescription drugs, the physicians who prescribe them, and the patients who misuse and mismanage their medications. A major component of the problem is American society itself. The simple fact that pharmaceuticals, medicine, and mental health are *businesses* in the United States, rather than *services* managed in the public interest predisposes American culture to exploitation and abuse.

Big Trouble in Big Pharma

In the 1990s, there was a broad push in the United States for physicians to take a more aggressive role in treating pain in patients. The movement adopted a marketing slogan, calling for pain to be recognized as the "fifth vital sign," which, the movement held, should be measured and estimated in *every* patient the same as a physician would check body temperature, pulse rate, respiration rate, and blood pressure (the four recognized "vital signs" of Western medicine). The Joint Commission, a US nonprofit organization that accredits healthcare programs, adopted the "fifth vital sign" framework in the late 1990s and, in 2000, began offering a continuing education program for doctors containing the results of questionable studies suggesting that opioid pain relievers carried no significant risk of addiction. According to a CNN report, the publication was partially funded by Purdue Pharma, one of the world's largest opioid manufacturers.[1] A 2003 report from the Government Accountability Office (GAO) revealed that Purdue Pharma had distributed 34,000 coupons for free OxyContin prescriptions to physicians, along with advertising swag like fishing hats and plush toys, in an effort to promote their products.[2]

Between 1996 and 2005, the pharmaceutical industry tripled spending on advertisements, with a fivefold increase in advertising direct to consumers. This intense marketing campaign had a major impact on physician and patient behavior. For instance, a 2003 study in the *Canadian Medical Association Journal*, found that US patients are more than twice as likely to request an advertised drug than patients in Canada, where direct-to-patient advertisement is prohibited. Advertisements and marketing materials are inherently manipulative, promoting positive aspects of a product while downplaying risks and dangers and the aggressive marketing of prescription drugs urged physicians to rely too much on pharmacological options while also creating a patient population that demanded certain kinds of treatments even when other treatments might be equally effective with lower levels of risk.[3]

Between 1999 and 2014, sales of opioid drugs quadrupled in America, with US patients accounting for more than four-fifths of the global supply. During this same period, news of America's growing prescription medication problem spread via investigative journalism and the manipulative, misleading practices of pharmaceutical companies was identified as a root cause of the problem. In a 2007 court case, executives at Purdue Pharma pled guilty to charges of misleading physicians, patients, and regulators about the addiction risk of OxyContin, which the company had marketed as a low-risk alterative to competing opioids like Percocet and Vicodin, and paid a $600 million fine. With increased scrutiny on drug companies, Department of Justice (DOJ) investigators found that drug companies offered benefits and even monetary payments to physicians who prescribed more of their opioid products. In December of 2016, executives at the drug company Insys Therapeutics were arrested for taking part in a conspiracy in which the company had been bribing physicians to prescribe the opioid fentanyl, which is 50 times more powerful and potentially more addictive than heroin.[4]

Between 2015 and 2017, state and municipal attorneys filed dozens of civil suits against drug manufacturers like Purdue Pharma and Johnson & Johnson, alleging that the companies irresponsibly marketed dangerous drugs, downplayed the risk of addiction, and engaged in unethical practices to dupe or bribe physicians into more frequently prescribing their products. In response, drug companies announced they were responding to the addiction crisis by developing new "slow release" opioid formulas that would be, in theory, more difficult to abuse. However, even as drug companies claimed to be taking responsibility, investigative reports indicated that the same companies were spending tens of millions to fund advocacy groups to fight against state efforts to limit prescriptions. The Associated Press and the Center for Public Integrity found, in a 2016 investigation, that pharmaceutical companies had trained and funded at least 1,350 lobbyists to fight against state and municipal efforts to limit opioid prescriptions.[5]

The Physician Factor

Physicians are the gateway between drug manufacturers and patients, charged with the ultimate responsibility of deciding when and how to dispense medications and when certain treatments are more appropriate than others. A majority of physicians attempt to adhere to ethical guidelines regarding the use of medication, though this is not always the case. The role that physicians have played in the prescription drug crisis is a function of many factors, including the fact that drug companies have promoted a culture of overprescription by misleading physicians with false research and/or data. In addition, the gross economic inequities of American healthcare with regard to treatment options and medical insurance limit the options available to physicians and result in overreliance on pharmacotherapy rather than more comprehensive types of treatment.

A 2012 report from the American Psychological Association found that health insurance payments to psychiatrists were higher and easier to obtain when medication was prescribed, rather than recommending therapy. The study found that physicians could earn twice to three times as much by prescribing medication than by recommending behavioral therapy as a treatment for anxiety or depression.[6] A combination of unethical drug manufacturer and medical insurance policies is thus one of the central pillars of the drug abuse epidemic, encouraging prescription drug use in situations where other therapeutic options might be more effective and less dangerous.

In a 1990 report in the *Western Journal of Medicine*, the authors identified four general "types" of doctors who have all played a role in creating and exacerbating prescription abuse problem; dated physicians, disabled physicians, dishonest physicians, and duped physicians. Dated physicians are those who are operating on out-of-date information about the efficacy of and/or potential risks of certain drugs. Disabled physicians are doctors whose judgment has been impaired by personal issues like drug addiction, depression, or mental illness, making it more difficult for such physicians to make responsible decisions with regard to their patients. Duped physicians are those who have essentially been misled by pharmaceutical companies and so, while attempting to act in their patients' best interests, may overprescribe potentially dangerous drugs without effectively portraying the potential dangers of abuse and addiction. Finally, the authors use the term dishonest physicians for those whose prescription habits are based on personal gain and who therefore, as the authors claim, "use their medical license to deal drugs," or purposefully overprescribe in an effort to earn higher payouts from medical insurance or drug companies.[7]

Physicians in all of the above categories contribute to the problem, but this occurs in conjunction with an evolving patient culture in the United States as patients increasingly demand fast, simple solutions to their problems. In some cases, physicians who refuse to dispense medication may lose their patients and patients may go "doctor shopping," trying numerous primary care physicians until they find one who will more readily dispense the medication they desire.

Even though physicians have contributed to the problem, they are also the most important actors in any legitimate effort to address the issue. Each year, more than 80 percent of Americans have contact with a healthcare professional, and this means that physicians have the best chance of detecting signs of abuse before it becomes addiction, or referring individuals with addiction to appropriate treatments. In addition, because there are patients who legitimately require opioids, depressants, and stimulants, there remains a pressing need for physicians who are able to responsibly dispense dangerous chemicals while ensuring that patients are well informed and prepared to cope with the potential dangers.[8]

The Healthcare Market

The effort to address drug addiction, both of prescription and illicit drugs, is hampered, in many ways, by the healthcare industry. Drug companies, insurance companies, and physicians compete for funding and resources in a crowded marketplace and this encourages a focus on short-term symptom-based treatment (which is less expensive) and discourages alternative or more comprehensive efforts to address public health issues. In the 1980s and '90s, Switzerland faced a similar opioid addiction crisis to the one affecting the United States in the twenty-first century and the Swiss government initially attempted to address the problem by enacting regulations to limit the supply of heroin and prescription opioids in the population.

This strategy, which is similar to current US policies, failed to reduce abuse rates and exacerbated the problem as addicts switched from pharmaceutical medication to heroin purchased through dangerous criminal sources. Realizing that the approach was counterproductive, the Swiss government tried a different strategy through a series of government-funded addiction clinics where medical professionals dispensed opioids to patients who were then asked to participate in behavioral, family, and lifestyle counseling programs. Over several years, Switzerland managed to completely eliminate prescription opioid overdoses and drastically reduced heroin use across the country.

The Swiss experiment was made possible by the fact that Switzerland's doctors, hospitals, and clinics are paid through tax revenues and medical care is therefore managed, by the government, as a public trust. By contrast, the United States healthcare system is a free market in which companies compete for consumers and in which the companies responsible for healthcare are motivated by profit rather than public welfare. In simple consumer markets, such as those marketing and selling consumer electronics or entertainment products, free-market competition results in innovation as companies are forced to put out better products to compete with their competitors. In complex markets, like education, healthcare, and agriculture, free-market competition does not benefit consumers and typically results in corporate exploitation.

Companies maximize profits by investing as little as possible in their products and charging the highest possible price to consumers. Medical insurance companies, therefore, urge patients towards low-cost treatment options and discourage, or refuse to cover, more comprehensive treatment programs even if such treatments are arguably better for patients. Therefore, an insurance plan might give patients a break on prescription medication, while covering only a fraction (if any) of the cost of mental health services that might be used to treat underlying issues motivating a patient's drug abuse. Alternative treatments for addiction, therefore, are often part of a boutique medical industry marketed to affluent patients and often unavailable to those at lower income levels, which includes the vast majority of substance abusers.

Legislators and public health advocates trying to work within the profit-driven US system often rely on regulation, arguing that drug and insurance companies must be forced to provide access to treatments that have been proven to have legitimate public health benefits. While such efforts can be successful, patients, legislators, and welfare advocates must repeatedly fight against the very nature of the industry in order to advance treatment and public welfare. Unless some future revolution fundamentally changes the US healthcare system, the antagonistic relationship between public welfare and corporate profit will continue to limit access to new treatments and will essentially slow the pace of change and inhibit the nation's ability to address most of the nation's most significant health crises.

Micah L. Issitt

Works Used

Lawson, Alex. "No Accident: Deadly Greed of Pharmaceutical Companies Drives the Heroin Epidemic." *Huffpost*. Huffington Post. Jan 20 2017. Web. 23 Aug 2017.

"Makers and Distributors of Opioid Painkillers Are under Scrutiny." *The Economist*. Economist. Apr 6 2017. Web. 22 Aug 2017.

Mandell, Brian F. "The Fifth Vital Sign: A Complex Story of Politics and Patient Care." *Cleveland Journal of Medicine*. June 2016. Vol. 83, No. 6, 400–01.

"Misuse of Prescription Drugs." *Drugabuse.gov*. National Institute on Drug Abuse (NIDA). 2016. Web. 22 Aug 2017.

Mulvihill, Geoff, Whyte, Liz Essley, and Ben Wieder. "Drugmakers Fought State Opioid Limits Amid Crisis." *AP*. Associated Press. Sep 18 2016. Web. 25 Aug 2017.

Smith, Brendan L. "Inappropriate prescribing." *APA*. American Psychological Association. 2012. Vol. 43, No. 6, 36.

Wesson, D.R. and D.E. Smith. "Prescription Drug Abuse: Patient, Physician, and Cultural Responsibilities." *Western Journal of Medicine*. May 1990. Vol. 152, No. 5, 613–16.

Notes

1. Mandell, "The Fifth Vital Sign: A Complex Story of Politics and Patient Care."
2. Lawson, "No Accident: Deadly Green of Pharmaceutical Companies Drives the Heroin Epidemic."
3. Smith, "Inappropriate Prescribing."
4. "Makers and Distributors of Opioid Painkillers Are under Scrutiny," *The Economist*.
5. Mulvihill, Whyte, and Wieder, "Drugmakers Fought State Opioid Limits Amid Crisis."
6. Smith, "Inappropriate Prescribing."
7. Wesson and Smith, "Prescription Drug Abuse: Patient, Physician, and Cultural Responsibilities."
8. "Misuse of Prescription Drugs," *Drugabuse.gov*.

The Selling of Attention Deficit Disorder

By Alan Schwarz

The New York Times, December 14, 2013

After more than 50 years leading the fight to legitimize attention deficit hyperactivity disorder, Keith Conners could be celebrating.

Severely hyperactive and impulsive children, once shunned as bad seeds, are now recognized as having a real neurological problem. Doctors and parents have largely accepted drugs like Adderall and Concerta to temper the traits of classic A.D.H.D., helping youngsters succeed in school and beyond.

But Dr. Conners did not feel triumphant this fall as he addressed a group of fellow A.D.H.D. specialists in Washington. He noted that recent data from the Centers for Disease Control and Prevention show that the diagnosis had been made in 15 percent of high school-age children, and that the number of children on medication for the disorder had soared to 3.5 million from 600,000 in 1990. He questioned the rising rates of diagnosis and called them "a national disaster of dangerous proportions."

"The numbers make it look like an epidemic. Well, it's not. It's preposterous," Dr. Conners, a psychologist and professor emeritus at Duke University, said in a subsequent interview. "This is a concoction to justify the giving out of medication at unprecedented and unjustifiable levels."

The rise of A.D.H.D. diagnoses and prescriptions for stimulants over the years coincided with a remarkably successful two-decade campaign by pharmaceutical companies to publicize the syndrome and promote the pills to doctors, educators and parents. With the children's market booming, the industry is now employing similar marketing techniques as it focuses on adult A.D.H.D., which could become even more profitable.

Few dispute that classic A.D.H.D., historically estimated to affect 5 percent of children, is a legitimate disability that impedes success at school, work and personal life. Medication often assuages the severe impulsiveness and inability to concentrate, allowing a person's underlying drive and intelligence to emerge.

But even some of the field's longtime advocates say the zeal to find and treat every A.D.H.D. child has led to too many people with scant symptoms receiving the diagnosis and medication. The disorder is now the second most frequent long-term diagnosis made in children, narrowly trailing asthma, according to a *New York Times* analysis of C.D.C. data.

Behind that growth has been drug company marketing that has stretched the image of classic A.D.H.D. to include relatively normal behavior like carelessness and impatience, and has often overstated the pills' benefits. Advertising on television and in popular magazines like *People* and *Good Housekeeping* has cast common childhood forgetfulness and poor grades as grounds for medication that, among other benefits, can result in "schoolwork that matches his intelligence" and ease family tension.

A 2002 ad for Adderall showed a mother playing with her son and saying, "Thanks for taking out the garbage."

The Food and Drug Administration has cited every major A.D.H.D. drug—stimulants like Adderall, Concerta, Focalin and Vyvanse, and nonstimulants like Intuniv and Strattera—for false and misleading advertising since 2000, some multiple times.

Sources of information that would seem neutral also delivered messages from the pharmaceutical industry. Doctors paid by drug companies have published research and delivered presentations that encourage physicians to make diagnoses more often that discredit growing concerns about overdiagnosis.

Many doctors have portrayed the medications as benign—"safer than aspirin," some say—even though they can have significant side effects and are regulated in the same class as morphine and oxycodone because of their potential for abuse and addiction. Patient advocacy groups tried to get the government to loosen regulation of stimulants while having sizable portions of their operating budgets covered by pharmaceutical interests.

Companies even try to speak to youngsters directly. Shire—the longtime market leader, with several A.D.H.D. medications including Adderall—recently subsidized 50,000 copies of a comic book that tries to demystify the disorder and uses superheroes to tell children, "Medicines may make it easier to pay attention and control your behavior!"

Profits for the A.D.H.D. drug industry have soared. Sales of stimulant medication in 2012 were nearly $9 billion, more than five times the $1.7 billion a decade before, according to the data company IMS Health.

Even Roger Griggs, the pharmaceutical executive who introduced Adderall in 1994, said he strongly opposes marketing stimulants to the general public because of their dangers. He calls them "nuclear bombs," warranted only under extreme circumstances and when carefully overseen by a physician.

Psychiatric breakdown and suicidal thoughts are the most rare and extreme results of stimulant addiction, but those horror stories are far outnumbered by people who, seeking to study or work longer hours, cannot sleep for days, lose their appetite or hallucinate. More can simply become habituated to the pills and feel they cannot cope without them.

Tom Casola, the Shire vice president who oversees the A.D.H.D. division, said in an interview that the company aims to provide effective treatment for those with the disorder, and that ultimately doctors were responsible for proper evaluations and prescriptions. He added that he understood some of the concerns voiced by the Food and Drug Administration and others about aggressive ads, and said that materials that run afoul of guidelines are replaced.

"Shire—and I think the vast majority of pharmaceutical companies—intend to market in a way that's responsible and in a way that is compliant with the regulations," Mr. Casola said. "Again, I like to think we come at it from a higher order. We are dealing with patients' health."

A spokesman for Janssen Pharmaceuticals, which makes Concerta, said in an email, "Over the years, we worked with clinicians, parents and advocacy groups to help educate health care practitioners and caregivers about diagnosis and treatment of A.D.H.D., including safe and effective use of medication."

Now targeting adults, Shire and two patient advocacy groups have recruited celebrities like the Maroon 5 musician Adam Levine for their marketing campaign, "It's Your A.D.H.D.—Own It." Online quizzes sponsored by drug companies are designed to encourage people to pursue treatment. A medical education video sponsored by Shire portrays a physician making a diagnosis of the disorder in an adult in a six-minute conversation, after which the doctor recommends medication.

Like most psychiatric conditions, A.D.H.D. has no definitive test, and most experts in the field agree that its symptoms are open to interpretation by patients, parents and doctors. The American Psychiatric Association, which receives significant financing from drug companies, has gradually loosened the official criteria for the disorder to include common childhood behavior like "makes careless mistakes" or "often has difficulty waiting his or her turn."

The idea that a pill might ease troubles and tension has proved seductive to worried parents, rushed doctors and others.

"Pharma pushed as far as they could, but you can't just blame the virus," said Dr. Lawrence Diller, a behavioral pediatrician in Walnut Creek, Calif. "You have to have a susceptible host for the epidemic to take hold. There's something they know about us that they utilize and exploit."

Selling to Doctors

Modern marketing of stimulants began with the name Adderall itself. Mr. Griggs bought a small pharmaceutical company that produced a weight-loss pill named Obetrol. Suspecting that it might treat a relatively unappreciated condition then called attention deficit disorder, and found in about 3 to 5 percent of children, he took "A.D.D." and fiddled with snappy suffixes. He cast a word with the widest net.

All.

For A.D.D.

A.D.D. for All.

Adderall.

"It was meant to be kind of an inclusive thing," Mr. Griggs recalled.

Adderall quickly established itself as a competitor of the field's most popular drug, Ritalin. Shire, realizing the drug's potential, bought Mr. Griggs's company for $186 million and spent millions more to market the pill to doctors. After all, patients can buy only what their physicians buy into.

As is typical among pharmaceutical companies, Shire gathered hundreds of doctors at meetings at which a physician paid by the company explained a new drug's value.

Like most psychiatric conditions, A.D.H.D. has no definitive test, and most experts in the field agree that its symptoms are open to interpretation by patients, parents and doctors.

Such a meeting was held for Shire's long-acting version of Adderall, Adderall XR, in April 2002, and included a presentation that to many critics, exemplifies how questionable A.D.H.D. messages are delivered.

Dr. William W. Dodson, a psychiatrist from Denver, stood before 70 doctors at the Ritz-Carlton Hotel and Spa in Pasadena, Calif., and clicked through slides that encouraged them to "educate the patient on the lifelong nature of the disorder and the benefits of lifelong treatment." But that assertion was not supported by science, as studies then and now have shown that perhaps half of A.D.H.D. children are not impaired as adults, and that little is known about the risks or efficacy of long-term medication use.

The PowerPoint document, obtained by the *Times*, asserted that stimulants were not "drugs of abuse" because people who overdose "feel nothing" or "feel bad." Yet these drugs are classified by the government among the most abusable substances in medicine, largely because of their effects on concentration and mood. Overdosing can cause severe heart problems and psychotic behavior.

Slides described side effects of Adderall XR as "generally mild," despite clinical trials showing notable rates of insomnia, significant appetite suppression and mood swings, as well as rare instances of hallucinations. Those side effects increase significantly among patients who take more pills than prescribed.

Another slide warned that later in life, children with A.D.H.D. faced "job failure or underemployment," "fatal car wrecks," "criminal involvement," "unwanted pregnancy" and venereal diseases, but did not mention that studies had not assessed whether stimulants decreased those risks.

Dr. Conners of Duke, in the audience that day, said the message was typical for such gatherings sponsored by pharmaceutical companies: Their drugs were harmless, and any traces of A.D.H.D. symptoms (which can be caused by a number of issues, including lack of sleep and family discord) should be treated with stimulant medication.

In an interview last month, Dr. Dodson said he makes a new diagnosis in about 300 patients a year and, because he disagrees with studies showing that many A.D.H.D. children are not impaired as adults, always recommends their taking stimulants for the rest of their lives.

He said that concern about abuse and side effects is "incredibly overblown," and that his longtime work for drug companies does not influence his opinions. He said he received about $2,000 for the 2002 talk for Shire. He earned $45,500 in speaking fees from pharmaceutical companies in 2010 to 2011, according to *Pro-Publica*, which tracks such payments.

"If people want help, my job is to make sure they get it," Dr. Dodson said. Regarding people concerned about prescribing physicians being paid by drug companies, he added: "They like a good conspiracy theory. I don't let it slow me down."

Many of the scientific studies cited by drug company speakers involved Dr. Joseph Biederman, a prominent child psychiatrist at Harvard University and Massachusetts General Hospital. In 2008, a Senate investigation revealed that Dr. Biederman's research on many psychiatric conditions had been substantially financed by drug companies, including Shire. Those companies also paid him $1.6 million in speaking and consulting fees. He has denied that the payments influenced his research.

Dr. Conners called Dr. Biederman "unequivocally the most published psychopharmacology maven for A.D.H.D.," one who is well known for embracing stimulants and dismissing detractors. Findings from Dr. Biederman's dozens of studies on the disorder and specific brands of stimulants have filled the posters and pamphlets of pharmaceutical companies that financed the work.

Those findings typically delivered three messages: The disorder was underdiagnosed; stimulants were effective and safe; and unmedicated A.D.H.D. led to significant risks for academic failure, drug dependence, car accidents and brushes with the law.

Dr. Biederman was frequently quoted about the benefits of stimulants in interviews and company news releases. In 2006, for example, he told Reuters Health, "If a child is brilliant but is doing just O.K. in school, that child may need treatment, which would result in their performing brilliantly at school."

This year, Dr. Biederman told the medical newsletter *Medscape* regarding medication for those with A.D.H.D., "Don't leave home without it."

Dr. Biederman did not respond to requests for an interview.

Most of Dr. Biederman's critics said that they believed his primary motivation was always to help children with legitimate A.D.H.D. and that risks of untreated A.D.H.D. can be significant. What concerned them was how Dr. Biederman's high-profile and unwavering promotion of stimulants armed drug companies with the published science needed to create powerful advertisements—many of which cast medications as benign solutions to childhood behavior falling far short of legitimate A.D.H.D.

"He gave them credibility," said Richard M. Scheffler, a professor of health economics and public policy at the University of California, Berkeley, who has written extensively on stimulants. "He didn't have a balance. He became totally convinced that it's a good thing and can be more widely used."

Building a Message

Drug companies used the research of Dr. Biederman and others to create compelling messages for doctors. "Adderall XR Improves Academic Performance," an ad in a psychiatry journal declared in 2003, leveraging two Biederman studies financed by Shire. A Concerta ad barely mentioned A.D.H.D., but said the medication would "allow your patients to experience life's successes every day."

Some studies had shown that stimulant medication helped some elementary school children with carefully evaluated A.D.H.D. to improve scores in reading and math tests, primarily by helping them concentrate. The concern, some doctors said, is that long-term, wider academic benefits have not been proved—and that ads suggesting they have can tempt doctors, perhaps subconsciously, to prescribe drugs with risks to healthy children merely to improve their grades or self-esteem.

"There are decades of research into how advertising influences doctors' prescribing practices," said Dr. Aaron Kesselheim of Brigham and Women's Hospital in Boston, who specializes in pharmaceutical ethics. "Even though they'll tell you that they're giving patients unbiased, evidence-based information, in fact they're more likely to tell you what the drug company told them, whether it's the benefits of the drugs or the risks of those drugs."

Drug company advertising also meant good business for medical journals—the same journals that published papers supporting the use of the drugs. The most prominent publication in the field, the *Journal of the American Academy of Child & Adolescent Psychiatry*, went from no ads for A.D.H.D. medications from 1990 to 1993 to about 100 pages per year a decade later. Almost every full-page color ad was for an A.D.H.D. drug.

As is legal and common in pharmaceutical marketing, stimulants' possible side effects like insomnia, irritability and psychotic episodes were printed in small type and dominated by other messages. One Adderall XR brochure included the recording of a man's voice reassuring doctors: "Amphetamines have been used medically for nearly 70 years. That's a legacy of safety you can count on." He did not mention any side effects.

Drug companies used sales representatives to promote the drugs in person. Brian Lutz, a Shire salesman for Adderall XR from 2004 to 2009, said he met with 75 psychiatrists in his Oakland, Calif., territory at least every two weeks—about 30 to 40 times apiece annually—to show them posters and pamphlets that highlighted the medicine's benefits for grades and behavior.

If a psychiatrist asked about issues like side effects or abuse, Mr. Lutz said, they were played down. He said he was told to acknowledge risks matter-of-factly for legal reasons, but to refer only to the small print in the package insert or offer Shire's phone number for more information.

"It was never like, 'This is a serious side effect, you need to watch out for it,'" Mr. Lutz recalled. "You wanted to give them more information because we're talking about kids here, you know? But it was all very positive."

A Shire spokeswoman said the company would not comment on any specific employee and added, "Shire sales representatives are trained to deliver fair and balanced presentations that include information regarding the safety of our products."

Mr. Lutz, now pursuing a master's degree and hoping to work in mental health, recalled his Shire work with ambivalence. He never lied or was told to lie, he said.

He said he still would recommend Adderall XR and similar stimulants for A.D.H.D. children and adults.

What he regrets, he said, "is how we sold these pills like they were cars, when we knew they weren't just cars."

Selling to Parents

In September 2005, over a cover that heralded Kirstie Alley's waistline and Matt Damon's engagement, subscribers to *People* magazine saw a wraparound advertisement for Adderall XR. A mother hugged her smiling child holding a sheet of paper with a "B+" written on it.

"Finally!" she said. "Schoolwork that matches his intelligence."

When federal guidelines were loosened in the late 1990s to allow the marketing of controlled substances like stimulants directly to the public, pharmaceutical companies began targeting perhaps the most impressionable consumers of all: parents, specifically mothers.

A magazine ad for Concerta had a grateful mother saying, "Better test scores at school, more chores done at home, an independence I try to encourage, a smile I can always count on." A 2009 ad for Intuniv, Shire's nonstimulant treatment for A.D.H.D., showed a child in a monster suit taking off his hairy mask to reveal his adorable smiling self.

"There's a great kid in there," the text read.

"There's no way in God's green earth we would ever promote" a controlled substance like Adderall directly to consumers, Mr. Griggs said as he was shown several advertisements. "You're talking about a product that's having a major impact on brain chemistry. Parents are very susceptible to this type of stuff."

The Food and Drug Administration has repeatedly instructed drug companies to withdraw such ads for being false and misleading, or exaggerating the effects of the medication. Many studies, often sponsored by pharmaceutical companies, have determined that untreated A.D.H.D. was associated with later-life problems. But no science determined that stimulant treatment has the overarching benefits suggested in those ads, the F.D.A. has pointed out in numerous warning letters to manufacturers since 2000.

Shire agreed last February to pay $57.5 million in fines to resolve allegations of improper sales and advertising of several drugs, including Vyvanse, Adderall XR and Daytrana, a patch that delivers stimulant medication through the skin. Mr. Casola of Shire declined to comment on the settlement because it was not fully resolved.

He added that the company's current promotional materials emphasize how its medications provide "symptom control" rather than turn monsters into children who take out the garbage. He pointed to a Shire brochure and web page that more candidly than ever discuss side effects and the dangers of sharing medication with others.

However, many critics said that the most questionable advertising helped build a market that is now virtually self-sustaining. Drug companies also communicated with parents through sources who appeared independent, from support groups to teachers.

The primary A.D.H.D. patient advocacy group, Children and Adults with Attention-Deficit/Hyperactivity Disorder, or Chadd, was founded in 1987 to gain greater respect for the condition and its treatment with Ritalin, the primary drug available at the time. Considerable funding was provided several years later by Ciba-Geigy Pharmaceuticals, Ritalin's primary manufacturer. Further drug company support helped create public service announcements and pamphlets, some of which tried to dispel concerns about Ritalin; one Chadd "fact sheet" conflicted with 60 years of science in claiming, "Psychostimulant drugs are not addictive."

A 1995 documentary on PBS detailed how Chadd did not disclose its relationship with drug companies to either the Drug Enforcement Administration, which it was then lobbying to ease government regulation of stimulants, or the Department of Education, with which it collaborated on an A.D.H.D. educational video.

Chadd subsequently became more open in disclosing its backers. The program for its 2000 annual convention, for example, thanked by name its 11 primary sponsors, all drug companies. According to Chadd records, Shire paid the group a total of $3 million from 2006 to 2009 to have Chadd's bimonthly magazine, *Attention*, distributed to doctors' offices nationwide.

Chadd records show that the group has historically received about $1 million a year, one-third of its annual revenue, from pharmaceutical company grants and advertising. Regarding his company's support, Mr. Casola said, "I think it is fair to call it a marketing expense, but it's an arm's-length relationship."

"We don't control what they do," he said. "We do support them. We do support broadly what they are trying to do in the marketplace—in society maybe is a better way to say it."

Advocates Answer

The chief executive of Chadd, Ruth Hughes, said in an interview that most disease-awareness groups receive similar pharmaceutical support. She said drug companies did not influence the group's positions and activities, and noted that Chadd receives about $800,000 a year from the C.D.C. as well.

"One pharma company wanted to get Chadd volunteers to work at their booth to sort of get peer counseling, and we said no, won't do that, not going there," Dr. Hughes said, adding, "It would be seen as an endorsement."

A.D.H.D. patient advocates often say that many parents resist having their child evaluated because of the stigma of mental illness and the perceived risks of medication.

To combat this, groups have published lists of "Famous People With A.D.H.D." to reassure parents of the good company their children could join with a diagnosis. One, in circulation since the mid-1990s and now posted on the psychcentral.com information portal beside two ads for Strattera, includes Thomas Edison, Abraham Lincoln, Galileo and Socrates.

The idea of unleashing children's potential is attractive to teachers and school administrators, who can be lured by A.D.H.D. drugs' ability to subdue some of their most rambunctious and underachieving students. Some have provided parents with pamphlets to explain the disorder and the promise of stimulants.

Susan Parry, who raised three boys in a top public school system on Mercer Island, outside Seattle, in the 1990s, said teachers pushed her into having her feisty son Andy evaluated for A.D.H.D. She said one teacher told her that her own twins were thriving on Ritalin.

Mrs. Parry still has the pamphlet given to her by the school psychologist, which states: "Parents should be aware that these medicines do not 'drug' or 'alter' the brain of the child. They make the child 'normal.'" She and her husband, Michael, put Andy on Ritalin. The Parrys later noticed that on the back of the pamphlet, in small type, was the logo of Ciba-Geigy. A school official told them in a letter, which they provided to the *Times*, that the materials had been given to the district by a Ciba representative.

> **Because studies have shown that A.D.H.D. can run in families, drug companies use the children's market to grow the adult one.**

"They couldn't advertise to the general public yet," said Michael Parry, adding that his son never had A.D.H.D. and after three years was taken off Ritalin because of sleep problems and heart palpitations. "But somebody came up with this idea, which was genius. I definitely felt seduced and enticed. I'd say baited."

Although proper A.D.H.D. diagnoses and medication have helped millions of children lead more productive lives, concerns remain that questionable diagnoses carry unappreciated costs.

"They were telling me, 'Honey, there's something wrong with your brain and this little pill's going to fix everything,'" said Micaela Kimball, who received the diagnosis in 1997 as a high school freshman in Ithaca, N.Y., and is now a freelance writer in Boston. "It changed my whole self-image, and it took me years to get out from under that."

Today, 1 in 7 children receives a diagnosis of the disorder by the age of 18. As these teenagers graduate into adulthood, drug companies are looking to keep their business.

The New Frontier: Adults

The studio audience roared with excitement two years ago as Ty Pennington, host of *The Revolution* on ABC, demonstrated how having adult A.D.H.D. felt to him. He staged two people struggling to play Ping-Pong with several balls at once while reciting the alphabet backward, as a crowd clapped and laughed. Then things got serious.

A psychiatrist on the program said that "the prison population is full of people with undiagnosed A.D.H.D." He told viewers, "Go get this diagnosis" so "you can skyrocket." He said that stimulant medication was effective and "safer than aspirin."

No one mentioned that Mr. Pennington had been a paid spokesman for Shire from 2006 to 2008. His Adderall XR video testimonials—the medication "literally changed my life" and "gave me confidence," he said in a 2008 ad—had drawn an F.D.A. reprimand for overstating Adderall's effects while omitting all risks.

Mr. Pennington said through a spokeswoman: "I am not a medical expert. I am a television host."

Many experts agree that the disorder was dismissed for too long as affecting only children. Estimates of the prevalence of adult A.D.H.D. in the United States—derived through research often backed by pharmaceutical companies—have typically ranged from 3 to 5 percent. Given that adults far outnumber children, this suggests that the adult market could be twice as large.

Because many doctors and potential patients did not think adults could have A.D.H.D., drug companies sold the concept of the disorder as much as their medications for it.

"The fastest-growing segment of the market now is the new adults who were never diagnosed," Angus Russell told Bloomberg TV in 2011 when he was Shire's chief executive. Nearly 16 million prescriptions for A.D.H.D. medications were written for people ages 20 to 39 in 2012, close to triple the 5.6 million just five years before, according to IMS Health. No data show how many patients those prescriptions represent, but some experts have estimated two million.

Foreseeing the market back in 2004, Shire sponsored a booklet that according to its cover would "help clinicians recognize and diagnose adults with A.D.H.D." Its author was Dr. Dodson, who had delivered the presentation at the Adderall XR launch two years before. Rather than citing the widely accepted estimate of 3 to 5 percent, the booklet offered a much higher figure.

"About 10 percent of adults have A.D.H.D., which means you're probably already treating patients with A.D.H.D. even though you don't know it," the first paragraph ended. But the two studies cited for that 10 percent figure, from 1995 and 1996, involved only children; no credible national study before or since has estimated an adult prevalence as high as 10 percent.

Dr. Dodson said he used the 10 percent figure because, despite several studies estimating adult rates as far lower, "once a child has A.D.H.D., he does for life. It doesn't go away with age."

The booklet later quotes a patient of his named Scarlett reassuring doctors: "If you give me a drink or a drug, I'll abuse it, but not this medication. I don't consider it a drug. Drugs get abused. Medication helps people have satisfying lives."

Shire's 2008 print campaign for adult A.D.H.D. portrayed a gloomy future to prospective patients. One ad showed a happy couple's wedding photo with the bride airbrushed out and "DIVORCED" stamped on it. "The consequences may be serious," the ad said, citing a study by Dr. Biederman supported in part by Shire. Although Dr. Biederman's study showed a higher rate of divorce among adults with the disorder, it did not assess whether stimulant treatment significantly deterred such consequences.

Questionable Quizzes

Adults searching for information on A.D.H.D. encounter websites with short quizzes that can encourage normal people to think they might have it. Many such tests are sponsored by drug companies in ways hidden or easily missed.

"Could you have A.D.H.D.?" beckons one quiz, sponsored by Shire, on the website everydayhealth.com. Six questions ask how often someone has trouble in matters like "getting things in order," "remembering appointments" or "getting started" on projects.

A user who splits answers evenly between "rarely" and "sometimes" receives the result "A.D.H.D. Possible." Five answers of "sometimes" and one "often" tell the user, "A.D.H.D. May Be Likely."

In a nationwide telephone poll conducted by the *Times* in early December, 1,106 adults took the quiz. Almost half scored in the range that would have told them A.D.H.D. may be possible or likely.

About 570,000 people took the EverydayHealth test after a 2011 advertisement starring Mr. Levine of Maroon 5 sponsored by Shire, Chadd and another advocacy group, according to the website Medical Marketing & Media. A similar test on the website for Concerta prompted L2ThinkTank.com, which assesses pharmaceutical marketing, to award the campaign its top rating, "Genius."

John Grohol, a Boston-area psychologist who licensed the test to Everyday-Health, said such screening tools do not make a diagnosis; they merely "give you a little push into looking into" whether you have A.D.H.D. Other doctors countered that, given many studies showing that doctors are strongly influenced by their patients' image of what ails them, such tests invite too many patients and doctors to see the disorder where it is not.

"I think it is misleading," said Dr. Tyrone Williams, a psychiatrist in Cambridge, Mass. "I do think that there are some people out there who are really suffering and find out that maybe it's treatable. But these symptoms can be a bazillion things. Sometimes the answers are so simple and they don't require prescriptions—like 'How about eight hours of sleep, Mom, because four hours doesn't cut it?' And then all their A.D.H.D. symptoms magically disappear."

Because studies have shown that A.D.H.D. can run in families, drug companies use the children's market to grow the adult one. A pamphlet published in 2008 by Janssen, Concerta's manufacturer—headlined "Like Parent, Like Child?"—claimed that "A.D.H.D. is a highly heritable disorder" despite studies showing that the vast majority of parents of A.D.H.D. children do not qualify for a diagnosis themselves.

A current Shire manual for therapists illustrates the genetic issue with a family tree: three grandparents with the disorder, all six of their children with it, and seven of eight grandchildren, too.

Insurance plans, increasingly reluctant to pay for specialists like psychiatrists, are leaving many A.D.H.D. evaluations to primary-care physicians with little to no training in the disorder. If those doctors choose to learn about the diagnostic process, they can turn to web-based continuing-education courses, programs often subsidized by drug companies.

A recent course titled "Unmasking A.D.H.D. in Adults," on the website Medscape and sponsored by Shire, featured an instructional video of a primary-care physician listening to a college professor detail his work-related sleep problems. After three minutes he described some attention issues he had as a child, then revealed that his son was recently found to have the disorder and was thriving in college on medication.

Six minutes into their encounter, the doctor said: "If you have A.D.H.D., which I believe you do, family members often respond well to similar medications. Would you consider giving that a try?"

The psychiatrist who oversaw the course, Dr. David Goodman of Johns Hopkins and the Adult Attention Deficit Disorder Center of Maryland, said that he was paid several thousand dollars to oversee the course by Medscape, not Shire directly, and that such income did not influence his decisions with patients. But as he reviewed the video in September, Dr. Goodman reconsidered its message to untrained doctors about how quickly the disorder can be assessed and said, "That was not an acceptable way to evaluate and conclude that the patient has A.D.H.D."

A Shire spokeswoman declined to comment on the video and the company's sponsorship of it.

Mr. Casola said Shire remains committed to raising awareness of A.D.H.D. Shire spent $1 million in the first three quarters of 2013, according to company documents, to support A.D.H.D. conferences to educate doctors. One this autumn found J. Russell Ramsay, a psychologist at the University of Pennsylvania's medical school, who also serves as a consultant and speaker for Shire, reading aloud one of his slides to the audience: "A.D.H.D.—It's Everywhere You Want to Be."

"We are a commercial organization trying to bring health care treatments to patients," Mr. Casola said. "I think, on balance, we are helping people."

Print Citations

CMS: Schwarz, Alan. "The Selling of Attention Deficit Disorder." In *The Reference Shelf: Prescription Drug Abuse*, edited by Betsy Maury, 105-116. Ipswich, MA: H.W. Wilson, 2017.

MLA: Schwarz, Alan. "The Selling of Attention Deficit Disorder." *The Reference Shelf: Prescription Drug Abuse*. Ed. Betsy Maury. Ipswich: H.W. Wilson, 2017. 105-116. Print.

APA: Schwarz, A. (2016). The selling of attention deficit disorder. In Betsy Maury (Ed.), *The reference shelf: Prescription drug abuse* (pp. 105-116). Ipswich, MA: H.W. Wilson. (Original work published 2013)

When the Mailman Unwittingly Becomes a Drug Dealer

By Arian Campo-Flores and Jon Kamp

The Wall Street Journal, **June 26, 2017**

Not long before Don Holman's son Garrett died from an overdose in February, he learned his 20-year-old had his drugs delivered directly to their Virginia home in the mail, in packages from foreign countries.

"Your drug dealer today is your mailman," said Mr. Holman. "If your kids are getting any packages in the mail whatsoever, you need to know what that is."

Fentanyl and other synthetic narcotics like U-47700, which was found in Garrett Holman's system, are now streaming into the U.S. through international parcels delivered by the U.S. Postal Service and private carriers like United Parcel Service Inc. and FedEx Corp., according to authorities. The deliveries are helping fuel an opioid crisis that claims tens of thousands of U.S. lives each year, prodding congressional lawmakers to propose tougher rules and new resources to try to stop the flow.

Seizures of fentanyl arriving by both international mail and express carriers reached nearly 37 kilograms in the U.S. overall in fiscal 2016, compared with 0.09 kilogram five years earlier, according to Customs and Border Protection data.

While Mexican drug cartels usually transport synthetic opioids like fentanyl in bulk by land across the southern U.S. border, many American dealers and users use the mail to receive smaller supplies of the drugs, officials say. In the past year, authorities have arrested such alleged dealers in cities including Cincinnati, Salt Lake City and Kearny, N.J.

Mail and private express services are "attractive options for smugglers," said Salvatore Ingrassia, acting assistant director for trade and cargo at CBP's New York field office. He said there has been a "significant increase" in synthetic opioids arriving in packages.

Customs officials rely on X-ray machines and visual scans to find the contraband at nine international mail facilities around the country. With 621.4 million international packages and mail pieces arriving through the U.S. Postal Service alone in fiscal 2016, it is like finding a needle in a haystack.

The chemicals are so lethal, drug-sniffing dogs aren't trained to identify them for fear of death.

"This manual process...coupled with the tremendous volume of inbound mail to the United States, creates a daunting task for CBP," said Robert Perez, the agency's

Seizures of fentanyl arriving by both international mail and express carriers reached nearly 37 kilograms in the U.S. overall in fiscal 2016, compared with 0.09 kilogram five years earlier, according to Customs and Border Protection data.

acting executive assistant commissioner for operations support, at a May Senate hearing on opioid mail shipments.

A measure sponsored by lawmakers including Sen. Sherrod Brown (D., Ohio) would provide customs officials with more screening equipment and lab resources to detect fentanyl arriving by mail or at ports of entry. Another bill in the Senate, sponsored by Ohio Republican Rob Portman, would require overseas shippers that use the U.S. Postal Service to provide certain pieces of information, transmitted electronically to CBP before parcels arrive in the country.

Sen. Portman's measure seeks to address a problem that customs officials and others have complained about for years: Unlike private carriers like FedEx and UPS, the Postal Service doesn't always provide CBP with advance data like a shipper's name and address and a description of contents. Run through software programs, the data can help flag warning signs such as an address or neighborhood known to be the origin of previous shipments of chemicals.

At the recent Senate hearing, a UPS official called advance data "the cornerstone of effective risk assessment." Mr. Perez from CBP also highlighted the data's importance.

The Postal Service says it is more limited than private carriers because it has to work with foreign postal operators. It has been pushing overseas operators to provide such information and now receives data for 40% to 50% of inbound packages, said Robert Cintron, the agency's vice president for network operations, at the hearing.

The Postal Service is obligated under international agreements to accept incoming mail from nearly every country, Mr. Cintron said. He added that the blanket requirements of Sen. Portman's bill are impractical and would undermine the Postal Service's ability to compete with private shippers.

Moreover, sellers routinely falsify the sender's name and address and the description of the contents, authorities say. On the receiving end, buyers often misrepresent themselves as well, and may use numerous mailboxes to evade detection.

"Though the express carriers typically require additional data to ship parcels, it is still rather difficult for these carriers and law enforcement to detect and intercept opioids," the White House Office of National Drug Control Policy wrote in a letter to the House Energy and Commerce Committee in March.

Spokespeople for UPS and FedEx said the companies comply with law enforcement's legal requirements on imports.

In the March arrest of alleged drug dealer Chukwuemeka Okparaeke, it was his unusual behavior at post offices in the Middletown, N.Y., area that helped tip off authorities.

They said the 28-year-old, known to online customers as "Fentmaster," dropped bags of envelopes in collection bins while wearing latex gloves. He also bought more than $7,500 worth of stamps at a time online.

Mr. Okparaeke ordered fentanyl variants online from vendors in China in one-kilogram quantities and had them shipped to a UPS store mailbox, according to authorities. He then repackaged the powder into two-milliliter plastic bags and shipped them through the post office to scores of customers around the U.S., authorities said. The envelopes had fictitious return addresses like "Middletown Sweets" and "North Jersey Plastics Co."

In April, a federal grand jury in New York indicted Mr. Okparaeke on charges including intent to import and distribute controlled substances. He pleaded not guilty. An attorney for Mr. Okparaeke declined to comment.

In March, word circulated in online drug forums that Fentmaster had been busted. "Do not order from Fentmaster," one participant wrote.

Print Citations

CMS: Campo-Flores, Arian, and Jon Kamp. "When the Mailman Unwittingly Becomes a Drug Dealer." In *The Reference Shelf: Prescription Drug Abuse*, edited by Betsy Maury, 117-119. Ipswich, MA: H.W. Wilson, 2017.

MLA: Campo-Flores, Arian, and Jon Kamp. "When the Mailman Unwittingly Becomes a Drug Dealer." *The Reference Shelf: Prescription Drug Abuse*. Ed. Betsy Maury. Ipswich: H.W. Wilson, 2017. 117-119. Print.

APA: Campo-Flores, A., & J. Kamp. (2017). When the mailman unwittingly becomes a drug dealer. In Betsy Maury (Ed.), *The reference shelf: Prescription drug abuse* (pp. 117-119). Ipswich, MA: H.W. Wilson. (Original work published 2017)

Alison's Story: How $750,000 in Drug "Treatment" Destroyed Her Life

By Warren Richey

The Christian Science Monitor, **May 9, 2017**

FORT LAUDERDALE, FLA.—When she enrolled in a South Florida drug treatment program in 2015, Alison Flory had high hopes of getting her life in order and starting anew.

But instead of receiving life-saving health care, the 23-year-old from a Chicago suburb found herself being recruited from one recovery residence to another as a string of shady drug treatment facilities systematically overcharged her mother's health insurance policy for expensive, unnecessary procedures and tests.

By October 2016, Alison was dead.

This is the story of how two troublesome national trends—booming drug addiction rates and widespread fraud in the health-care industry—conspired to destroy a young woman's life.

The US is in the midst of an epidemic of drug addiction and fatal overdoses with more than 52,000 deaths in 2015—and the numbers are rising. The carnage is fueled in part by the widespread legal distribution of opiates to medical patients, easy availability of cheap heroin, as well as an ever-expanding lineup of other types of prescription drugs and synthetic intoxicants ripe for abuse.

The crisis is creating a broad new spectrum of Americans struggling with addiction—from suburban high school students, to young adults, to white-collar office workers, to grandmothers on Medicare.

At the same time, America is facing an epidemic of fraud in the health-care industry. Experts estimate that the government and private insurance companies lose $100 billion each year to health-care scams and fraudulent claims. (That is more than the entire GDP of 131 of the world's 195 countries. It would place 24th on the Fortune 500 list of largest US corporations, ahead of Boeing, Microsoft, and Bank of America.)

Some Americans cynically dismiss health-care fraud as something less than a major crime problem, federal investigators say. It is just money from the government or money from deep-pocket insurance companies, these cynics suggest.

But when greed replaces much needed health care for the most vulnerable in society, experts say, the result can be —even fatal.

This is Alison's story.

Over a 15-month period in 2015 and 2016, Alison moved nine times to different drug treatment centers. It was largely the work of fellow addicts—young men—who were paid to lure her and others away from their current treatment program. They did so with the promise of free rent, free use of a scooter, and other benefits—including possible romance—if the patient agreed to enroll in a particular treatment program and live in a recovery residence or sober home associated with that treatment program.

Sobriety had nothing to do with it. It is an open secret among addicts enrolled in South Florida treatment facilities that hundreds of suburban homes posing as drug-free recovery residences are little more than co-ed flop houses where the use of drugs is permitted and sometimes encouraged.

Rather than promoting health and healing, the business model that supports this multimillion-dollar health-care fraud involves warehousing addicts in fake sober homes to facilitate the perpetual fleecing of their parents' insurance policies.

Many of the addicts are complicit in the scam, using their parents' insurance benefits like a credit card to fund a work-free and responsibility-free South Florida lifestyle while hiding behind a false façade of "treatment."

For individuals struggling under the weight of addiction with poor judgment, low self-esteem, and inadequate coping skills, this scam and the associated lifestyle is the antithesis of rehabilitation.

"This goes beyond anything I could ever imagine, that so many people are so selfish and heartless," Alison's mother, Jennifer Flory, said in an interview.

At first, Ms. Flory was relieved that under the Affordable Care Act a parent's health insurance policy extends to their children up to age 26—including requiring open-ended coverage for drug treatment programs.

A mother of five, Flory was working in a job she didn't particularly like, but she resolved to remain in that job because it came with a generous health insurance plan that she couldn't otherwise afford. "I thought [having health insurance covering Alison] was a blessing. I thought, I have to keep this job until Alison is out of treatment," she said.

Now, two years later, she has a different perspective. "Oh my God, if I would have just lost my job and not had insurance, she would still be alive."

Evidence of Fraud

Throughout her daughter's ordeal, evidence of fraud arrived almost daily at Flory's house in Illinois. But she didn't know what to look for.

"I would get bills and bills and bills in the mail and half of the time I would just throw them in a drawer," she said. "I just thought, 'Oh cool, Alison is getting treatment.'"

Many of the statements were for expensive drug tests at sophisticated laboratories. Random spot tests cost $5 to $10 each and can be performed once a week or less.

> **This is the story of how two troublesome national trends—booming drug addiction rates and widespread fraud in the health care industry— conspired to destroy a young woman's life.**

In contrast, under the fraudulent business model that has taken root in South Florida and elsewhere, certain treatment programs are collecting their patient's urine three times a week and sending it to a lab for highly sophisticated testing. Instead of $5 to $10, these tests cost anywhere from $1,000 to $4,000, or more.

Such bills are routinely being sent out and they are routinely being paid by insurance companies. They fuel an insurance-funded web of bribes and kickbacks with a steady stream of payoffs flowing between treatment centers, patient recruiters, sober homes, and laboratory operators, according to law enforcement officials.

During Alison's 15 months in drug treatment, her mother estimates her insurance company was billed $750,000. It is not clear how much of that was actually paid by the company.

In a single day, she says, her insurance was once charged $10,000 from a treatment center that her daughter may or may not have attended for that one day. "She never told me anything about it," Flory says.

For Flory, her daughter's experience has produced more questions than answers.

"My question to the treatment centers is this: So you guys have billed my insurance almost $750,000 and my daughter is dead. You mean to tell me that $750,000 cannot get a person to a stable point in life to be able to function?"

How Patients Are Recruited

Alison's story begins with a tragedy eight years ago, in May 2009, when she was in high school. Shortly after she broke up with her boyfriend, he threw himself in front of a speeding train. Alison was at his side in the hospital when he was pronounced dead. She was 17.

The pain and guilt nearly crushed her, according to her mother. A friend wanted to help and gave her some pills to make her feel better. That is the moment the door opened to addiction.

After graduating from high school, Alison studied video-game design and art in college. Then she worked at a fabric store, as a dance instructor, and at the front desk of a hotel.

By 2015, Alison's mother recognized that her daughter had a drug problem. Alison admitted her addiction and said she wanted her life back. She enrolled in a drug treatment program in Pompano Beach, Fla.

Once in Florida, she improved and seemed to be firmly on the path to recovery. After being released from detox, she moved to an intensive out-patient program (IOP) at a drug treatment center where she received counseling, therapy, and drug testing.

As an out-of-state patient, she needed to find a place to live during the treatment. That is where sober homes and halfway houses enter the picture. Such recovery residences are usually a group house in a suburban neighborhood shared by other recovering addicts. Legitimate recovery residences charge their patients rent and do not permit co-ed housing.

At some point during this second-level of treatment, Alison attended an anti-addiction group meeting where she was approached by an attractive young man who suggested that she move to a different treatment center and into a co-ed recovery residence where she wouldn't have to pay any rent.

"She ended up admitting [later] that she was following him [for potential romantic reasons], but what she didn't realize is that the guy was getting paid," says Flory. "So it was never in her best interest, ever."

In retrospect, it was a turning point. It took Alison off a road to recovery and put her instead on a path toward relapse after relapse after relapse.

A Shady Treatment Center

By switching, she was leaving behind a reputable and successful treatment program to enroll in something called Reflections Treatment Center in Margate, Fla.

Reflections paid patient recruiters and brokers to identify young patients whose parents' insurance policies could be systematically overcharged. Scores of unscrupulous treatment centers in South Florida are conducting the same insurance scam, but law enforcement and other officials say Reflections appears to have been the worst of the worst.

Reflections was run by Kenneth "Kenny" Chatman, a convicted felon who had served time in federal prison for stealing credit card numbers. He registered Reflections in his wife's name to conceal his own involvement.

Others in the drug-treatment community saw what he was doing.

"Everyone knows Chatman was a [problem], I mean basically we all knew," says Richard Riccardi, owner of Fellowship Living Facilities, which runs long-established, legitimate recovery residences in Margate and Fort Lauderdale.

FBI agents raided and shut down Reflections in December. Mr. Chatman was arrested and later pleaded guilty to health-care fraud. He also admitted that he engaged in sex trafficking by recruiting some of his addicted female patients to work in the sex industry.

John Lehman, president of the Florida Association of Recovery Residences, says Chatman showed up on his radar several years ago. "All the kids that were living in various [recovery] houses in Palm Beach and Broward Counties would be transported to Reflections for 'treatment,'" he says. "But none of them were getting any treatment. It was a joke."

In 2014, Mr. Lehman began pushing for an investigation. Eventually he went to the *Palm Beach Post*. Reporters began writing news stories about Chatman and corruption in the drug treatment and sober home industry. The *Post* reported that drug treatment had become a $1 billion business in Palm Beach County, the county's fourth-largest industry.

The stories sparked a public outcry that prompted criminal investigations. A Sober Homes Task Force was set up to identify legislative and other solutions.

But in September, just as federal agents were zeroing in on Chatman's alleged scams, his wife, Laura, applied for a license to open a second drug treatment facility. To Lehman's disbelief, the Florida Department of Children and Family Services granted a provisional license.

"Everyone on the planet knew that this guy should be shut down, yet they make application and are issued another provisional license," Lehman says.

A Systemic Problem

It wasn't just Chatman and Reflections. The proliferation of overbilling and sober home scams in Florida have made it difficult for legitimate recovery residences to stay in business.

There are 958 licensed drug treatment centers in Florida and roughly 3,000 legitimate recovery residences in the state. Lehman estimates that 6,000 to 7,000 houses claiming to be sober homes are really drug dens or flop houses.

At any one time there are as many as 10,000 patients enrolled in clinical drug treatment services in Florida. Of those, 75 percent are from out of state, he says.

Most will seek to live in a recovery residence in Florida rather than return home immediately after detox treatment, creating a market of addicts that is exploited by corrupt treatment centers. They pay kickbacks of $400 to $500 per week to sober homes for each insured resident who signs up for treatment, Lehman says.

The need for housing is the leverage that these treatment centers use to obtain new patients and gain access to their parents' insurance benefits, officials say. Insurance companies will pay for drug treatment, but not forever. When the coverage lapses, the fraudsters need a way to extend the insurance gravy train.

Shady treatment centers often give their clients two options: Hit the road or "take what is behind Door No. 2," says Lehman.

He says the option behind "Door No. 2" sounds something like this: "It says here on your medical chart you are a heroin user. You go out and have a weekend party with your friends and you shoot lots of heroin and then you go back to detox and when you get out of detox you can come back into the [IOP] program and your insurance benefits will be reset because it will be a new episode of care. And we can bill your insurance company and therefore you can have all the housing you want."

It sets up a cycle of recovery and relapse.

"I have met people on the street and they have been down here for two or three years on the spin cycle under two or three different policies," says Maureen Kielian, Florida director of Steered Straight, an anti-addiction group, and a member of the Sober Homes Task Force.

Ms. Kielian says there is a huge downside to drug treatment insurance scams. "It keeps those seeking recovery sick," she says. "It just keeps them sick, and they are dying."

Consequences: Overdose Deaths

Between 2012 and 2015, the number of overdose deaths more than doubled in Palm Beach County, where many of the treatment centers and recovery residences are located. The county medical examiner is still compiling the total for 2016, but the expectation is that it will almost double again from 307 to nearly 600 overdose deaths in 2016.

"It is horrific," says Al Johnson, chief assistant in the Palm Beach State Attorney's Office, who heads the Sober Homes Task Force.

Johnson says his office receives frequent phone calls from parents worried about their children in treatment. One said she was sure her son wouldn't survive the year. She wanted to come to Florida to see him one last time.

Another parent called and said her daughter had relapsed and she didn't know where she was but that she was sure she was in a "bad place." Johnson adds: "Our investigator said, 'Ma'am, get on an airplane, come down, get your daughter, and take her home.'"

The point of the task force is to save the legitimate treatment centers and recovery residences and weed out the bad actors, Johnson says. "Let's clean up the industry so this truly is the place to go for effective, productive treatment," he says. "There are good providers that are dedicated not to a profit motive but to recovery."

There are signs of a potential turnaround. "I was told by the code enforcement chief in Delray Beach that 40 houses have closed down," Johnson says, referring to flop houses.

How Reflections Was Shut Down

One of the biggest problems faced by addicts and their family members is trying to differentiate between legitimate providers and corrupt providers.

"It's disgusting, these people and what they do," says Flory. "Alison's case was particularly horrible because she got wrapped up in the Kenny Chatman thing," she says.

"She got into every sad thing I think there was," Flory says of her daughter's experience in South Florida.

She partly blames herself. "I told her to trust the people who were looking over her. I told her she needs to not make decisions on her own. Let the people around her who care about her and are treating her, the doctors and so forth, let them help her to make decisions."

The mother adds: "Little did I know I was telling her to put all her trust and faith into these people who were taking advantage of her. That's what got me, there is so much more to it than just a young girl making bad choices."

Among those people was Chatman.

On March 15, he appeared in federal court in West Palm Beach in handcuffs and leg irons. Prosecutors said he and his companies received fraudulent insurance reimbursement payments of between $9.5 million and $25 million.

According to a signed statement as part of his guilty plea, Chatman and others recruited some of his female patients residing in sober homes into prostitution. They advertised on websites like Craig's List and Backpage.com.

The statement adds: "The defendant and co-conspirators provided controlled substances to these addicted patients to induce them to perform sexual acts."

Implicit in this arrangement was Chatman's power to also withhold controlled substances from drug-dependent women. Those who were noncompliant with Chatman's wishes could face debilitating symptoms of sudden drug withdrawal, loss of income, and eviction from the sober home. In essence, they could be dumped on the street, sick and homeless.

By contrast, those who complied were not required to attend drug treatment sessions and submit to drug testing—but their insurance policies were billed as if they had, according to the signed statement.

At one female-only sober home, near West Palm Beach, Chatman confiscated cell phones, screwed down the windows, and prohibited the women from leaving the house, according to court documents.

Chatman could have faced up to life in prison on the sex trafficking charge, but with federal sentencing guidelines he will likely spend 12 ½ to 15 years in prison under his plea agreement. His sentencing is set for May 17.

Chatman wasn't the only one responsible for the fraud at Reflections.

The medical director at Reflections was Donald Willems. During his tenure at Reflections, Dr. Willems was under indictment in state court on pending racketeering conspiracy charges for allegedly helping to run an opiate pill mill in Pompano Beach a few years earlier.

On March 23, Willems pleaded guilty in the Chatman case. He admitted that he used his position as a licensed physician to falsely declare that the excessive drug testing and other treatments at Reflections were medically necessary and thus covered by health insurance policies.

In addition to excessive drug tests, he authorized expensive saliva, DNA, and allergy testing, regardless of whether patients had allergies or any need for such tests.

Despite his actions in the Chatman case and the pending charges in the 2012 pill mill case, Willems' medical license remained in good standing with a "Clear/Active" listing right up to the day of his guilty plea.

Barry Gregory, a licensed mental health counselor, worked as the clinical director at Reflections. In a YouTube video shot in September 2015, Dr. Gregory said Reflections was licensed to provide three different levels of care. "We really believe our job is to save lives and that is what we are doing," he says on the video.

On Feb. 16, Gregory pleaded guilty to conspiring to commit health-care fraud. In a signed statement as part of his guilty plea, Gregory admitted that he knew that Chatman was telling patients that they were allowed to continue to use drugs while they were clients at the treatment center.

"As many as 90 percent of the patients [at Reflections] continued to use controlled substances while purportedly obtaining treatment," Gregory said in the statement.

October 14, 2016

In August 2016, Alison moved with her boyfriend into her last sober home, this one a yellow three-bedroom ranch-style house on NW 33rd Avenue in Lauderdale Lakes.

The neighborhood had seen better days. Two years ago, the community of 35,000 was named one of the 10 most dangerous towns in Florida. Crack cocaine was being sold in the parking lot of a convenience store a few blocks from the sober home.

But Alison had a reason to move in. She could live there rent-free, and was also being paid $350 a week. According to her mother, the payment was for her work as a "house manager." She was also enrolled at Reflections and supposedly was attending treatment sessions three times a week. This was her second stint as a patient at Reflections.

Flory confirms that her insurance was being billed during that period for treatments and drug tests.

The sober home on NW 33rd Avenue was rented by a man who lived next door and ran the sober home. He had a van and would transport the clients to their treatment sessions at Reflections. According to Alison's mother, sometimes Chatman himself would arrive in a van to pick up Reflections clients.

At some point in the early morning hours of Oct. 14, Alison and one of her housemates, Nicole De La Pena, decided to smoke crack cocaine. Earlier, they made a purchase down the street, according to an account Nicole gave to her mother, Johanna.

What neither Alison nor Nicole could know was that the crack cocaine they were about to smoke was laced with carfentanil.

> **The issue of selecting a treatment center and recovery residence arises at a time of crisis not only in the life of the addict, but also in the lives of those affected family members who are attempting to help the addict. In other words, the addict isn't the only one whose life is in turmoil.**

Three weeks earlier, the Drug Enforcement Administration had issued a nationwide warning about carfentanil, a synthetic opiate said to be 10,000 times more powerful than morphine. The DEA warned that mere skin contact could cause an overdose in a paramedic or police officer responding to an emergency. A dose of carfentanil about the size of a grain of salt would likely be fatal to a human, experts say.

Alison was last seen alive by her boyfriend at 4 a.m. when he saw her asleep in her bed and still breathing.

Later that morning around 8:30 a.m., the man who ran the sober home arrived to take clients to their treatment sessions at Reflections. He was unable to awaken Alison.

According to a recording of the 911 call, it took the house manager 37 seconds to vocalize a muffled, "Hello."

"Your phone dialed 911. Do you have an emergency," the operator asked.

"Yes, I am trying to figure out right now," the manager responded. "Um, um, I have, I have, I have someone in here and she's—we're trying to wake her up but I don't feel no pulse."

At no point during the 911 call was the manager able to state the address of his sober home or even the nature of the emergency despite requests from the emergency operator. The call lasted one minute and 48 seconds.

Some advocates for reform of the sober home industry say that those who run sober homes should be trained in CPR and maintain a stock of naloxone, an antidote for opiate overdoses.

It is not clear that this would have saved Alison's life on the morning of Oct. 14, but experts say it might have.

When paramedics arrived, they were unable to revive Alison. She was pronounced dead at 9:08 a.m.

The medical examiner's report says Alison died of carfentanil and cocaine toxicity.

Police photos taken inside Alison's room in the sober home shortly after her death show the presence of three postage-stamp sized pink plastic bags with white residue inside. Two were on the floor near her closet, one was inside a shoe. They are the type of bags that are used to sell street quantities of illegal drugs.

In addition, the photos reveal a five-inch glass tube with smoke residue inside and seven pills in a cluster on the night stand beside the bed.

'"All They Care about Is the Money"

Flory says there is no way to measure the pain caused to parents and other family members of addicts lost to drug addiction. "It is the most horrible thing I would imagine ever having to go through, losing my oldest kid," Flory says.

"We talked, we confided in each other, we hung out, we had the same sense of humor," she says of her daughter. "She was literally my best friend."

Until Alison's experience in South Florida, Flory said she never really considered the full cost of fraud in the American health-care system.

"I just thought it didn't really affect anybody. Yeah, insurance fraud is making people's premiums go up, but that's it," Flory says. "I didn't know it was killing people."

At some point during her ordeal in the South Florida spin cycle, Alison apparently figured it out. In a moment of candor she told her mother it was fraud, that it was all a gigantic scam. "All they care about is the money," Alison said, according to her mother.

"I told her, no, that's not true," Flory said she replied to her daughter. "She told me that these people are just greedy and selfish and they just want to make money. I said that is ridiculous."

The mother adds: "I just thought she was trying to be dramatic. But yeah, she is laughing now. She is looking down and saying, 'I told you so.'"

Flory says she is telling Alison's story for one reason—to save other lives.

"The most important thing is to understand what is happening and put an end to it," she says. "To find a solution so that other people don't have to go through this."

MAY 10, 2017 FORT LAUDERDALE, FLA.—Five days after losing her daughter to a drug overdose in a South Florida sober home, Jennifer Flory found herself standing before a task force set up to investigate sober homes.

"My daughter passed away on Thursday night and I'm coming here to get her stuff—and her—and to find out why she died," the grieving mother from Illinois told the assembled group in West Palm Beach.

Months later, she said her public appearance so soon after her daughter's passing was aimed at helping other parents and other addicts avoid the pitfalls that took her daughter's life.

"Alison knows that I love her and care about her and miss her terribly. But that can wait," she said in an interview with the *Monitor*. "Right now there is an urgent need for people to be helped and saved."

With more than 140 people dying every day in the US from drug overdoses, addiction treatment has become a growth industry across the country. South Florida, in particular, is a national destination for those seeking treatment.

It isn't just Florida's warm and sunny weather. Those suffering under addiction are targeted by aggressive marketing tactics featuring national advertising and patient recruiters.

In the process, Florida has also become a prime location for unscrupulous drug treatment centers that seek to recruit young addicts covered by their parents' insurance policies. Many of the "patients" are allowed to continue to use drugs while the treatment center overcharges their parents' insurance policy for unnecessary drug tests and other unneeded services.

Federal, state, and local authorities are cracking down, but the insurance scams continue.

Flory says chief among her mistakes was assuming that everyone in the drug treatment industry was honest and actually cared about the well-being of her daughter.

"I think people need to know, there are scam artists out there," she says. "Don't just send your kid to Florida and expect a miracle."

Two years ago, that's what Flory did with Alison.

"I didn't know the industry wasn't [closely] regulated. I didn't know that addiction treatment wasn't under the supervision of a doctor at all times," Flory says. "I was picturing white lab coats and stuff like that. I didn't know. I didn't know any of it."

Instead of being helped along a road to recovery to a new life, Flory's daughter was recruited away from an effective drug treatment program and lured into a sham program.

As reported in the first part of this two-part series, the program, Reflections Treatment Center in Margate, Fla., was set up largely as a mechanism to overcharge health insurance policies for unnecessary tests and treatments at inflated prices. As the operators of the treatment center grew richer, Flory's daughter experienced relapse after relapse while living in a fake "sober home" where illicit drug use was permitted.

It was in one such sober home where, on Oct. 14, Alison and one of her housemates, Nicole De La Pena, smoked crack cocaine laced with the synthetic opiate carfentanil. Alison passed out and never woke up. Nicole spent a week in the hospital and is suffering from memory loss.

Although Reflections was later raided by the FBI and shut down, many other treatment centers and sober homes in South Florida are continuing to operate under a similar business model based on insurance fraud.

Criminal investigations are ongoing. And a special task force is exploring how to reform the sober home industry to weed out bad actors.

In the meantime, parents are continuing to struggle to identify legitimate and effective treatment centers and recovery residences. Flory and other mothers of addicts are part of an informal support network that offers help and advice to those seeking to identify quality treatment centers and avoid the fraudsters.

Key Questions Parents Should Ask

Flory and Johanna De La Pena, Nicole's mother, both offer the same essential piece of advice to parents or loved ones of an addict seeking treatment: Talk to other moms of addicts.

Both of them say that parents and others researching rehab programs are at a significant disadvantage when trying to differentiate legitimate treatment centers and recovery residences from the bad actors in the industry.

The issue of selecting a treatment center and recovery residence arises at a time of crisis not only in the life of the addict, but also in the lives of those affected family members who are attempting to help the addict. In other words, the addict isn't the only one whose life is in turmoil.

These vulnerable family members are confronted by a well-organized, well-funded, and in some cases highly deceptive marketing effort designed to attract and recruit new patients. Sometimes they offer free airfare to Florida, a tactic that experts say should raise red flags to family members.

"I would have never sent her [to Florida] if I knew then what I know now," Ms. De La Pena said in an interview. "I would have picked a different state. I would have researched the facilities more. I would have gotten references."

She says when her daughter agreed to enter treatment in Florida, she was so desperate to do something to help her daughter that she did not fully investigate the drug treatment industry.

"At the time my daughter was sent off to Florida I was still kind of in denial about her addiction," De La Pena says. "In my hometown, we don't really talk about this."

Experts stress that not all drug treatment centers in Florida are engaged in health-care fraud. There are many long-established, reputable, and effective treatment facilities in the state. One key piece of advice offered by many experts and many parents of addicts: Find a reputable treatment center and stay there. Resist patient recruiters, they say.

The difficulty is being able to ignore fancy advertisements and slick website presentations to identify a truly reputable treatment center. Equally important is the ability to identify legitimate recovery residences and bypass fake sober homes, flop houses, and drug dens.

Addiction recovery specialists suggest parents and other loved ones ask a few key questions:

- Is the recovery residence certified by the Florida Association of Recovery Residences? If not, look elsewhere.

- Does the sober home offer residents free rent and money for food? Experts say residents should pay their own way. Offers of free rent or other benefits can be evidence of illegal patient brokering.

- Is the recovery residence coed? Experts say sober homes should be segregated by gender and not facilitate dating-type relationships between patients, which in the early stages of drug treatment can take the focus off recovery and make relapse more likely.

- Is the staff of the sober home trained in CPR? Do they have a supply of naloxone in the house for use as an emergency antidote in the event of an overdose?

- Are random drug tests performed? How much do they cost? Such tests should cost $5 to $10.

- Are referral fees paid to the sober home from a drug treatment center if residents enroll at that center? If so, it suggests the presence of an illegal kickback scheme, specialists say.

Parents Need Fortitude, Strategy

For some parents, dealing with a child who is an addict requires not only fortitude but strategy and cunning.

After spending a week at her daughter's bedside at a South Florida hospital following Nicole's overdose in October, De La Pena decided it would be best to take her daughter home to Texas.

She arranged for security officers to accompany them from the hospital to the airport until they safely boarded their flight. As they entered the line for TSA screening, Nicole saw an opening.

"She just started running and I couldn't get to her," De La Pena says. Nicole apparently wanted to be with her boyfriend, who was also in a drug treatment program.

It took two months of pleading on the telephone before Nicole agreed to return to her mother's house in Texas. Soon, Nicole began plotting her return to Florida.

De La Pena refused to pay for a flight to Florida. But that didn't stop Nicole's boyfriend from pulling strings to arrange a "free" Texas-Florida flight.

"These kids already know that they can get free flights back to Florida, so when she was here she was already planning it," De La Pena says.

The mother says she was able to intercept and stop attempts by two different treatment centers to send a free ticket to Nicole. It is a common recruitment tactic to offer to pay for airfare to Florida if the would-be patient has health insurance and is willing to enroll in their treatment program.

Maureen Kielian is the Florida director of the anti-drug group Steered Straight and a member of the Sober Homes Task Force. She says there is a relatively easy way to determine if a treatment center is engaging in an illegal activity such as patient brokering—offering something to a prospective patient in exchange for their agreement to enroll in a particular treatment program.

"If they are being offered anything free, they are being brokered," she says. "The way to think about it is if my son had leukemia, would this be happening?" she says. "Would they be flying you in for treatment? Would they be offering you free anything? No."

After dealing with her daughter's overdose, De La Pena knew about patient brokering and was twice able to intercept and block free plane tickets meant for Nicole.

> One key piece of advice offered by many experts and many parents of addicts: Find a reputable treatment center and stay there. Resist patient recruiters, they say.

"Then one of them did purchase her a ticket," she says. "It was late at night when I saw it and I personally contacted the person and told them they better cancel. They were really ugly and rude. So I told them I am canceling my insurance because I know that is the only reason they wanted her out there. They said, no, we've already verified the coverage." De La Pena upped the pressure. She told them what they were doing was illegal. They disagreed.

After the telephone call ended, De La Pena sent them a text message with the business card of an official with an anti-fraud task force in South Florida. She repeated her statement that what they were doing was illegal. "Within minutes he texted me back, saying that he had canceled the flight," she says.

"The next morning, my daughter did not know that I had canceled the flight," she says. "I was asleep at six in the morning when she got a ride to the airport."

De La Pena sent a text message to her daughter who, by then, was stranded at the airport. The message: Give your mom a call when you are ready for a ride home. Nicole called her grandmother for a ride.

The time away from Florida has been good for her daughter, De La Pena says. Nicole has a job and has been drug-free for three months. The mother says it is easier to fight off patient recruiters when they think there is no insurance policy to fleece.

A Fast Way to Stop the Fraud

Flory says she believes any chance her daughter Alison had for recovery was lost amid the ongoing fraud in South Florida. "I think she was doomed by the people who were supposed to help her," she says.

Flory has hired a lawyer to investigate a possible lawsuit against one or more of the drug treatment centers Alison attended.

The lawyer, Susan Ramsey of West Palm Beach, says the increased law enforcement scrutiny of the treatment industry in recent months is causing some people to close their doors and move on.

"There are those who are going to pull up their shingle and go find some other scam. I think that is happening," she says. "But the struggle is going to continue for some years."

One development that Ms. Ramsey says might trigger a rapid cleansing of the treatment industry would be if insurance companies launched their own investigation into past practices and demanded their money back from shady treatment centers and laboratories that overbilled.

"That is what they need to do," she says. "That would stop this pretty darned fast."

At one point De La Pena got the same idea. She called her insurance company and asked them to block a South Florida treatment center from billing more charges to her health insurance plan. "They declined to do that," she says.

She called a fraud investigator with the insurance company. He never called back.

"I Know the Warning Signs"

Flory says she will always feel an emptiness from the loss of Alison, her oldest child. But in a cruel twist, her struggle dealing with an addicted child is not over yet.

Four months after Alison's fatal overdose, her 20-year-old son came to her with a heart-breaking admission.

"I'm doing heroin and I need help or else I'm going to die," she says he told her. That's not all. "He wanted to go to Florida. That wasn't my idea, but he said that's where he wanted to be."

He enrolled in a South Florida drug treatment facility.

"So at first it looks like I'm doing the same thing all over again, expecting a different result," Flory says. "But now that I know how it works… I have people watching out for him. If I knew then what I know now, I would have seen what Alison was falling into."

This time will be different, she says. "I know what to expect. If he is going to get into trouble, I know what the warning signs are and I am going to have him watched like a hawk by all the people I have met. I have a big network of people now who live (in South Florida) because I've made it my business to know them."

If there is any one rule she will enforce with her son that she did not enforce with Alison it is that he will enroll in a legitimate, high-quality program and remain in it.

"You don't move," Flory says. "You don't make any decisions about that. He knows that he is not allowed to make those decisions."

Print Citations

CMS: Richey, Warren. "Alison's Story: How $750,000 in Drug 'Treatment' De-
stroyed Her Life." In *The Reference Shelf: Prescription Drug Abuse*, edited by
Betsy Maury, 120-134. Ipswich, MA: H.W. Wilson, 2017.

MLA: Richey, Warren. "Alison's Story: How $750,000 in Drug 'Treatment' De-
stroyed Her Life." *The Reference Shelf: Prescription Drug Abuse*. Ed. Betsy Maury. Ipswich: H.W. Wilson, 2017. 120-134. Print.

APA: Richey, W. (2017). Alison's story: How $750,000 in drug "treatment" destroyed
her life. In Betsy Maury (Ed.), *The reference shelf: Prescription drug abuse* (pp.
120-134). Ipswich, MA: H.W. Wilson. (Original work published 2017)

Drug-Company Payments Mirror Doctors' Brand-Name Prescribing

By Charles Ornstein, Ryann Grochowski Jones, and Mike Tigas
NPR Morning Edition, March 17, 2016

Doctors have long disputed the accusation that the payments they receive from pharmaceutical companies have any relationship to how they prescribe drugs.

There's been little evidence to settle the matter, until now.

A *ProPublica* analysis has found that doctors who receive payments from the medical industry do indeed prescribe drugs differently on average than their colleagues who don't. And the more money they receive, the more brand-name medications they tend to prescribe.

We matched records on payments from pharmaceutical and medical device makers in 2014 with corresponding data on doctors' medication choices in Medicare's prescription drug program.

Doctors who got money from drug and device makers prescribed a higher percentage of brand-name drugs overall than doctors who didn't, our analysis showed. Even those who simply got meals from companies prescribed more brand-name drugs, on average.

Moreover, as payments increased, brand-name prescribing rates tended to as well.

Doctors who received more than $5,000 from companies in 2014 typically had the highest brand-name prescribing percentages. Among internists who received no payments, for example, the average brand-name prescribing rate was about 20 percent, compared to about 30 percent for those who received more than $5,000.

ProPublica's analysis doesn't prove industry payments sway doctors to prescribe particular drugs, or even a particular company's drugs. Rather, it shows that payments are associated with an approach to prescribing that, writ large, benefits drug companies' bottom line.

"It again confirms the prevailing wisdom ... that there is a relationship between payments and brand-name prescribing," said Dr. Aaron Kesselheim, an associate professor of medicine at Harvard Medical School who provided guidance on early versions of *ProPublica's* analysis. "This feeds into the ongoing conversation about the propriety of these sorts of relationships. Hopefully we're getting past the point where people will say, 'Oh, there's no evidence that these relationships change physicians' prescribing practices.'"

Numerous studies show that generics, which must meet rigid Food and Drug Administration standards, work as well as name brands for most patients. Brand-name drugs typically cost more than generics and are more heavily advertised. Although some medications do not have exact generic versions, there usually is a similar one in the same category. In addition, when it comes to patient satisfaction, there isn't much difference between brands and generics, according to data collected by the website Iodine, which is building a repository of user reviews on drugs.

There's wide variation from state to state when it comes to what proportion of prescribers take industry money, our analysis found. The share of doctors taking payments in Nevada, Alabama, Kentucky and South Carolina was at least twice as high as in Vermont, Minnesota, Wisconsin and Maine.

But overall, payments are widespread. Nationwide, nearly 9 in 10 cardiologists who wrote at least 1,000 prescriptions for Medicare patients received payments from a drug or device company in 2014, while 7 in 10 internists and family practitioners did.

Doctors nowadays almost have to go out of their way to avoid taking payments from companies, according to Dr. Richard Baron, president and chief executive of the American Board of Internal Medicine. And those who do probably have greater skepticism about the value of brand-name medications. Conversely, doctors have to work to cultivate deep ties with companies—those worth more than $5,000 a year—and such doctors probably have a greater receptiveness to brand-name drugs, he said.

"You have the people who are going out of their way to avoid this, and you've got people who are, I'll say, pretty committed and engaged to creating relationships with pharma," Baron said. "If you are out there advocating for something, you are more likely to believe in it yourself and not to disbelieve it."

Physicians consider many factors when choosing which medications to prescribe. Some treat patients for whom few generics are available. A case in point is doctors who care for patients with HIV/AIDS. Others specialize in patients with complicated conditions who have tried generic drugs without success.

Holly Campbell, a spokeswoman for the Pharmaceutical Research and Manufacturers of America, the industry trade group, said in a statement that many factors affect doctors' prescribing decisions. A 2011 survey commissioned by the industry found that more than 9 in 10 physicians felt that a "great deal of their prescribing was influenced by their clinical knowledge and experience," Campbell said in a written statement.

"Working together, biopharmaceutical companies and physicians can improve patient care, make better use of today's medicines and foster the development of tomorrow's cures," she wrote. "Physicians provide real-world insights and valuable feedback and advice to inform companies about their medicines to improve patient care."

Individual doctors who received large payments from industry and had above-average prescribing rates of brand-name drugs said they are acting in patients' best interest.

"I do prefer certain drugs over the others based on the quality of the medication and also the benefits that the patients are going to get," said Dr. Amer Syed of Jersey City, N.J., who received more than $66,800 from companies in 2014 and whose brand-name prescribing rate was more than twice the mean of his peers in internal medicine. "My whole vision of practice is to keep the patients out of the hospital."

A 2011 survey commissioned by the industry found that more than 9 in 10 physicians felt that a "great deal of their prescribing was influenced by their clinical knowledge and experience," Campbell said in a written statement.

Dr. Felix Tarm, of Wichita, Kan., likewise prescribed more than twice the rate of brand-name drugs compared with internal medicine doctors nationally. Tarm, who is in his 70s, said he's on the verge of retiring and doesn't draw a salary from his medical practice, instead subsidizing it with the money he receives from drug companies. He said he doesn't own a pharmacy, a laboratory or an X-ray machine, all of which other doctors use to increase their incomes.

"I generally prescribe on the basis of what I think is the best drug," said Tarm, who received $11,700 in payments in 2014. "If the doctor is susceptible to being bought out by a pharmaceutical company, he can just as easily be bought out by other factors."

A third doctor, psychiatrist Alexander Pinkusovich of Brooklyn, N.Y., also prescribed a much higher proportion of brand-name drugs than his peers in 2014 while receiving more than $53,400 from drug companies. He threatened to call the district attorney if a reporter called again. "Why are you doing a fishing expedition?" he asked. "You know that I didn't do anything illegal, so good luck."

ProPublica has been tracking drug company payments to doctors since 2010 through a project known as Dollars for Docs. Our first lookup tool included only seven companies, most of which were required to report their payments publicly as a condition of legal settlements. The tool now covers every drug and device company, thanks to the Physician Payment Sunshine Act, a part of the 2010 Affordable Care Act. The law required all drug and device companies to publicly report their payments. The first reports became public in 2014, covering the last five months of 2013; 2014 payments were released last year.

The payments in our analysis include promotional speaking, consulting, business travel, meals, royalties and gifts, among others. We did not include research payments, although those are reported in the government's database of industry spending, which it calls Open Payments.

Separately, *ProPublica* has tracked patterns in Medicare's prescription drug program, known as Part D, which covers more than 39 million people. Medicare pays for at least 1 in 4 prescriptions dispensed in the country.

This new analysis matches the two data sets, looking at doctors in five large medical specialties: family medicine, internal medicine, cardiology, psychiatry and ophthalmology. We only looked at doctors who wrote at least 1,000 prescriptions in Medicare Part D.

Dr. David W. Parke II, chief executive of the American Academy of Ophthalmology, suggested that many payments made to ophthalmologists don't relate to drugs they prescribe in Medicare Part D, and instead may be related to drugs administered in doctors' offices or devices and implants used in eye surgery. As a result, he said, it may be unfair to presume that industry payments are associated with prescribing in Part D.

Still, he said, *ProPublica's* analysis points to areas that specialty societies may want to look at. "In some cases, there are very appropriate and clinically valid reasons" for doctors who are outliers in their prescribing, he said. "For others, education may very easily result in prescribing change leading to substantive savings for patients, employers and society."

Dr. Kim Allan Williams Sr., president of the American College of Cardiology, said he believes relationships between companies and doctors are circular. The more physicians learn about a new drug's "differentiating characteristics," he said, the more likely they are to prescribe it. And the more they prescribe it, the more likely they are to be selected as speakers and consultants for the company.

"That dovetails with improving your practice, and yes, you are getting paid to do it," he said.

Williams said new drugs are, at least in part, responsible for a significant decrease in cardiovascular mortality in the past three decades.

"If you're not making strides in this highly competitive area, if you don't have a product that's better, it's not going to fly," he said. "So the fact that there's this high relationship in cardiology [between doctors and companies] may in fact be driving the progress that we're making."

Print Citations

CMS: Ornstein, Charles, Grochowski Jones, Ryann, and Mike Tigas. "Drug-Company Payments Mirror Doctors' Brand-Name Prescribing." In *The Reference Shelf: Prescription Drug Abuse*, edited by Betsy Maury, 135-138. Ipswich, MA: H.W. Wilson, 2017.

MLA: Ornstein, Charles, Grochowski Jones, Ryann, and Mike Tigas. "Drug-Company Payments Mirror Doctors' Brand-Name Prescribing." *The Reference Shelf: Prescription Drug Abuse*. Ed. Betsy Maury. Ipswich: H.W. Wilson, 2017. 135-138. Print.

APA: Ornstein, C., Grochowski Jones, R., & M. Tigas. (2017). Drug-company payments mirror doctors' brand-name prescribing. In Betsy Maury (Ed.), *The reference shelf: Prescription drug abuse* (pp. 135-138). Ipswich, MA: H.W. Wilson. (Original work published 2016)

Opioid Rx Abuse Probe Sees a Record 31 Doctors Hit with Sanctions in New Jersey

By Elizabeth Llorente
Fox News, March 9, 2017

Dr. George Beecher took the oath to do no harm.

But the New Jersey physician did plenty of harm, according to Middlesex County prosecutors. And his alleged weapon was the addictive painkiller oxycodone.

Beecher, who was indicted last summer, was said to have prescribed a staggering 60,000 tablets of oxycodone to more than two dozen people he never even examined or met.

"He was ruthless, he made my son into an addict," said David Delmonaco, whose son, Robert, was one of the people who got prescriptions for oxycodone from Beecher even though he never met with the doctor. "My son started taking it, he was injured in the military, he had pain, and he quickly got addicted. This doctor just kept writing prescriptions, the highest dosage, three days in a row, and the pharmacy kept filling it."

Beecher's case is scheduled to go for a status conference on April 7, according to Middlesex County court officials. He is being represented by attorney Robert Galantucci, who could not be reached for comment Thursday.

Beecher is one of a record 31 doctors who New Jersey authorities sanctioned in the past 12 months, saying they overprescribed painkillers and other narcotics. New Jersey has pursued criminal charges against some, and imposed sanctions including suspension and taking away their license to practice.

The crackdown on unscrupulous doctors is part of a concerted effort led by New Jersey Gov. Chris Christie's administration to fight the opioid epidemic on multiple fronts—law enforcement, medical and a preventive educational campaign.

Other states also are working to address the opioid prescription epidemic that claims an average of 44 lives every day.

More than 600 legislative bills addressing opioid prescriptions are pending in 49 states this year, according to the American Academy of Family Physicians. Last year, there were 1,000.

Such legislative actions may have saved Robert Delmonaco. Once a healthy U.S. Army officer and Kean University student who made it into the National Honor Society, he committed suicide in the fall of 2014 at the age of 21.

"That Dr. Beecher did it all for money," said his father, who still breaks down when speaking of his son's tragic experience.

New Jersey, like many other U.S. states, has been hit by an opioid epidemic that led to nearly 1,600 documented overdoses in 2015, an increase of 21 percent over 2014, according to state medical records.

"It represents the largest number of doctors who have been sanctioned since we've been doing this," New Jersey Attorney General Chris Porrino told *Fox News* about the sanctions against doctors. "It's a very serious problem. Because so many people become addicted through the [initially legal] use of prescription opioids, we feel one very important part of our efforts to prevent addiction is to ferret out doctors who are not following the rules."

> **The medical industry acknowledges that opioid addiction has become an epidemic, and that health professionals must do their part to more responsibly handle painkiller prescriptions.**

In New Jersey, authorities learned of many of the wayward doctors through a prescription monitoring program that allows for the tracking of how medication is being prescribed, which doctor is prescribing it and to whom it is being written, Porrino said.

"So, we can determine whether someone is doctor-shopping, or whether in certain cases a particular physician is prescribing in a way that raises a red flag," he said.

Doctors who irresponsibly write prescriptions for such potentially dangerous addictive medications such as opioids, often for the money to be made, in essence are drug dealers in white coats, authorities say.

"Why they do it is a good question," Porrino said. "It's our view that doctors who are doing this are violating not just the law, but their oath and the trust that their patients put in them. Some of them do it for the insurance money they get based on visits, some of them get paid in cash for doing it. Very often it's driven by a desire for financial gain."

The stakes are too high, say government authorities and physicians, as well as the many people who have fallen victim to addiction, and their loved ones.

"Four out of five heroin addicts walking the streets started with prescription pain medications," Porrino said.

Last week, a grand jury indicted one of the 31 doctors, Byung Kang, 77, who is charged with selling prescriptions for high-dose oxycodone pills to people he knew were addicts and to drug dealers, the attorney general's office said.

Kang was indicted in connection with the oxycodone overdose death of 26-year-old Michael Justice.

The attorney general's statement about Kang's indictment said that he sold 90-count prescriptions for 30 milligram oxycodone pills to "numerous patients for $150 or $200 when the patients had no medical need for the potent pain pills…Kang's own records allegedly revealed that he knew many of those patients were addicted to oxycodone or were reselling the pills."

A year and a half before Michael Justice's death, his mother pleaded with Kang to stop prescribing the pills to her son, the attorney general's statement about the case said. She threatened to report him to police, but Kang continued writing the young man prescriptions "without medical justification" until his death, the statement said.

Beecher was one of the most egregious cases. He and seven other people, who were not doctors, were indicted last year on charges they operated a million-dollar prescription pill ring, authorities said.

Beecher also was indicted for a 2013 death under the state's "strict liability" law that allows drug dealers to be charged with a first-degree crime after a fatal overdose. The victim, Jason Stoveken, 30, died of an overdose from painkillers traced back to Beecher.

Jason Stoveken's father, Andrew Stoveken, who ran a hearing aid company and shared an office suite with Beecher, also is scheduled to have a status conference at the Middlesex County courthouse in April. His attorney, Steven Altman, could not be reached.

Andrew Stoveken was among seven people charged in a separate indictment last year that accused them of involvement in distributing and selling the pills Beecher prescribed.

Authorities said Beecher knowingly wrote the prescriptions for oxycodone and Xanax for Stoveken that killed him.

"We allege that even after a young man died from narcotics that Dr. Beecher falsely prescribed, Beecher and the victim's own father, defendant Andrew Stoveken, callously continued to profit by supplying tens of thousands of oxycodone pills to drug dealers," Porrino said in a statement.

Still mired in the pain over his son's death, David Delmonaco recalls how his former wife, his son's mother, pleaded with Beecher and the pharmacy that handled the prescriptions to stop because they were harming Robert.

Delmonaco said they denied they were doing anything wrong, and were dismissive.

Lawyers wanted to charge more than they could afford to take action against Beecher, he said.

Delmonaco said there's plenty about Gov. Chris Christie's administration he does not approve, but he is thankful for the tough response New Jersey officials are applying to the crisis that led to the death of Robert, who had been in and out of rehab.

"No one would do anything," Delmonaco said of the pleas that were ignored. "Nothing was done until Christie and the attorney general."

The medical industry acknowledges that opioid addiction has become an epidemic, and that health professionals must do their part to more responsibly handle painkiller prescriptions.

That involves a delicate balance, they say, between not prescribing them gratuitously, while at the same time keeping them accessible to the many Americans who experience debilitating pain and genuinely need them to function and to get through the day.

Some health professionals and patients who rely or have relied on painkillers criticized the Christie administration's recent signing of a measure that, among other things, imposes a five-day limit on initial opioid prescriptions—a dramatic drop from the 30-day time period.

New Jersey officials have said that people with chronic pain and cancer, for instance, will not be denied the dosage and amount of opioids they need.

"The pendulum can swing too far one way or too far the other," said Dr. George E. Woody, a psychiatry professor at the University of Pennsylvania who specializes in substance abuse issues. "There clearly are situations which are criminal cases, and then there are other cases whether it's just a lack of knowledge or sloppiness" in prescribing opioids.

"These are valuable drugs" for alleviating agonizing pain, Woody said. "They've been around for hundreds of years, they're old medicines and they're very useful, they make a huge difference in the lives of many people."

The American Academy of Family Physicians states on its website that it deems it a priority to find "solutions to the crisis of pain management and opioid abuse."

At the same time, it notes, "We recognize that long-acting and extended-release opioids are powerful drugs that require oversight, but these drugs can be controlled without unduly limiting their proper use. Creating additional prescribing barriers for primary care physicians would limit patient access when there is a legitimate need for pain relief."

The crisis has presented the medical profession with a challenge to rethink longtime practices, said Dr. Alan Schwartzstein, a practicing family physician who is vice speaker of the Congress of Delegates for the American Academy of Family Physicians.

"Doctors prescribed opioids in the past as they felt was appropriate," Schwartzstein told *Fox News*. "Around the early 2000's, there was a push to prescribe medicine for chronic pain. We were not adequately treating pain. We have to balance appropriately managing pain, and protecting the public from addiction and overdoses."

Print Citations

CMS: Llorente, Elizabeth. "Opioid Rx Probe Sees a Record 31 Doctors Hit with Sanctions in New Jersey." In *The Reference Shelf: Prescription Drug Abuse*, edited by Betsy Maury, 139-143. Ipswich, MA: H.W. Wilson, 2017.

MLA: Llorente, Elizabeth. "Opioid Rx Probe Sees a Record 31 Doctors Hit with Sanctions in New Jersey." *The Reference Shelf: Prescription Drug Abuse*. Ed. Betsy Maury. Ipswich: H.W. Wilson, 2017. 139-143. Print.

APA: Llorente, E. (2017). Opioid Rx probe sees a record 31 doctors hit with sanctions in New Jersey. In Betsy Maury (Ed.), *The reference shelf: Prescription drug abuse* (pp. 139-143). Ipswich, MA: H.W. Wilson. (Original work published 2017)

4

A Search for Solutions—Treatment

Credit: Photo by Whitney Hayward/Portland Press Herald via Getty Images

Amy Alexander has been a patient at CAP Quality Care clinic for eight years, which offers methadone treatment to patients as a part of their substance recovery program in Westbrook, ME. Alexander said methadone, in combination with other therapies during her recovery, has allowed her to function in her daily life after struggling with opiate addiction for years.

Treatment and Wellness

Drug abuse and addiction are mental health diseases that require treatment, though often addicts and abusers are treated more as criminals than patients. In the 1980s, the United States adopted an almost entirely criminal-justice-based approach to combating drug abuse and this approach proved remarkably ineffective despite decades of application and refinement. Public support for the criminalization of drug use and abuse has waned significantly and a 2014 Pew Research report found that two-thirds of Americans favored treatment, rather than jail, for heroin and cocaine users.[1] The National Institute on Drug Abuse (NIDA) lists both drug addiction and drug abuse as mental health issues and officially recommends that addiction should be treated, overall, as a disease rather than a crime. Gradually, the American public, and the American government, has adjusted to the idea that drug addicts and users are also sufferers, individuals for whom drug use is often a way to address complex underlying problems and vulnerabilities. It is the effort to advance treatment that is the most difficult and yet the only potentially lasting solution for drug abuse and addiction.

Some studies have suggested that interdisciplinary pain management, which may involve strategies to address the physiological, sensory, cognitive, and social/familial aspects of pain and may therefore require the involvement of physicians, therapists, and neurological specialists, provides better results than treatment with pain relievers alone. With increased scrutiny on the use of prescription drugs, as well, it will become more and more important that physicians take responsibility for responsible prescriptive practices while still advocating for the needs of patients for whom potentially dangerous drugs may be the only available solution.

The Search for Alternatives

One way to address the prescription drug problem is to find alternatives that can help patients suffering from disorders commonly treated using potentially addictive drugs. For instance, as much as 30 percent of the US population suffers from chronic pain and, in some cases, opioid pain relievers are considered the only effective option for pain control. Estimates indicate that between 1 and 8 percent of chronic pain sufferers using opioids may develop addiction, but the misuse and diversion of prescribed opioids frequently occurs, exacerbating the problem. Even if opioids were not physically and psychologically addictive, there are many other problems with the use of opioids, including digestive, behavioral, and motor control side effects and the fact that the body gradually becomes inured to the effects of opioids, making the drugs less effective over time and motivating patients to increase to potentially dangerous dosages.[2] Some studies have suggested that a more nuanced and comprehensive strategy for pain management, involving a combination of cognitive, behavioral, social, and physiological treatments to address the many varied impacts of pain, is more effective than treatment with pain relievers alone. While promising, alternative treatment programs involving interdisciplinary teams are unlikely to be covered by average insurance plans and so, for now, will likely be available only to a select group of patients. Physicians must play a role in helping alternative therapies and approaches reach mainstream acceptance by advocating for patients and taking the initiative to learn about and apply lessons from emerging research.

It is likely that, in the future, chemists will discover ways to use chemical altera- tion to reduce or eliminate the risk of addiction. Researchers working in 2016 and 2017 have already discovered a promising approach that may signal a new direction in pain medication. A 2017 paper in the journal *Science* reported on the results of a new series of studies in which researchers altered the opioid Fentanyl such that the molecule would only become active when absorbed into tissues with low pH (high acidity). Tissues that are damaged, and so might be causing pain, have lower pH levels and so by modifying opioids to work only in low-pH environments, research- ers were able to create an opioid that worked only at the site of injury and did not affect the central nervous system (CNS) as a whole. In theory, opioids modified in this way would not activate neural pathways that lead to addiction and would not produce the euphoric effect that has made opioids popular as a recreational drug and so would be unlikely to contribute to the illicit drug trade.[3] While the develop- ment of nonaddictive opioids could be a revolution in the future, it typically takes many years for a new drug to pass through clinical trials and into general use and subsequent testing may reveal as yet unknown complications with pH-altered mol- ecules. Such developments then, while promising, will do little to help address the problems of the present.

There is another substance that is widely available, nonaddictive, and has been shown to be helpful in the treatment of pain, depression, and many other ailments that are often treated using dangerous drugs. The substance is cannabis, or medical marijuana, a flowing plant that has been used for thousands of years as both a rec- reational drug and a medical aid in the treatment of pain, digestive problems, and numerous other common maladies. The problem is, marijuana acquired a cultural stigma during the many years in which the substance was classified as an illicit sub- stance and many Americans still fear that marijuana poses a threat to public health and welfare.

Research on marijuana use for pain, though still in its infancy, has produced positive and promising results. A 2014 study in the *Journal of the American Medical Association (JAMA)* found that states with medical marijuana laws, in which mari- juana can be used to supplement opioids in the treatment of pain, have had a 25 percent decrease in opioid overdoses.[4] A 2015 study in *JAMA* revealed that cannabi- noids were 30 percent more effective than placebos in pain management[5] and other studies suggest that patients treated with both opioids and cannabis require lower doses of opioids and can effectively reduce opioid use over time. A 2016 report in the journal *Health Affairs* demonstrated that, in states where medical marijuana is legal, doctors prescribe an average of 1,800 fewer doses of painkillers each year.[6]

With studies indicating that marijuana is a safer alternative and an effective way to reduce, if not eliminate, the use of opioids, some legislators and medical professionals are lobbying to eliminate remaining state laws prohibiting the use of marijuana in medicine. These legislators and lobbyists, like Massachusetts Senator Elizabeth Warren, who has advocated for legalizing marijuana as a supplement in pain treatment, represent the vast majority of the American people. Polls in 2017 indicate that 88 percent of Americans support medical marijuana use and 61 percent support legalizing marijuana in general, whether for medical or recreational purposes.[7]

Efforts to legalize marijuana as a medical aid have also been hampered by lobbying on behalf of pharmaceutical companies. This is because, even if pharmaceutical companies produce and distribute marijuana, the companies stand to earn far less from marijuana than from continuing to sell opioid pain relievers, antianxiety pills, and synthetic stimulants. These companies then support the political careers of a small number of politicians who have effectively blocked medical marijuana legislation on the dubious basis of public health concerns. Economic manipulation coupled with the insidious effects of decades of campaigning to portray marijuana as a dangerous "gateway drug" that leads to the use of heavier, addictive drugs (despite no legitimate evidence to support this) have not only slowed the legalization of marijuana as a medical aid but have also hampered research into the effectiveness of marijuana treatment.

The Mental Health Approach

Whether or not alternative drugs can be found, there are many who believe that the use of dangerous drugs could be curtailed if physicians and patients alter their basic approach to treating certain disorders. For instance, patients using potentially addictive antianxiety drugs, in many cases, respond just as well if treated with behavioral and psychotherapy. A combination of limited medication coupled with therapy might be the most effective treatment for anxiety and depression and yet such treatment options are, for many Americans, prohibitively expensive and not covered by medical insurance plans. Expanding medical health coverage and requiring insurance companies to fund mental health treatment at lower rates could therefore provide a powerful tool to addressing the roots of addiction.

Whether taking CNS depressants, stimulants, or opioid pain relievers, the potential for addiction and abuse is a function of a person's well-being and mental health. Individuals who suffer from anxiety, depression, and high levels of stress, whether related to an existing and/or diagnosable mental health problem or entirely environmental are more likely to abuse and so to develop dependency on prescription drugs *or* illicit substances. A variety of life stressors, such as marriage or employment difficulties, poverty, abuse, past and current trauma, and many other factors, place individuals at a higher risk for abuse and eventual dependency as individuals use prescription or illicit drugs as self-treatment for the discomforts of their lives.

The high rate of abuse and addiction in the United States, compared to other nations in which potentially addictive substances are regularly prescribed, indicates that there is something unique about US society that makes Americans especially susceptible to abuse. Studies indicating that Americans are more depressed and more prone to anxiety than people living in many other developed nations may hold the answer to this puzzle, essentially suggesting that the US population as a whole is suffering from an abundance of stress, anxiety, and depression-related issues and thus is especially prone and vulnerable to addiction and drug abuse.

In a 2016 article in *Scientific American*, author Maia Szalavitz argues that reducing opioid addiction requires addressing the risk factors that predispose people to addiction and abuse, such as unemployment, childhood trauma, and mental illness.[8] Studies of heroin abuse indicate, for instance, that two-thirds of abusers reported some childhood trauma, such as the death of a parent or child abuse.[9] A 2015 study in *Drug and Alcohol Dependence* indicated that 50 percent of those suffering from opioid addiction had diagnosable mental health or personality disorders.[10]

A variety of studies have likewise demonstrated that poverty, economic insecurity, unemployment, and social marginalization are extremely important risk factors in the drug abuse cycle. Individuals who are unemployed or who earn low incomes are more than three times more likely to develop an addiction than individuals in higher economic strata and studies additionally show that those at lower income levels are less likely to locate and succeed in treatment programs after developing a drug abuse problem. It has been argued that it is not simply a coincidence that the collapse of the white middle class in the United States, bringing about higher levels of depression, job insecurity, unemployment, and hopelessness, has coincided with growth of the opioid addiction crisis and state data indicates that opioid addiction is more prevalent in communities suffering from high levels of economic distress.

While it might be tempting to believe that the prescription drug epidemic can be solved by tightening regulations on drug companies or penalizing doctors for overprescribing drugs, or even by developing new nonaddictive alternatives, such efforts are ultimately futile, addressing the supply side of the equation, but not the demand. Many of those who abuse and become addicted to drugs begin using intoxicants in an attempt to "self-medicate" against the pains and pressures of their daily lives. As long as there is a population living in poverty and despair, the precipitating conditions will remain and there will be those who seek chemical solutions.

Micah L. Issitt

Works Used

"America's New Drug Policy Landscape." *Pew Research*. Pew Foundation. Apr 2 2014. Web. 24 Aug 2017.

Bachhuber, Marcus A., Saloner, Brendan, and Chinazo O. Cunningham, et al. "Medical Cannabis Laws and Opioid Analgestic Overdose Mortality in the United States, 1999-2010." *JAMA*. Journal of the American Medical Association. Oct 2014. Vol. 174, No. 10, 1668–73.

Bogdanowicz, Karolina M., et al. "Double Trouble: Psychiatric Comorbidity and Opioid Addiction—All-Cause and Cause-Specific Mortality." *Drug and Alcohol Dependence*. Mar 1 2015. Vol. 148, 85-92.

Darke, Shane. "Pathways to Heroin Dependence: Time to Re-appraise Self-Medication." *Addiction*. Apr 2013. Vol. 108, No. 4, 659–67.

De Pinto, Jennifer, Backus, Fred, Khanna, Kabir, and Anthony Salvanto. "Marijuana Legalization Support at All-Time High." *CNS News*. Apr 20 2017. Web. 23 Aug 2017.

Mole, Beth. "Early Study Suggests New Opioid Is Non-addictive, Works Only Where It Hurts." *Arstechnica*. Mar 4 2014. Web. 22 Aug 2017.

Sifferlin, Alexandra. "Can Medical Marijuana Help End the Opioid Epidemic?" *Time*. Time Inc. Jul 28 2016. Web. 22 Aug 2017.

Szalavitz, Maia. "Opioid Addiction Is a Huge Problem, but Pain Prescriptions Are Not the Cause." *Scientific American*. Nature America, Inc. May 10 2016. Web. 23 Aug 2017.

Volkow, Nora D. and Thomas McLellan. "Opioid Abuse in Chronic Pain—Misconceptions and Mitigation Strategies." *NEJM*. New England Journal of Medicine. Mar 31 2016. Web. 22 Aug 2017.

Whiting, Penny F., Wolff, Robert F., and Sohan Deshpande, et al. "Cannabinoids for Medical Use: A Systematic Review and Meta-analysis." *JAMA*. Journal of the American Medical Association. 2015. Vol. 313, No. 24, 2456–73.

Notes

1. "America's New Drug Policy Landscape," *Pew Research*.
2. Volkow and McLellan, "Opioid Abuse in Chronic Pain—Misconceptions and Mitigation Strategies."
3. Mole, "Early Study Suggests New Opioids Is Non-addictive, Works Only Where It Hurts."
4. Bachhuber, Saloner, and Cunningham, et al., "Medical Cannabis Laws and Opioid Analgesic Overdose Mortality in the United States, 1999-2010."
5. Whiting, Wolff, and Deshpande, et al., "Cannabinoids for Medical Use: A Systematic Review and Meta-analysis."
6. Sifferlin, "Can Medical Marijuana Help End the Opioid Epidemic?"
7. De Pinto, Backus, Khanna, and Salvanto, "Marijuana Legalization Support at All-Time High."
8. Szalavitz, "Opioid Addiction Is a Huge Problem, but Pain Prescriptions Are Not the Cause."
9. Darke, "Pathways to Heroin Dependence: Time to Re-appraise Self-Medication."
10. "Bogdanowicz, et al, "Double Trouble: Psychiatric Comorbidity and Opioid Addiction—All-Case and Cause-Specific Mortality."

A Primary Care Doctor Delves into the Opioid Epidemic

By Monique Tello, MD, MPH
Harvard Health Publications, **February 20, 2017**

Our nephew Christopher died of a heroin overdose in October 2013. It had started with pain pills and experimentation, and was fueled by deep grief. He was charismatic, lovable, a favorite uncle, and a hero to all the children in his life. His death too young was a huge loss to our family. I have always felt that I didn't do enough to help prevent it, and perhaps, in a way, even contributed.

Good Intentions with Unintended Consequences

My medical training took me through several big-city hospitals where addiction and its consequences were commonplace. Throughout all of it, great emphasis was placed on recognizing "the fifth vital sign," i.e., pain, and treating it.

I distinctly remember as a medical student wearing a little pin with the word "PAIN" and a line across it. One was considered a bad doctor if they didn't ask about and treat pain.

And so, treat we did. This medical movement, combined with the mass marketing of OxyContin and a swelling heroin trade, has created the current opioid epidemic.

It generally starts with pain pills: Percocet, Vicodin, Oxycodone or OxyContin, either prescribed or given or bought. Quickly, a person finds that she or he needs more and more of the drug to get the same effect. Almost overnight, they need the drug just to feel normal, to stave off

> **There's a great need for doctors willing and able to treat opioid use disorder.**

the horror of withdrawal. Street heroin is cheaper and easier to come by than pills, and so, people move on to the next level. Just like Christopher.

Recent data from the Centers for Disease Control (CDC) and the National Institute for Drug Abuse (NIDA) show that deaths from overdose of opioids have been rising every year since 1999. (OxyContin came to market in 1996). Deaths from heroin overdose have recently spiked: a 20% increase from 2014 to 2015. And most recently we're seeing fentanyl, an extremely potent synthetic opioid, where even a few small grains can kill.

So, if we doctors helped everyone get into this mess, we should help them get out of it, no?

Needed: Treatment That Works

As the opioid epidemic has exploded, so has the demand for treatment. But treatment is almost impossible to come by. The U.S. is short almost 1 million treatment slots for opioid addiction treatment. And not all treatments offered are that effective.

The "traditional" treatment of detoxification, followed by referrals to individual therapy or group support (think Narcotics Anonymous), may work well for some, but the data suggest that there are more effective approaches. In fact, a growing body of evidence very strongly supports medication, combined with therapy and group support, as the most effective treatment currently available.

"Detox" followed by therapy has consistently shown poor results, with more than 80% of patients relapsing, compared to treatment with medications, with only 15% relapsing. Medications, specifically methadone and buprenorphine, can help prevent withdrawal symptoms and control cravings, and can help patients to function in society. Suboxone (a combination of the drugs buprenorphine and naloxone) has many advantages over methadone. It not only prevents withdrawal and controls cravings, but also blocks the effects from any illicit drug use, making it more difficult for patients to relapse or overdose. In addition, while methadone can only be prescribed through certified clinics, any primary care provider who completes a training course can prescribe Suboxone. That means treatment for opioid use disorders could be much more widely available.

Basically, treatment with medications, and especially Suboxone, is effective, and safer than anything else we have to offer. Yes, relapses can occur, but far less frequently than with traditional treatment. And death from heroin overdose? Far, far less.

Biases against Treating Opioid Use Disorder with Medications

Despite their effectiveness, there is stigma associated with treating substance use disorders with medication. I admit that I had my own doubts as well. People say, as I did, "Oh, you're just replacing one drug with another." But a lot of hard science has accumulated since 2002, when the FDA approved Suboxone for the treatment of opioid addiction.

Think about it. Is shooting street heroin that's cut with God knows what, using needles infected with worse, really the same as using a well-studied, safe, and effective daily oral medication? Some may claim "Oh, you're just creating another addiction." Would you tell someone with diabetes who depends on insulin that they're "addicted"? Then why say that to someone with opioid use disorder who depends on Suboxone? This is literally the reasoning that played out in my head as I have learned about treating opioid addiction, or, more correctly stated, opioid use disorder.

Stepping Up

I've decided that it's time to do something. There's a great need for doctors willing and able to treat opioid use disorder. In 2016, surgeon general Vivek Murthy issued a strident call to action to all U.S. healthcare providers, asking them to get involved.

This issue has been on my mind and soul since Christopher's death, so I started educating myself, and contacted our hospital's substance use disorders specialist with my motivation and concerns. In the few months since then, I've taken the training course to become a licensed prescriber, and am working with the team to begin treating a small group of patients.

In my 16 years of clinical training and practice, I have witnessed all of this first-hand: the blatant, medically rationalized over-prescription of pain meds, the stigma and undertreatment of opioid use disorder, and the unnecessary, premature death of a really good kid. I'm just starting off on this, and I'm still learning, but my hope is to keep another family from experiencing unnecessary loss.

Print Citations

CMS: Tello, Monique. "A Primary Care Doctor Delves into the Opioid Epidemic." In *The Reference Shelf: Prescription Drug Abuse*, edited by Betsy Maury, 153-155. Ipswich, MA: H.W. Wilson, 2017.

MLA: Tello, Monique. "A Primary Care Doctor Delves into the Opioid Epidemic." *The Reference Shelf: Prescription Drug Abuse*. Ed. Betsy Maury. Ipswich: H.W. Wilson, 2017. 153-155. Print.

APA: Tello, M. (2017). A primary care doctor delves into the opioid epidemic. In Betsy Maury (Ed.), *The reference shelf: Prescription drug abuse* (pp. 153-155). Ipswich, MA: H.W. Wilson. (Original work published 2017)

The Doctors Who Started the Opioid Epidemic

By Paul A. Offit

The Daily Beast, April 1, 2017

On January 16, 2016, Gina Kolata and Sarah Cohen, writing for the *New York Times,* offered up some grim news: "The rising death rates for young white adults make them the first generation since the Vietnam War years of the mid-1960s to experience higher death rates in early adulthood than the generation that preceded it." The reason: opioid addiction. The biggest culprit: doctors. By refusing to accept their inability to separate pain relief from addiction, physicians have long suffered the sin of hubris—and their patients have paid the price.

It started with humankind's first medicine.

About 6,000 years ago, the Sumerians discovered opium. One of the first clinicians to recommend it was Hippocrates, the Father of Modern Medicine, who used opium to treat nausea. But it was an unknown contemporary of Hippocrates named Diagoras of Melos who first noticed that many of his fellow Greeks had become addicted to the drug.

Diagoras's warnings were ignored.

Opium users became opium addicts.

In 1803, Frederich Sertürner, a 20-year-old German chemist, purified opium's most active and most abundant ingredient. He called it morphium after the Greek God of Dreams. Sertürner hoped that by purifying opium's main ingredient, he could separate pain relief from addiction. While conducting his studies, Sertürner became addicted to the drug. Like Diagoras of Melos, he warned against its use. Again, no one listened. In 1827, the German pharmaceutical company Merck began mass-producing Sertürner's drug.

Opium addicts became morphine addicts.

In 1874, C.R. Alder Wright chemically modified morphine to produce diacetylmorphine. He fed it to his dog, which became violently ill and frighteningly hyperactive. Wright published his findings in an obscure scientific journal. For 20 years, no one noticed the powerful drug that Wright had created.

In 1895, Heinrich Dreser, a chemist working for a pharmaceutical company in the Rhineland named Bayer, discovered Wright's paper. Dreser found that diacetylmorphine entered the brain five times more efficiently than morphine. He reasoned that because lesser quantities of this drug could relieve pain, it would be less

> **On June 16, 2016, at its annual meeting in Chicago, the American Medical Association (AMA) urged physicians to eliminate pain as the fifth vital sign.**

addictive. He tested diacetylmorphine on a few workmen in his company and a handful of local patients. After four weeks of observation, no one appeared to be addicted—at last, a non-addictive, potent painkiller. Bayer named the drug for its heroic properties.

Morphine addicts became heroin addicts.

In the early 1900s, German researchers chemically modified thebaine, another component of opium. They called it oxycodone. In the early 1950s, oxycodone entered the United States. The most potent, most addictive, and most deadly preparation of oxycodone was OxyContin, which was manufactured by Purdue Pharmaceuticals and licensed in 1995. Purdue later hoped to reduce the number of daily doses by offering a time-released preparation. However, by chewing the product, users could bypass the time-released mechanism and ingest as much as 160 milligrams of oxycodone at one time, a potentially lethal dose.

Although many doctors had learned to fear opioids, two events liberalized their use in the United States. (Products derived directly from the opium poppy are called opiates; morphine is an opiate. Chemical modifications of opiates are called opioids; heroin and oxycodone are opioids.)

In 1967, Cicely Saunders, a nurse working at St. Luke's Hospital for the Dying in East London, founded the hospice movement. Saunders believed that terminally ill patients shouldn't have to spend their last few days crying out in pain. To avoid this suffering, she offered large quantities of painkillers. Saunders' ideas crossed the ocean. In 1984, the United States Congress passed the Compassionate Pain Relief Act, making it legal to treat terminally ill patients with heroin.

In 1985, Russell Portenoy, a New York City pain specialist, argued that our compassion for people in pain shouldn't be limited to those with terminal illnesses. No one should be allowed to suffer. He believed that American physicians needed to get over their fear of painkillers, what he called their "opiophobia." Portenoy insisted that, if used correctly, opioids wouldn't cause addiction. Under Russell Portenoy's influence, pain became the fifth vital sign (in addition to heart rate, temperature, blood pressure, and respiratory rate).

Heroin addicts became opioid addicts.

During the past year, doctors, public health officials, and lawmakers have finally taken steps to stem the tide of America's growing opioid crisis.

On March 15, 2016, the Centers for Disease Control and Prevention (CDC) issued a series of restrictive guidelines. The CDC recommended that doctors should prescribe opioids: (1) only after non-prescription painkillers and physical therapies have failed; (2) in quantities not to exceed a three-day supply for short-term pain or a seven-day supply for chronic pain (for which patients have typically been given a one-month supply with refills); and (3) only when improvement is significant.

On June 16, 2016, at its annual meeting in Chicago, the American Medical Association (AMA) urged physicians to eliminate pain as the fifth vital sign. "We have taken ownership of [the problem]," said AMA president Andrew Gurman. "And physicians have taken ownership of being part of the solution."

On January 1, 2017, lawmakers for the Commonwealth of Pennsylvania took the CDC's guidelines one step further—turning its recommendations into law. Unless treating patients with cancer or in palliative care, physicians working in hospital emergency departments, urgent care centers, or in-patient units in Pennsylvania were not allowed to prescribe opioids in excess of a seven-day supply nor allowed to prescribe refills. Further, when prescribing opioids to minors, physicians were required to counsel the patient or parents about the risks of addiction and obtain written consent, unless the situation was a medical emergency.

In his book, *1984*, George Orwell wrote, "Of pain you could wish only one thing: that it should stop. Nothing in the world is so bad as physical pain. In the face of pain there are no heroes." In the face of a powerful addiction, there are also no heroes.

Today, the United States, which contains 5 percent of the world's population, uses 80 percent of the world's painkillers.

Print Citations

CMS: Offit, Paul A. "The Doctors Who Started the Opioid Epidemic." In *The Reference Shelf: Prescription Drug Abuse*, edited by Betsy Maury, 156-158. Ipswich, MA: H.W. Wilson, 2017.

MLA: Offit, Paul A. "The Doctors Who Started the Opioid Epidemic." *The Reference Shelf: Prescription Drug Abuse*. Ed. Betsy Maury. Ipswich: H.W. Wilson, 2017. 156-158. Print.

APA: Offit, P.A. (2017). The doctors who started the opioid epidemic. In Betsy Maury (Ed.), *The reference shelf: Prescription drug abuse* (pp. 156-158). Ipswich, MA: H.W. Wilson. (Original work published 2017)

Can We Curb the Opioid Abuse Epidemic by Rethinking Chronic Pain?

By Richard Gunderman

The Conversation, January 8, 2016

Over the last few decades, medicine has witnessed a sea change in attitudes toward chronic pain, and particularly toward opioids. While these changes were intended to bring relief to many, they have also fed an epidemic of prescription opioid and heroin abuse.

Curbing abuse is a challenge spilling over into the 2016 political campaigns. Amid calls for better addiction treatment and prescription monitoring, it might be time for doctors to rethink how to treat chronic pain.

Ancient Roots, Modern Challenges

A class of drugs that includes morphine and hydrocodone, opioids get their name from opium, Greek for "poppy juice," the source from which they are extracted.

In fact, one of the earliest accounts of narcotic addiction is found in Homer's *Odyssey*. One of the first places Odysseus and his beleaguered crew land on their voyage home from Troy is the land of the Lotus-Eaters. Some of his men eat of the Lotus, lapsing into somnolent apathy. Soon the listless addicts care for nothing but the drug and weep bitterly when Odysseus forces them back to their ships.

For decades in the U.S., physicians resisted prescribing opioids, in part for fear that patients would develop dependency and addiction. Beginning in the 1980s and 1990s, this began to change.

Based on experiences with end-of-life care, some physicians and drug companies began saying that opioids should be used more liberally to relieve chronic pain. They argued that the risks of addiction had been overstated.

Since 2001, the Joint Commission, an independent group that accredits hospitals, has required that pain be assessed and treated, leading to numerical pain rating scales and the promotion of pain as medicine's "fifth vital sign." Doctors and nurses now routinely ask patients to rate the severity of their pain on a scale of zero to 10.

While it is impossible to measure the burden of pain strictly in dollars, it has been estimated that the total health care cost attributable to pain ranges from US$560 billion to $635 billion annually, making it an important source of revenue for many health professionals, hospitals and drug companies.

More Prescriptions for Opioids Have Fed Abuse

Today it is estimated that 100 million people in the U.S. suffer from chronic pain—more than the number with diabetes (26 million), heart disease (16 million) and cancer (12 million). Many who suffer from chronic pain will be treated with opioids.

In 2010 enough prescription painkillers were prescribed to medicate every American adult every four hours for one month. The nation is now in the midst of an epidemic of opioid abuse, and prescription medications far outrank illicit drugs as causes of drug overdose and death.

It is estimated that 5.1 million Americans abuse painkillers, and nearly two million Americans suffer from opioid addiction or dependence. Between 1999 and 2010, the number of women dying annually of opioid overdose increased five times. The number of fatalities each day from opioid overdoses exceeds that of car accidents and homicides.

In response, the Drug Enforcement Agency and a number of state legislatures have tightened restrictions on opioid prescribing.

For instance, patients must have a written prescription to obtain Vicodin and doctors can't call prescriptions in. The downside, of course, is that many patients must visit their physicians more often, a challenge for those who are seriously ill.

Some patients seek multiple prescriptions for opioids so that they can turn a profit selling extra pills. The increase in prescription opioid misuse is also linked to an increase in the number of people using heroin.

A sea change in pain treatment helped create the opioid abuse epidemic, and another sea change in how doctors view chronic pain could help curb it.

Looking beyond Physical Pain

In a recent article in the *New England Journal of Medicine*, two physicians from the University of Washington, Jane Ballantyne and Mark Sullivan, argue that physicians need to reexamine the real strengths and weaknesses of opioids. While these drugs can be very effective in relieving short-term pain associated with injuries and surgery, the authors say "there is little evidence supporting their long-term benefit."

One of the reasons opioids have become so widely used today, the authors suggest, has been the push to lower pain intensity scores, which often requires "escalating doses of opioids at the expense of worsening function and quality of life." Merely lowering a pain score does not necessarily make the patient better off.

They point out that the experience of pain is not always equal to the amount of tissue damage. In some cases, such as childbirth or athletic competition, individuals may tolerate even excruciating degrees of pain in pursuit of an important goal. In other situations, lesser degrees of pain—particularly chronic pain—can prove unbearable, in part because it is experienced in the setting of helplessness and hopelessness.

Instead of focusing strictly on pain intensity, they say, physicians and patients should devote greater attention to suffering. For example, when patients better understand what is causing their pain, no longer perceive pain as a threat to their lives and know that they are receiving effective treatment for their underlying condition, their need for opioids can often be reduced. This means focusing more on the meaning of pain than its intensity.

> **Doctors and nurses now routinely ask patients to rate the severity of their pain on a scale of zero to 10.**

This helps to explain why one group of patients, those with preexisting mental health and substance abuse problems ("dual diagnosis patients"), are particularly poorly served by physicians who base opioid doses strictly on pain intensity scores. Such patients are more likely to be treated with opioids on a long-term basis, to misuse their medications, and to experience adverse drug effects leading to emergency room visits, hospitalizations, and death—often with no improvement in their underlying condition.

The point is that pain intensity scores are an imperfect measure of what the patient is experiencing. When it comes to chronic pain, say the authors, "intensity isn't a simple measure of something that can be easily fixed." Instead patients and physicians need to recognize the larger psychological, social and even spiritual dimensions of suffering.

For chronic pain, Ballantyne and Sullivan argue, one of the missing links is conversation between doctor and patient, "which allows the patient to be heard and the clinician to appreciate the patient's experiences and offer empathy, encouragement, mentorship, and hope."

If the authors are right, in other words, patients and physicians need to strike a new and different balance between relying on the prescription pad and developing stronger relationships with patients.

One problem, of course, is that many physicians are not particularly eager to develop strong relationships with patients suffering from chronic pain, substance abuse and/or mental illness. One reason is the persistent widespread stigma associated with such conditions.

It takes a doctor with a special sense of calling to devote the time and energy necessary to connect with such patients, many of whom can prove particularly difficult to deal with.

In too many cases today, it proves easier just to numb the suffering with a prescription for an opioid.

Print Citations

CMS: Gunderman, Richard. "Can We Curb the Opioid Abuse Epidemic by Rethinking Chronic Pain?" In *The Reference Shelf: Prescription Drug Abuse*, edited by Betsy Maury, 159-162. Ipswich, MA: H.W. Wilson, 2017.

MLA: Gunderman, Richard. "Can We Curb the Opioid Abuse Epidemic by Rethinking Chronic Pain?" *The Reference Shelf: Prescription Drug Abuse*. Ed. Betsy Maury. Ipswich: H.W. Wilson, 2017. 159-162. Print.

APA: Gunderman, R. (2017). Can we curb the opioid abuse epidemic by rethinking chronic pain? In Betsy Maury (Ed.), *The reference shelf: Prescription drug abuse* (pp. 159-162). Ipswich, MA: H.W. Wilson. (Original work published 2016)

The Painkillers That Could End the Opioid Crisis

By Adam Piore

MIT Technology Review, **August 11, 2016**

It happens every time James Zadina publishes a new paper or receives a write-up: the phone in his New Orleans laboratory begins to ring. The e-mails flood his inbox. The messages come from people all around the nation telling him how much they hurt.

"I get calls saying, 'I have this terrible pain. When's your medicine coming?'" Zadina says. "And my response is, 'I can't give it to you now. I'm working as fast as I can.'

That's all I can say. But it's difficult."

For the last 20 years, Zadina, a researcher at the Tulane School of Medicine and the Southeast Louisiana Veterans Health Care System, has been on the front lines of a battle to defeat an ancient human adversary: physical pain. But lately his work has taken on new urgency. As opioid-related deaths and addiction in the United States reach epidemic proportions, Zadina has been attempting to engineer a new kind of painkiller that wouldn't have the devastating side effects often caused by commonly prescribed drugs such as Oxycontin.

His pursuit is difficult because the very mechanisms that make those pills good at dulling pain are the ones that too often lead to crippling addiction and drug abuse. Like their close chemical cousin heroin, prescription opioids can cause people to become physically dependent on them. Researchers have been trying for decades to "separate the addictive properties of opiates from the pain-reducing properties," says David Thomas, an administrator at the National Institute on Drug Abuse and a founding member of the NIH Pain Consortium. "They kind of go together."

But Zadina believes he is getting close to decoupling them. Just this past winter, he and his team published a study in *Neuropharmacology* reporting that they had treated pain in rats without causing the five most common side effects associated with opioids, including increased tolerance, motor impairment, and respiratory depression, which leads to most opioid-related deaths. The next step is to test it in humans.

It's just one of a number of efforts that aim to end the long-term damage that is being caused by relieving people of agony. Up to 8 percent of patients prescribed narcotic painkillers for chronic pain will become addicted, according to the National

Institute of Drug Abuse. That's why it used to be relatively difficult for patients to obtain opioids such as codeine to treat pain, Thomas says. That began to change in the 1990s. New opioids such as Oxycontin (and new marketing campaigns by pharmaceutical companies) arrived to meet the earnest demands of pain doctors and patient advocates who argued that many people with chronic pain—which afflicts an estimated 100 million Americans—were needlessly suffering.

But the pendulum has swung so far that opioids have become the default drug even when there might be better alternatives. Dan Clauw, director of the Chronic Pain and Fatigue Research Center at the University of Michigan, says that too many doctors now are essentially telling patients, "Well, I was taught that opioids would always work in any kind of pain, and if the pain's bad enough and you're desperate enough, I'll try this class of drugs even if I am concerned about the risk of addiction."

The consequences have been devastating. In 2014, the number of deaths from opioid overdoses in the United States topped 18,000, about 50 a day—more than three times the number in 2001. And that doesn't even take into account painkiller addicts who have turned to heroin to soothe their cravings. Officials at the Centers for Disease Control and Prevention recently compared the scale of the problem to the HIV epidemic of the 1980s.

Developing any kind of better painkiller is very hard largely because pain takes complex pathways in our bodies. The signals that reach the brain and are interpreted as pain sometimes come from a problem on the periphery, or the surface, of our bodies, like when you get a cut. Other times the source of the pain signals is deeper: from damage to our nerves, which can happen with a really bad wound or, say, a back injury. And researchers such as Clauw are now finding evidence that much pain comes from a third type of situation: misfiring in the brain.

However, the presence of these different pain mechanisms also means there are a few different ways to try to solve the opioid problem. While Zadina and other scientists try to remove the dangerous properties from opioids, other new painkillers might target altogether different mechanisms in the body.

Make It Stop

The main way to kill pain is simply to reduce the signals that the body feeds to the brain.

Nearly all our tissues have what are known as "nociceptive" nerve endings, tiny fibers whose job is to collect information and convey it back to the central nervous system and into the brain for processing. These fibers act as pain sensors. Some of the nerve endings respond to pressure, which causes them to send electrical impulses to the spinal cord so we actually feel hurt. Other kinds of nerve endings respond to changes in temperature, generating pain signals when things get too hot or cold. When we sustain an injury, inflammatory cells are recruited to the site and release at least a dozen different chemicals aimed at triggering other cells to come in and fight off pathogens, clean up debris, and begin rebuilding. But these inflammatory cells also cause the nerve endings at the site of the injury to fire more pain signals. In this type of localized injury, such as a sprained ankle or twisted knee, ice or anti-inflammatory drugs such as ibuprofen can be enough to tamp down the pain signals.

But sometimes—after a severe injury, an amputation, or diabetic nerve damage, for example—nerve fibers or the cells from which they originate physically change. Deep inside them, some genes can get turned on or off. That changes the number or type of active cellular machines known as sodium channels—proteins that stick out of the cells and regulate their ability to generate electrical impulses. Nerve cells talk to each other by means of these electrical impulses, and the sudden activity of extra sodium channels can cause a nerve to fire machine-gun-like bursts "spontaneously, even when there are no threatening stimuli," explains Stephen Waxman, a professor of neurology at Yale University who directs the Center for Neuroscience and Regeneration Research at a Veterans Affairs hospital in Connecticut. Those bursts leave people in extreme pain. One common cause is chemotherapy. "Sometimes that pain is so bad people say 'I can't stand it,'" Waxman says. "'I would rather die from cancer than have the pain associated with treatment.'"

"I'm working as fast as I can," Zadina says. "That's all I can say. But it's difficult."

There are nine kinds of sodium channels; the numbing medicine you get in the dentist's office works by locally blunting all of them. That wouldn't work as a general pain medication, because some of these channels are present in the brain and central nervous system. But Waxman is part of a cadre of researchers hunting for ways to target just one key sodium channel. He discovered its importance by studying people who have a rare genetic mutation that prevents them from making this particular channel. Even though the channel is not found everywhere in the human body, they essentially go through life feeling no pain. Conversely, people born with a hyperactive version of it feel as though "lava has been poured into their bodies," Waxman says.

A drug developed by Pfizer, based on Waxman's discoveries, has been tested on five patients, and similar painkillers are in development. Theoretically at least, these would not have major side effects.

Which brings us back to opioids.

Flipping a Switch

Our peripheral nerves, where we pick up pain signals, lead back to the spinal column, where they connect with nerve cells that carry messages into the central nervous system and to neurons in the brain, at which point we feel the pain.

This is where all opioids, from Oxycontin to heroin and morphine, work their magic. They do so by binding to what are known as mu receptors at the junctions where nerve cells meet. That essentially flips a switch that reduces the ability of these cells to fire. So when nerve fibers at the periphery of the body send pain signals up to the brain for processing, the neurons that would normally make us feel this pain don't respond.

"Opioids don't touch the pain source; they only turn off the appreciation of the pain in the brain," says Lewis Nelson, a professor of emergency medicine at New

York University School of Medicine, who sat on a panel that recently recommended opioid guidelines for the Centers for Disease Control. "A small dose of an opioid just changes the sensation from being something that is quite irritating to being something that you don't seem to care about as much."

Mu receptors respond not only to painkilling drugs but also to "endogenous opioids," natural signaling agents produced by our bodies—like the endorphins that are released during exercise, producing the so-called "runner's high." The problem is that the body doesn't seem to respond to drugs such as heroin and Oxycontin in the same way it does to the endogenous substances.

Unlike endogenous opioids, pain drugs often activate specialized cells in the central nervous system, known as glia. Glia clean up cellular debris in the body and help regulate the response to injuries to the central nervous system. But when activated, they produce inflammatory substances—which can cause the body to register more pain signals. Many researchers, in fact, believe this increased activation of glial cells may be what causes the dangerous buildup of tolerance that makes opioids less effective over time, so that a patient needs higher doses to feel their effects. Eventually those higher doses can cause deadly respiratory problems.

The main way to kill pain is simply to reduce the signals that the body feeds to the brain.

All this might be avoided if Zadina can finally develop a synthetic opioid more like the body's own substances—one that hits the mu receptors without activating glial cells. In the 1990s, he and his team isolated a previously undiscovered neurochemical in the brain, a pain-numbing substance they named endomorphin. He has been attempting ever since to perfect synthetic versions of it.

One of those versions was the drug that Zadina tested on rats in the study reported this past winter in *Neuropharmacology*. Like some of his previous compounds, this version appeared to be as good as or possibly better than morphine at relieving the animals' pain without causing the worst side effects. Now he is in talks with several investors and biotech companies interested in turning it into a pill for people. Once he and his collaborators raise the money to start their own company, or ink a deal with a licensing partner, they intend to seek approval for early-stage human trials. "You never know until you actually put it in humans," he says.

Zadina's drug would still be likely to activate the reward areas of the brain, and it might generate a mild high that could predispose some to addiction. But the rapid escalation of tolerance that opioids normally cause—and the physical withdrawal symptoms people endure when they stop taking them—would probably be removed from the equation. "I want to take away the dilemma that both patients and physicians face, of 'Do I treat this pain adequately and risk addiction or do I treat the pain inadequately because I don't want to use opioids?'" Zadina says. "That's what drives me."

But even if his new drug succeeds, neither it nor new sodium-channel painkillers are likely to treat a type of pain we weren't even sure existed until recently—pain that does not seem to respond at all to opioids. Michigan's Clauw has been studying this kind of pain for the past 20 years. From brain imaging studies, he has determined that it is caused by misfiring in the brain rather than a problem at the site where the pain seems to be coming from. He contends that this is the most common reason for pain in younger people suffering from conditions that have long confounded doctors, including fibromyalgia, certain headaches, and irritable bowel syndrome. What should those patients take instead of the opioids they are often prescribed? Many of them, Clauw argues, should be on drugs that can actually halt the misfiring by boosting neurotransmitters. Some drugs originally developed as antidepressants achieve this.

The NIH's Thomas points to Clauw's research as evidence that opioids today are simply overprescribed.

"If you get in a car accident, get wounded in battle, your arm gets blown up or something, and you're in really severe pain, they will knock out severe pain pretty darn quickly," says Thomas. "But right now they're being used for all sorts of other cases where they're probably not beneficial to the patient in the long run."

Print Citations

CMS: Piore, Adam. "The Painkillers That Could End the Opioid Crisis." In *The Reference Shelf: Prescription Drug Abuse*, edited by Betsy Maury, 163-167. Ipswich, MA: H.W. Wilson, 2017.

MLA: Piore, Adam. "The Painkillers That Could End the Opioid Crisis." *The Reference Shelf: Prescription Drug Abuse*. Ed. Betsy Maury. Ipswich: H.W. Wilson, 2017. 163-167. Print.

APA: Piore, A. (2017). The painkillers that could end the opioid crisis. In Betsy Maury (Ed.), *The reference shelf: Prescription drug abuse* (pp. 163-167). Ipswich, MA: H.W. Wilson. (Original work published 2016)

How Medical Marijuana Could Help End the Opioid Epidemic

By Eric Killelea
Rolling Stone, March 29, 2017

Rio Arriba County, just north of Santa Fe, New Mexico, has long struggled with some of the highest rates of drug overdoses in the United States. Between 2010 and 2014, at least 78 people died from overdoses for every 100,000, compared with 24 instate and 14 across the nation. Heroin and other opioids—highly effective painkillers that include oxycodone, hydrocodone and fentanyl—have been consuming the small, high desert communities in the Southwest. The state has introduced harm-reduction efforts—like syringe exchange services, overdose training and the distribution of naloxone, an injection that can reverse the effects of an overdose—but New Mexicans are searching for ways to cut ties with opioid abuse altogether.

On March 17th, two days after Attorney General Jeff Sessions told law enforcement that marijuana is "only slightly less awful" than heroin, the New Mexico State Senate passed HB 527, a GOP-sponsored House bill aimed at modernizing the state's strategies to combat multigenerational opioid abuse. "We're hoping to make things easier on the patients enrolled in the program," says state House Minority Leader Rep. Nate Gentry. "Medical cannabis has great potential as an opioid replacement drug and we want to move people away from being prescribed highly addictive opiates."

Medical marijuana is legal in New Mexico. The state is among 28 others and the District of Columbia where people can legally use cannabis to treat a host of state-determined qualifying conditions like cancer, glaucoma, AIDS/HIV, PTSD and chronic pain. Jessica Gelay, coordinator at Drug Policy Alliance's New Mexico office, says the state has licensed 35 dispensaries for 33,000 patients since medical marijuana became legal in 2007. "The program is established," says Gelay. "People continue to use marijuana here and lessen the stigma." Now, Republican Governor Susana Martinez has until April 7th to decide whether her state becomes the first-ever to legalize the use of medical marijuana to treat opioid addiction.

Martinez, a former prosecutor turned two-term governor, has long been opposed to marijuana legislation. But the fate of the bill remains uncertain because of bipartisan support and a statewide effort to curtail the opioid crisis, while Martinez finishes her final year allowed in office. "I hope the governor recognizes medical marijuana as a tool to help save lives," says Gelay. "No other solution is working.

Overdose death rates are still going up. Naloxone works, but we need to find a more proactive solution. It's pretty clean cut, and she would be such a hero if she signed the bill." If Martinez vetoes the measure, advocates can direct final pleas to Lynn Gallagher, the Secretary of the New Mexico Department of Health, to sign a petition separate from the legislative process aimed to add opioid addiction to the state's existing 21 conditions of medical marijuana use.

The author of the petition is Anita Willard Briscoe, a psychiatric nurse practitioner with a private practice in Albuquerque. Briscoe grew up in Espanola, a largely Hispanic and Latino city in Rio Arriba, settled by the Spanish in 1598 and more recently taken over by devastating drugs. "Heroin took over this area starting in the 1940s with the Lowrider culture and then in the 1970s with Vietnam veterans," says Briscoe. "I saw it absolutely ravage my hometown. I had a lot of high school classmates who died." Briscoe became a registered nurse in 1977 and a psychiatric nurse in 1992. In 2005, she became a nurse practitioner because she saw medical professionals "misdiagnosing people, over-prescribing pills, and patients were suffering as a result." After the state legalized medical marijuana in 2007, a colleague showed her its ability to help patients with PTSD and she started referring patients to the state Medical Cannabis Program in 2009.

Last year, Briscoe teamed up with her "cannabis prescribing colleagues"—two other psychiatric nurse practitioners and one psychiatrist—to collect self-reported data from 400 patients, and they found that many were "successful at quitting opiates using cannabis." Between 2015 and 2016, Briscoe observed that 25 percent of her patients reported being able to "kick" opioids with marijuana. "They state it calms down their cravings, relaxes their … anxiety and is helping to keep them off opioids," Briscoe wrote in November to the Department of Health's medical advisory committee, which approved the petition and passed it onto Gallagher. "If they are in pain, cannabis is helping relieve their pain, often to the point that they don't need opiates anymore."

A 2014 study published in *JAMA Internal Medicine*, which examined data between 1999 and 2010, found that states with medical marijuana laws had 25 percent lower annual opioid overdose death rate compared to states without such laws. Briscoe's team is not looking to replace the use of methadone and Suboxone with marijuana completely, but rather to use cannabis as "an adjunct to treatment."

New Mexicans are not the only people searching for alternative ways to ward off opioid-related deaths. Last year, the Maine Department of Health and Human Services denied a petition drafted by a medical marijuana caregiver requesting to add opioid addiction to the state's list of qualifying conditions, citing the "lack of rigorous human studies" and the "lack of any safety or efficacy data." Advocates admit direct evidence is needed, but they contend that funding is limited since marijuana is federally listed as a Schedule 1 drug, on par with LSD and heroin. In the meantime, they turn to a Centers of Disease Control report to make their point on the safety of marijuana, comparing the 33,000 Americans who died from prescription painkillers and heroin overdoses in 2015 to the number of people who died that year from using cannabis: zero.

Earlier this year, the National Academy of Sciences, in a 395-page report, refuted the "gateway drug" theory that using marijuana can lead to opioid addiction and instead found evidence of cannabis having therapeutic and health benefits. Joe Schrank, a social worker who worked at various detox centers and clean houses, is now practicing the report's findings at High Sobriety treatment center in Los Angeles, where he offers clients medical and therapeutic sessions, and daily doses of marijuana to treat a variety of addictions.

Schrank, who has been sober for 20 years and doesn't smoke marijuana, says his most recent efforts started with the death of his friend Greg Giraldo, the comedian who died in 2010 after accidentally overdosing from prescription drugs in a hotel. As Schrank tells it, he suggested that Giraldo use pot instead of cocaine or painkillers weeks before his death—unpopular advice in the rehab world. "I think Greg's death was the moment I said, 'Fuck this, if people can get better smoking pot rather than using cocaine and Valium, I'm going to help,'" says Schrank. After Giraldo's death, Schrank began working with addiction psychiatrist Dr. Scott Bienenfeld and former Drug Policy Alliance law and policy expert Amanda Reiman, who lectures at her alma mater UC-Berkeley on marijuana issues. Schrank has found success since opening the treatment center in January 2017. "Having worked in rehab for many years, my first thought is, 'Why didn't we do this years ago?'" says Schrank. "One of the barriers in entry to treatment is detox. Many people are afraid of it. It's difficult to break this step. But when they're told, 'Hey, you can smoke pot.' It softens the blow."

According to Bienenfeld, heroin, morphine, Oxycontin, oxycodone and Vicodin activate the opioid system in the brain, causing a sense of extreme pleasure, sedation, numbing and euphoria—well above and beyond what normal pleasure feels like from food and sex. Side effects of opiates include analgesia and respiratory depression. "Opiates kill you in overdose by cutting off the brain's sense that it needs oxygen, thus the reflex to breathe is cut off and people die of respiratory failure," says Bienenfeld. "Combining opiates with other drugs like alcohol and sleeping pills makes it easier to overdose." Still, opioids seem to have a profound ability to reduce anxiety and depression in some people. These drugs rapidly induce a physical dependence and users become hooked quickly and need more of the drug to get high, and if they stop the drug abruptly, they experience withdrawal, which contrary to its uncomfortable feeling is usually not life-threatening. Marijuana stimulates cannabinoid receptors in the brain and causes mild psychedelic effects and a range of other feelings such as calmness, paranoia, anxiety and hunger—which can alleviate the symptoms of withdrawal.

But Schrank says others in the rehab business criticize High Sobriety as a "money-making scheme" for charging $42,500 a month. "Cardiologists make money and so do lawyers," says Schrank. "I'm a socialist and I fucking hate it. I don't like class systems. I don't like that suburban white kids go to rehab and black kids go to jail. We're trying to get insurance companies to accept what we do." It would be great to have "the blessing from a scholarly journal," says Schrank, who adds that he has clients telling him they haven't shot heroin in years because of cannabis. But as Bienenfeld notes in an email, "There are no actual data or studies that prove marijuana treats opioid addiction, but there are studies to suggest it may be a viable option."

Though marijuana is not fatal in overdose, Bienenfeld notes that people can have intense reactions. "There seems to be an association between cannabis use and psychotic mental illness in people who either have an underlying psychotic disorder, or a strong family history of schizophrenia, therefore it can be risky," says Bienenfeld. Yet he believes that's no reason to stop their treatments.

Schrank and Bienenfeld believe their position is controversial because established addiction treatment programs like Alcoholics Anonymous are against using any intoxicants in sobriety. "The 12-step advice to fight the opiate epidemic is to go to more 12-step meetings and programs," says Bienenfeld. But, he notes, the statistics show that approach isn't working. "People are dying by the tens of thousands per year due to the opiate epidemic. If this was Zika Virus, the National Guard would be called in and it would be panic in the streets. Nobody would oppose trying experimental approaches based on research trends and medical anecdotes."

> "I hope the governor recognizes medical marijuana as a tool to help save lives," says Gelay. "No other solution is working. Overdose death rates are still going up. Naloxone works, but we need to find a more proactive solution. It's pretty clean cut, and she would be such a hero if she signed the bill."

The established medical community is less sure. The position of the Philadelphia-based Treatment Research Institute, a nonprofit organization focused on substance abuse treatment reform and policy, is that until there is research to conclusively prove the connection, the experimental treatment is too risky. "Until there is research that deems safe and successful outcomes for the use of FDA-approved, marijuana-derivative medications to treat a substance abuse disorder it does not align with the currently available FDA-approved Medication Assisted Treatments for Opioid Use Disorders," writes TRI spokeswoman Debra Snyder in email. (Snyder declined to comment on the High Sobriety treatment protocols specifically.)

Thomas McLellan, founder of TRI and a former deputy drug czar under the Obama administration, believes that the pending New Mexico bill is misguided: "The United States has the safest, most effective medications in the world," writes McLellan. "We should not approve something as serious and important as medications by voice vote." But such beliefs are not helping existing opioid addicts clean up, according to Bienenfeld, who adds that marijuana is already preventing new addictions from forming.

Even though there is a lot of support, New Mexico's bill is going to face problems since Governor Martinez seems uncertain on the potential benefits of marijuana. Earlier this year, she supported legislators killing a measure seeking to join

Colorado, Nevada, California, Washington, Alaska, Maine, Massachusetts and the District of Columbia in the legalization of recreational marijuana. In New England, where lawmakers are reviewing cannabis regulation in the wake of legalizing recreational use in two of four states last year, legislators are also trying to figure out how to reduce high rates of opioid-related deaths. As thousands of people in Massachusetts have already been using cannabis as a replacement to prescription opioids, Integr8 Health, a Maine-based medical marijuana physicians practice, has reporting an uptick in patients using marijuana to manage chronic pain. A 2016 study published in *Health Affairs Journal* supports the trends, finding that Medicare patients received fewer prescriptions for pain and other conditions between 2010 and 2013, as states adopted medical marijuana laws. "We're finding strong evidence that approving medical cannabis can be effective in preventing people from using opiates," says W. David Bradford, a health economist at the University of Georgia, who published the findings with his daughter, a master's student Ashley C. Bradford. The research duo expects to publish a follow-up study in the summer that has "promising results" supporting marijuana's replacement of prescription drugs among Medicaid patients.

"The clinical community has passed the Reefer Madness stage," adds W. David Bradford. "Opioid addiction is killing over 600 people a week. That's more than two 747 planes crashing every week. There's no single solution to that problem, but we haven't really seen the beginning of the deaths that are rooted in this country and anything we can do to slow that down we just have to take advantage of."

What will become of New Mexico, a state that has the opportunity to set new standards in the prevention and treatment of opioid addiction? Briscoe, who has gained attention from drug policy groups seeking help with drafting petitions in Arizona, Oregon, New York, New Jersey and Maine believes the move will save lives in her hometown of Espanola and elsewhere in New Mexico. "This will help the state's children if the parents aren't hooked on prescription pills and heroin," says Briscoe. "It will help our economy, because they will get on their feet and get jobs. Crime will go down. This is a simple solution to our heroin problem. There is no reason not to sign off on this."

Print Citations

CMS: Killelea, Eric. "How Medical Marijuana Could Help End the Opioid Epidemic." In *The Reference Shelf: Prescription Drug Abuse*, edited by Betsy Maury, 168-172. Ipswich, MA: H.W. Wilson, 2017.

MLA: Killelea, Eric. "How Medical Marijuana Could Help End the Opioid Epidemic." *The Reference Shelf: Prescription Drug Abuse*. Ed. Betsy Maury. Ipswich: H.W. Wilson, 2017. 168-172. Print.

APA: Killelea, E. (2017). How medical marijuana could help end the opioid epidemic. In Betsy Maury (Ed.), *The reference shelf: Prescription drug abuse* (pp. 168-172). Ipswich, MA: H.W. Wilson. (Original work published 2017)

What's Really Causing the Prescription Drug Crisis?

By Johann Hari

Los Angeles Times, January 12, 2017

There are two quite different stories about why there is a prescription drug crisis in the United States, and why opioid-related deaths have quadrupled since 1999. At some level, you are probably aware of both. Earlier this year, I interviewed people in the New Hampshire towns worst affected by this crisis—from imprisoned addicts to grieving families. Even the people who were living through it would alternate between these stories, without seeing that, in fact, they clash, and imply the need for different solutions.

Thousands of lives depend on which of these tales is correct.

Here's the first story. It has been endorsed by some excellent journalists and broadcasters, from Sam Quinones to HBO's John Oliver. It goes, in crude summary, like this: Starting in the late 1990s, a handful of pharmaceutical corporations promoted prescription opiates as the solution to America's physical pain. Large numbers of people then started to take these drugs—and because Oxycontin and Percocet and the rest have such powerful chemical hooks, many found themselves addicted. Big Pharma is like the drug-pusher in a Reagan-era public service announcement, waiting at America's metaphorical playground gate with a drug you can't resist.

This narrative leads to a clear solution: Restrict prescription opiates and prevent addicts from taking them. Since the drug caused the problem, ending access to the drug humanely will end the problem.

Although this is a coherent story, put forward by serious and thoughtful people, there are some key facts that don't fit. Here's one: Doctors in many parts of the world—including Canada and some European countries—prescribe more powerful opiates than their peers in the United States. In England, if, say, you get hit by a car, you may be given diamorphine (the medical name for heroin) to manage your pain. Some people take it for long periods. If what we've been told is right, they should become addicted in huge numbers.

But this doesn't occur. The Canadian physician Gabor Maté argues in his book *In the Realm of Hungry Ghosts* that studies examining the medicinal use of narcotics for pain relief find no significant risk of addiction. I've talked with doctors in Canada and Europe about this very issue. They say it's vanishingly rare for a patient given diamorphine or a comparably strong painkiller in a hospital setting to develop an addiction.

Given that really powerful opiates do not appear to systematically cause addiction when administered by doctors, we should doubt that milder ones do. In fact, only 1 in 130 prescriptions for an opiate such as Oxycontin or Percocet in the United States results in addiction, according to the National Survey on Drug Use and Heath.

So what's really happening? The second, clashing story goes, again, crudely, like this: Opiate use is climbing because people feel more distressed and disconnected, and are turning to anesthetics to cope with their psychological pain.

Addiction rates are not spread evenly across the United States, as you would expect if chemical hooks were the primary cause. On the contrary, addiction is soaring in areas such as the Rust Belt, the South Bronx and the forgotten towns of New England, where people there say they are lonelier and more insecure than they have been in living memory.

This phenomenon isn't new. After a collapse in people's sense of status, meaning or community, an addiction epidemic often follows. In England in the 18th century, for example, huge numbers were driven out of the countryside into urban slums. Then came a mass outbreak of alcoholism—it was called the Gin Craze—and many drank themselves to death. At the time, commentators blamed the evil booze peddlers. If only they hadn't sold the gin in the first place, they said, none of this would have happened; gin hijacks people and destroys them.

Blunt restriction of prescription drugs will actually increase deaths, just as the war on illegal drugs has.

When we look back, we can see that gin couldn't have been the true source of the problem. Gin is legal today, and it is not causing social collapse. It was a symptom, a way of trying to survive in an unbearable environment. Gin caused problems, certainly. But if gin hadn't been invented, people would have turned to another intoxicant, or simply been suicidally depressed.

It might seem as if these two stories are compatible. Can't we argue that distress has made more people vulnerable to addiction—and that Big Pharma was responsible for stepping in with a dangerous drug?

But acting on the drug pusher story will only make things worse. The first victims would be the vast majority of users who do not develop an addiction, and who would be plunged into needless pain.

The consequences would be even more shattering for those rare few—1 in 130 cases—who do have an addiction problem. Doctors have explained to me that when they have to cut off patients abruptly, the distress the patient is trying to numb is still there, so they buy illegal drugs on the black market. Oxycontin is mostly not available from dealers, so many will end up using contaminated street heroin instead, which is far more dangerous.

Blunt restriction of prescription drugs will actually increase deaths, just as the war on illegal drugs has.

If, however, you act on the second story, you come to a different solution—one that has been tried with remarkable success.

In the 1980s and '90s, the Swiss had a serious opiate epidemic. They tried harsh crackdowns on sellers, and the problem got worse. They tried herding addicted people into a park and letting them use street drugs there, which produced scenes of chaos.

Then, starting in the early 2000s, Switzerland assigned addicted people to clinics where they were given opiates under supervision by a nurse. Crucially, they were also given extensive social support to turn their lives around, including therapy and help finding a job or housing. They gave you the drug, and at the same time, they dealt with the underlying pain that made you feel you needed the drug in the first place.

Patients can stay on that program for as long as they like, there's no pressure to cut back, but almost everyone chooses to stop after a few years. One of the psychiatrists in the clinic in Geneva told me why. It's because their lives get better, so they are in less psychological distress. Since the program began, there have been zero overdose deaths on legal opiates in Switzerland. None. That's why 70% of Swiss people voted to keep this approach.

We can't solve the opioid crisis if we continue to simplistically blame the drugs, or the people who supply them. That's a misunderstanding of what is really going wrong. Every day that we refuse to act on the second, more sophisticated story, another 78 Americans overdose on opiates.

Print Citations

CMS: Hari, Johann. "What's Really Causing the Prescription Drug Crisis?" In *The Reference Shelf: Prescription Drug Abuse*, edited by Betsy Maury, 173-175. Ipswich, MA: H.W. Wilson, 2017.

MLA: Hari, Johann. "What's Really Causing the Prescription Drug Crisis?" *The Reference Shelf: Prescription Drug Abuse*. Ed. Betsy Maury. Ipswich: H.W. Wilson, 2017. 173-175. Print.

APA: Hari, J. (2017). What's really causing the prescription drug crisis? In Betsy Maury (Ed.), *The reference shelf: Prescription drug abuse* (pp. 173-175). Ipswich, MA: H.W. Wilson. (Original work published 2017)

After Medical Marijuana Legalized, Medicare Prescriptions Drop For Many Drugs

By Shefali Luthra
NPR, July 6, 2016

Prescription drug prices continue to climb, putting the pinch on consumers. Some older Americans appear to be seeking an alternative to mainstream medicines that has become easier to get legally in many parts of the country.

Research published Wednesday found that states that legalized medical marijuana—which is sometimes recommended for symptoms like chronic pain, anxiety or depression—saw declines in the number of Medicare prescriptions for drugs used to treat those conditions and a dip in spending by Medicare Part D, which covers the cost on prescription medications.

Because the prescriptions for drugs like opioid painkillers and antidepressants—and associated Medicare spending on those drugs—fell in states where marijuana could feasibly be used as a replacement, the researchers said it appears likely legalization led to a drop in prescriptions. That point, they said, is strengthened because prescriptions didn't drop for medicines such as blood-thinners, for which marijuana isn't an alternative.

The study, which appears in *Health Affairs*, examined data from Medicare Part D from 2010 to 2013. It is the first study to examine whether legalization of marijuana changes doctors' clinical practice and whether it could curb public health costs.

The findings add context to the debate as more lawmakers express interest in medical marijuana. This year, Ohio and Pennsylvania passed laws allowing the drug for therapeutic purposes, making it legal in 25 states, plus Washington, D.C. The approach could also come to a vote in Florida and Missouri this November. A federal agency is considering reclassifying medical marijuana under national drug policy to make it more readily available.

Medical marijuana saved Medicare about $165 million in 2013, the researchers concluded. They estimated that, if medical marijuana were available nationwide, Medicare Part D spending would have declined in the same year by about $470 million. That's about half a percent of the program's total expenditures.

Shefali Luthra, *NPR*, The Henry J. Kaiser Family Foundation, July 6, 2016. Creative Commons License 4.0

That is an admittedly small proportion of the multibillion-dollar program. But the figure is nothing to sneeze at, said W. David Bradford, a professor of public policy at the University of Georgia and one of the study's authors.

We wouldn't say that saving money is the reason to adopt this. But it should be part of the discussion," he added. "We think it's pretty good indirect evidence that people are using this as medication."

The researchers found that in states with medical marijuana laws on the books, the number of prescriptions dropped for drugs to treat anxiety, depression, nausea, pain, psychosis, seizures, sleep disorders and spasticity. Those are all conditions for which marijuana is sometimes recommended.

The study's authors are separately investigating the effect medical marijuana could have on prescriptions covered by Medicaid, the federal-state health insurance program for low-income people. Though this research is still being finalized, they found a greater drop in prescription drug payments there, Bradford said.

> **In states that legalized medical uses of marijuana, painkiller prescriptions dropped—on average, the study found, by about 1,800 daily doses filled each year per doctor.**

If the trend bears out, it could have other public health ramifications. In states that legalized medical uses of marijuana, painkiller prescriptions dropped—on average, the study found, by about 1,800 daily doses filled each year per doctor. That tracks with other research on the subject.

Marijuana is unlike other drugs, such as opioids, overdoses of which can be fatal, said Deepak D'Souza, a professor of psychiatry at Yale School of Medicine, who has researched marijuana. "That doesn't happen with marijuana," he added. "But there are whole other side effects and safety issues we need to be aware of."

Study author Bradford agreed: "Just because it's not as dangerous as some other dangerous things, it doesn't mean you want to necessarily promote it. There's a lot of unanswered questions."

Because the federal government classifies marijuana as a Schedule I drug, doctors can't technically prescribe it. In states that have legalized medical marijuana, they can only write patients a note sending them to a dispensary.

Insurance plans don't cover it, so patients using marijuana pay out of pocket. Prices vary based on location, but a patient's recommended regimen can cost as much as $400 per month. The Drug Enforcement Agency is considering changing that classification—a decision is expected sometime this summer. If the DEA made marijuana a Schedule II drug, the move would put it in the company of drugs such as morphine and oxycodone, making it easier for doctors to prescribe and more likely that insurance would cover it.

To some, the idea that medical marijuana triggers cost savings is hollow. Instead, they say it is cost shifting. "Even if Medicare may be saving money, medical marijuana doesn't come for free," D'Souza said. "I have some trouble with the idea that this is a source of savings."

Still, Bradford maintains that if medical marijuana became a regular part of patient care nationally, the cost curve would bend because marijuana is cheaper than other drugs.

Lester Grinspoon, an associate professor emeritus of psychiatry at Harvard Medical School, who has written two books on the subject, echoed that possibility. Unlike with many drugs, he argued, "There's a limit to how high a price cannabis can be sold at as a medicine." He isn't associated with the study.

And, in the midst of the debate about its economics, medical marijuana still sometimes triggers questions within the practice of medicine.

"As physicians, we are used to prescribing a dose. We don't have good information about what is a good dose for the treatment for, say, pain," D'Souza said. "Do you say, 'Take two hits and call me in the morning?' I have no idea."

Print Citations

CMS: Luthra, Shefali. "After Medical Marijuana Legalized, Medicare Prescriptions Drop For Many Drugs." In The Reference Shelf: Prescription Drug Abuse, edited by Betsy Maury, 176-178. Ipswich, MA: H.W. Wilson, 2017.

MLA: Luthra, Shefali. "After Medical Marijuana Legalized, Medicare Prescriptions Drop For Many Drugs." *The Reference Shelf: Prescription Drug Abuse.* Ed. Betsy Maury. Ipswich: H.W. Wilson, 2017. 176-178. Print.

APA: Luthra, S. (2017). After Medical Marijuana Legalized, Medicare Prescriptions Drop For Many Drugs. In Betsy Maury (Ed.), *The reference shelf: Prescription drug abuse* (pp. 176-178). Ipswich, MA: H.W. Wilson. (Original work published 2017)

5

A Search for
Solutions—Policy

Credit: Photo by John Moore/Getty Images

Michael Botticelli, U.S. National Drug Control Policy Director, speaks at the 'Fed Up!' rally to end the opioid epidemic on September 18, 2016 in Washington, DC. Activists and family members of people who have died in the opioid and heroin epidemic gathered on the National Mall to march to the Capitol Building. Some 30,000 people die each year due to heroin and painkiller pill addicton. Speakers called for Congress to provide $1.1 billion for the Comprehensive Addiction and Recovery Act, which Congress passed in July without funding.

The Policy Approach: Restricting Supply and Legalizing Treatment

In the history of global efforts to fight drug abuse and addiction, the most common approach is to rely on law enforcement and government policies to reduce the supply of dangerous drugs. The logic behind this approach is simple; reducing the supply of drugs will create fewer potential addicts and so, over time, reduce the scope of the problem. In practice, limiting supply typically fosters black market production and sale industries and motivates the use of more dangerous drugs, thus deepening the problem. The failure of the alcohol prohibition in the 1930s and the equally ineffective "War on Drugs" from the 1980s to the present, provide examples of how policy solutions tend to be ineffective. In the United States, consumers and government agencies are also addressing the problem through civil and criminal litigation, attempting to force drug companies to pay for unethical corporate promotion and punishing executives and physicians who have knowingly and unethically contributed to the problem. Finally, legislators can attempt to alleviate the problem by changing laws so as to make it more likely that individuals suffering from abuse and addiction can safely seek help.

Fighting Big Pharma

Pharmaceutical companies have been one of the primary architects of the prescription drug crisis in that the companies have deemphasized or misrepresented the risks and potential benefits of certain dangerous drugs in an effort to boost sales and profits. Essentially, pharmaceutical company manipulation urged physicians to treat pain, depression, and anxiety as diseases, rather than symptoms of underlying issues, and so to use pharmaceutical agents as a treatment though a wealth of research suggests that such treatments do not address the underlying causes of a patient's discomfort and/or dysfunction.[1]

In May of 2017, the state of Ohio filed civil suit against five major drug companies, Purdue Pharma, Endo Health Solutions, Teva Pharmaceutical Industries, Johnson & Johnson, and Allergan for misrepresenting the risks and exaggerating the benefits of opioids for treating chronic pain.[2] The Ohio case was one of many similar suits filed since 2015 and, in 2016 alone, at least 25 states, cities, and counties filed civil cases against drugstores, manufacturers, and distributors of opioid medication. In some cases, such suits have resulted in drug companies adopting new policies and/or firing senior executives and so the civil litigation effort has resulted in measurable effects for the companies that played a role in the problem. State governments involved in suits also claimed that their goal was to force drug companies to pay for the costs accrued in the effort to combat and treat addiction.[3]

While civil litigation might help cities and states recoup public funds used to combat addiction, such efforts are unlikely to change drug company behavior over the longer term because executives and employees in the industry are judged (and their continued employment is based) on their capability to advance company earnings and not (in most cases) by the humanitarian impact of their work. The opioid controversy is only one of many drug industry controversies that demonstrates this facet of the industry. For instance, when the drug company Mylan purchased the right to distribute epinephrine shots to treat severe allergic reactions, the company, realizing that the need for such medications created an obligated consumer base, raised the price of epinephrine prescriptions from $94 to over $609. While an organization or advocacy group responsible for public health or welfare might argue that lifesaving medications should be made available at the lowest cost possible, this perspective is fundamentally at odds with the goal of maximizing corporate profit margins. Faced with public outrage, Mylan later agreed to offer a $300 generic alternative, which was advertised as a "humanitarian" decision on the part of the company despite the fact that the $300 version still represented a 200 percent price increase on a lifesaving medication that had not been improved in any way that might have justified the increased cost.[4]

Monitoring Patients and Doctors

Another way in which policy makers are attempting to address prescription drug abuse is by monitoring or regulating physician prescribing habits and monitoring patient behavior to better identify individuals at risk for addiction or abuse. Much of this effort essentially seeks to reverse changes in physician behavior resulting from the 1990–2000 push towards overprescription. Part of this effort also involves education, producing reliable, updated data for doctors and patients on the realistic benefits and potential problems with using potentially dangerous medications.

In 2016, the Centers for Disease Control and Prevention (CDC) updated their official guidelines on the use and potential hazards of opioid pain relievers. The new CDC guidelines, which have been distributed to physicians, hospitals, and other medical professionals across the country, are intended to guide physicians' decisions regarding opioid analgesics. Among other changes, the CDC updated information on the danger of opioid abuse and addiction and provided guidelines to help physicians recognize patient behavior that might indicate abuse.[5] A similar effort, aimed at a different subset of the population, is underway through the National Institute on Drug Abuse (NIDA), which has begun funding educational programs delivered through schools and community groups explaining the dangers of opioid use and addiction.

One of the most widely debated proposed measures to combat prescription addiction involves creating or forcing physicians to utilize databases used to monitor prescriptions given to patients. The so-called "prescription drug monitoring programs," allow a physician to see whether a patient requesting a certain medication had received a prescription for the same or a similar medication in the past. Such an effort is meant to combat "doctor shopping," in which patients with drug addiction problems visit a number of different primary care physicians until they find one willing to prescribe their desired medication. Proponents hope that more widespread use of such databases will help physicians discover signs of addiction at earlier stages. New York became the first state to require physicians to use drug monitoring databases in 2012 and similar legislation has been proposed in a number of other states. However, some physicians object to the practice, arguing that policing patient behavior is not a doctor's role and that the database system is inefficient and time-consuming and reduces time available for patient interaction.[6]

Similarly, some argue that drug abuse screenings should become a common practice for physicians. The screening system SBIRT (Screening, brief intervention, and referral for treatment), which is covered by Medicaid, Medicare, and many other insurance programs, has been proven effective in detecting drug abuse in patients and modifications on the system have been developed to detect abuse of different types of drugs and in different patient populations (teens, young adults, elderly, etc.). While SBIRT screenings are widely known and available, the use of such systems is not standard for general practitioners.[7]

In 2016, the state of Maine took a more aggressive step, creating the toughest opioid prescription law in the nation, which limits physicians to prescribing 100 milligrams per day, with exceptions for cancer treatment, hospice care, and a few other conditions. The Maine law stirred some controversy and met with resistance from chronic pain patients and physicians specializing in pain treatment, who argued that many individuals with incurable conditions would not be able to reduce consumption to meet the maximum dose limit.[8] Though controversial, the Maine law has been widely touted as a success and it is therefore likely that other states will consider similar legislation in coming years.

Limiting Damage

Policy solutions to the prescription drug problem are not only aimed at limiting the supply of dangerous drugs in the community but also on altering or amending laws to make it more likely or possible for those suffering from drug abuse and/or addiction to seek help. Individuals who are illegal drug users, and their friends/family, are in a difficult position, caught between the need for help and the fear of criminal penalties for engaging in illegal activities.

As of 2017, 40 states and the District of Columbia have enacted "Good Samaritan" laws that grant immunity from prosecution for a person who is overdosing on a drug, or suspects someone else of overdosing, if he or she calls police or emergency services. Idaho, Wyoming, Texas, Kansas, Missouri, Indiana, Arizona, South Carolina, and Maine, have no immunity laws and so individuals who contact emergency services in the case of a suspected overdose might be subject to criminal charges. While legislators in some of the above states have proposed Good Samaritan legislation, it remains to be seen whether state legislatures will approve such measures in the future.

Another program that skirts the line of legality are the "needle exchange" programs that allow intravenous drug users to exchange used needles for clean ones without any legal penalty. Such programs have been proven effective in preventing the spread of disease through sharing needles and public health professionals operating needle exchange programs have used such programs to interact with users and to attempt to steer them towards treatment options. However, opposition to such programs come from those who prefer an absolutist criminal justice approach to drug use and only a small number of states have thus legalized needle exchange programs.[9]

A related issue involves the legality of "emergency treatment" drugs like Naloxone, which is available as an inhalant and in several other forms, and can reverse respiratory suppression, which is the most common cause of overdose-related death. In 2001, the state of New Mexico passed a law that provided immunity to doctors who gave out or prescribed Naloxone for patients suspected of being at risk for drug abuse in an attempt to expand the availability of the drug in needy populations. Critics argue that giving out Naloxone encourages abuse and that physicians suspecting drug addiction or abuse should instead notify criminal authorities. However, laws meant to expand Naloxone availability have proven successful. In 2014, it was reported that more than 150,000 nonmedical professionals had received information or Naloxone rescue kits resulting in more than 26,000 cases in which Naloxone was used to reverse an overdose.[10]

There is also a controversy surrounding the drug buprenorphine, available in the prescription form, Suboxone, which reduces the intensity of opioid cravings and has been demonstrated to prevent relapses following rehabilitation. Suboxone does not produce an opioid "high" if taken in pill form, but some reports indicate that when snorted, injected, or combined with benzodiazepines (a potentially fatal combination in itself), it is possible for addicts to use Suboxone as an intoxicant.[11]

Despite risks, the use of tapering medication, also known as "medically assisted treatment," is the standard for opioid addiction around the world and, despite failings, treatment-based programs are far more effective in practice than abstinence-only programs, which are favored in the United States. Studies show that as many as 90 percent of patients treated in abstinence-only programs will relapse, compared to around 31 percent of those who have access to tapering medications to reduce and control cravings. Despite these findings, a majority of Americans prefer abstinence-only programs and many see an inherent illogic to using drugs to treat drug addiction, despite indications that the effort is simply more successful. However, despite low availability and support, there are many physicians and treatment specialists that are lobbying for expanded availability of tapering medications and who have been promoting global research suggesting that such medications, despite risks, could be an important and effective tool in the current addiction epidemic.[12]

Micah L. Issitt

Works Used

Almendrala, Anna. "Needle Exchanges Are Vital, but There's Major Stigma around Them: Here's Why." *Huffpost*. Huffington Post. Mar 27 2015. Web. 25 Aug 2017.

"CDC Guidelines for Prescribing Opioids for Chronic Pain." *CDC*. Centers for Disease Control and Prevention. Mar 18 2016. Web. 25 Aug 2017.

"Drug Overdose Immunity and Good Samaritan Laws." *NCSL*. National Conference of State Legislatures. Jun 5 2017. Web. 25 Aug 2017

Dwyer, Colin. "Ohio Sues 5 Major Drug Companies for 'Fueling Opioid Epidemic.'" *NPR*. National Public Radio. May 31 2017. Web. 24 Aug 2017.

Higham, Scott and Lenny Bernstein. "Drugmakers and Distributors Face Barrage of Lawsuits over Opioid Epidemic." *The Washington Post*. Nash Holdings. Jul 4 2016. Web. 24 Aug 2017.

MacGillis, Alec. "The Wonder Drug." *Slate*. Slate Inc. Feb 9 2015. Web. 25 Aug 2017.

Macy, Beth. "Addicted to a Treatment for Addiction." *The New York Times*. New York Times Co. May 28 2016. Web. 27 Aug 2017.

McGraw, Daniel J. "How Big Pharma Gave America Its Heroin Problem." *PSMag*. Pacific Standard. Nov 30 2015. Web. 23 Aug 2017.

Rapaport, Lisa. "Another Look at the Surge in EpiPen Costs." *Reuters*. Reuters News Agency. Mar 27 2017. Web. 24 Aug 2017.

Rettner, Rachael. "Prescription Drug Problem Sparks Debate over Solutions." *LiveScience*. Purch. Jun 21 2012. Web. 25 Aug 2017.

"Screening, Brief Intervention, and Referral to Treatment (SBIRT)." *SAMHSA*. Substance Abuse and Mental Health Services Administration. 2016. Web. 25 Aug 2017.

Wight, Patty. "Intent on Reversing Its Opioid Epidemic, a State Limits Prescriptions." *NPR*. National Public Radio. Aug 23 2017. Web. 25 Aug 2017.

Notes

1. McGraw, "How Big Pharma Gave America Its Heroin Problem."
2. Dwyer, "Ohio Sues 5 Major Drug Companies for 'Fueling Opioid Epidemic.'"
3. Higham and Bernstein, "Drugmakers and Distributors Face Barrage of Lawsuits over Opioid Epidemic."
4. Rapaport, "Another Look at the Surge in EpiPen Costs."
5. "CDC Guidelines for Prescribing Opioids for Chronic Pain," *CDC*.
6. Rettner, "Prescription Drug Problem Sparks Debate over Solutions."
7. "Screening, Brief Intervention, and Referral to Treatment (SBIRT), *SAMHSA*
8. Wight, "Intent on Reversing Its Opioid Epidemic, a State Limits Prescriptions."
9. Almendrala, "Needle Exchanges Are Vital, But There's Major Stigma Around Them. Here's Why."
10. "Drug Overdose Immunity and Good Samaritan Laws," *NCSL*.
11. Macy, "Addicted to a Treatment for Addiction."
12. MacGillis, "The Wonder Drug."

Researchers Use Black-Market Drug Website to Gauge Public Health

By Felice J. Freyer

The Boston Globe, April 18, 2015

On Friday, someone in New Bedford paid a dealer $2 for a 5-milligram hydrocodone pill, a price deemed "cheap" in the busy black market for prescription opioids. That same day in Winchendon, a person spent $5 on a 30-milligram Adderall, rated "not bad" for the popular stimulant.

The sales are illegal. But that didn't stop buyers and sellers from reporting the transactions on StreetRx.com, a five-year-old website that offers a glimpse into the shadowy world of illicit drug sales at a time when an epidemic of opioid abuse rampages through the Northeast.

Anyone can visit StreetRx to learn about drug prices, and anyone can post information and rate the deals. Hundreds of people around the country contribute reports every day—voluntarily and anonymously.

Researchers are using StreetRx data to gauge the effectiveness of public policy, track changes in the market, and learn more about the people who obtain drugs this way, in the hope of helping them and deterring others. Law enforcement officials check the prices to inform officers buying undercover.

Although it peers into the black market, StreetRx is far removed from the street: It bears a respectable dot-com address and an academic pedigree.

And to the unending surprise of its creators, the website is booming.

"Of all the crowd-sourcing projects I've been involved with, this is the most successful," said John S. Brownstein of Boston Children's Hospital, a cofounder of the site. "It's not been promoted. It's a completely grass-roots data entry."

StreetRx is one of several projects by Epidemico, an informatics company established in 2007 by disease-trackers and data scientists from Children's, Harvard Medical School, and the Massachusetts Institute of Technology.

The website, which includes links to resources such as treatment programs and drug-disposal sites, receives 2,500 unique visitors each day and logs 4,000 to 5,000 drug-price reports per month.

"It's an innovative approach to try to harness the information age to advance public health," said Dr. Caleb Alexander, codirector of the Johns Hopkins Center for Drug Safety and Effectiveness, who is not involved with StreetRx but has used its data in his research.

For example, when the maker of OxyContin changed the formulation so it would be harder to crush for snorting or injection, StreetRx showed that the price of the new OxyContin dropped.

> **The website, which includes links to resources such as treatment programs and drug-disposal sites, receives 2,500 unique visitors each day and logs 4,000 to 5,000 drug-price reports per month.**

"It really shows the value of these abuse-deterrent formulations. People definitely don't like them as well," said Dr. Richard C. Dart, director of the Rocky Mountain Poison and Drug Center in Denver, who helped found StreetRx. On Friday, StreetRx presented data to pharmaceutical companies and federal regulators that compared three types of drug formulations intended to deter abuse, showing which is most effective.

The website is primarily focused on prescription drugs because they come in precise dosages whose prices can be easily compared. Heroin sales are sometimes reported on StreetRx, but quantities and potency can be inexact, making price comparisons difficult.

To use StreetRx, people fill out an online form with the name of the drug, the formulation (such as pill or tablet), price per unit, dose, date, and location of the sale, and source of the price information—whether personal experience or word of mouth.

Anyone can click on others' purchases to rate the price as "cheap," "not bad," "reasonable," "pricey," or "overpriced." People who use the site do not identify themselves, and StreetRx says it has no way of tracing them.

The website also cannot verify the accuracy of any individual post. But an Epidemico study found that, overall, the prices jibe with what is seen in law enforcement surveys and on websites that sell illegal drugs.

StreetRx started with conversations between Dart and the three cofounders of Epidemico, Nabarun Dasgupta, Clark Freifeld, and Brownstein. Dart heads the RADARS System (Researched Abuse, Diversion, and Addiction-related Surveillance), which tracks drug abuse, misuse, and diversion for pharmaceutical companies.

Dart wanted data that were up-to-date and included more drugs, to supplement what RADARS was learning from surveys of law enforcement officials. He was familiar with Epidemico's work at the forefront of a growing trend to mine online sources for public health purposes.

Epidemico launched StreetRx in 2010. It is part of the RADARS System, which is funded by pharmaceutical companies. The companies pay a yearly subscription fee to track illegal use of their drugs, as a way to meet federal regulations requiring drug makers to ensure that their products' benefits outweigh the risks. Subscribers are barred by contract from access to the raw data or any role in the website's design or related research.

StreetRx got off to a slow start. It took more than a year for the site to attract significant numbers. Now, it is slowly expanding into seven other countries.

Why do people post drug prices on StreetRx? "Who knows?" said the site's project manager, Chris Menone. The people reporting on StreetRx are probably a small subset of those buying drugs on the black market, he said, and there's no way to know how representative they are. "We can't know anything about them. We have no demographic information. That's a challenge; it's also a necessity," he said.

Recently, StreetRx started posing questions to users, an experiment to study the link between health behavior and prices, said Dasgupta, the Epidemico cofounder. Today, at the bottom of the form used to enter price information, they are asked, "When did you last see a doctor?"

Those who have seen a clinician recently are more likely to be people who sought treatment for pain, who may have fallen into substance misuse after being prescribed opioid painkillers, health experts believe.

StreetRx's growing trove of data has caught the attention of public health researchers hungry for information about an otherwise inaccessible population.

Alexander, of Johns Hopkins, traced the connection between drugs sold at pharmacies and those sold on the street.

In an as-yet unpublished study, Alexander and colleagues looked at the prices of 10 drugs that can lead to addiction or abuse. They compared the out-of-pocket costs for the drugs bought in pharmacies with their street prices as listed on StreetRx.

In areas where costs were low in the pharmacies, costs were lower on the street as well. Pharmacy prices also tended to be lower in areas where pharmacies were selling higher volumes of the 10 drugs.

"Our findings add to growing evidence that a key driver of the epidemic [of opioid abuse] is the incredible volume of opioids dispensed in the United States," Alexander said.

Other researchers see great potential in StreetRx to inform public policy. Dara Lee Luca, a visiting assistant professor at Harvard's John F. Kennedy School of Government, plans to study how street prices of opioids and heroin changed after Florida abruptly shut down pain clinics that were overprescribing.

And Margie Skeer, assistant professor of public health and community medicine at Tufts University School of Medicine, is seeking funding to open discussion forums on StreetRx. Skeer would pose questions to drug users, such as how they first got involved with drugs—information that could inform prevention efforts.

Print Citations

CMS: Freyer, Felice J. "Researchers Use Black-Market Drug Website to Gauge Public Health." In *The Reference Shelf: Prescription Drug Abuse*, edited by Betsy Maury, 187-190. Ipswich, MA: H.W. Wilson, 2017.

MLA: Freyer, Felice J. "Researchers Use Black-Market Drug Website to Gauge Public Health." *The Reference Shelf: Prescription Drug Abuse*. Ed. Betsy Maury. Ipswich: H.W. Wilson, 2017. 187-190. Print.

APA: Freyer, F. J. (2017). Researchers use black-market drug website to gauge public health. In Betsy Maury (Ed.), *The reference shelf: Prescription drug abuse* (pp. 187-190). Ipswich, MA: H.W. Wilson. (Original work published 2015)

Are Pharmaceutical Companies to Blame for the Opioid Epidemic?

By Alana Semuels
The Atlantic, June 2, 2017

Opioid abuse is rampant in states like Ohio, where paramedics are increasingly spending time responding to overdoses and where coroners' offices are running out of room to store bodies. In 2012, there were 793 million doses of opioids prescribed in the state, enough to supply every man, woman, and child, with 68 pills each. Roughly 20 percent of the state's population was prescribed an opioid in 2016. And Ohio leads the nation in overdose deaths.

Who is responsible for this? Some attorneys general and advocates are now asking in court whether the pharmaceutical companies who marketed the drugs and downplayed their addictive nature can be held legally responsible for—and made to pay for the consequences of—the crisis. This may not be such an outlandish idea; in fact, there's a good precedent. In 1998, the tobacco industry, 46 states, and six other jurisdictions entered into the largest civil-litigation settlement agreement in U.S. history. State attorneys general had sued tobacco companies, arguing that the companies should take up the burden of paying for the costs of treating smoking-related diseases. In the settlement, which left the tobacco industry immune from future state and federal suits, the companies agreed to make annual payments to the states, in perpetuity, to fund public-health programs and anti-smoking campaigns.

Now, as a new public-health crisis ravages states, Ohio's Attorney General Mike DeWine filed a lawsuit Wednesday against a handful of pharmaceutical companies, including Purdue Pharma, Teva Pharmaceuticals, and Johnson & Johnson. The lawsuit accuses the companies of spending millions on marketing campaigns that "trivialize the risks of opioids while overstating the benefits of using them for chronic pain." The companies, the lawsuit alleges, lobbied doctors to influence their opinions about the safety of opioids, "borrowing a page from Big Tobacco."

The lawsuit follows similar recent lawsuits in Illinois, Mississippi, four counties in New York, and Santa Clara and Orange Counties in California. Last month, the Cherokee Nation filed a lawsuit against distributors and pharmacies in tribal court over the opioid epidemic. In January, the city of Everett, Washington, filed a lawsuit against Purdue Pharma, the makers of OxyContin, alleging that the company knew the drug was being funneled into the black market but did nothing to stop it.

"What you're getting now is a lot more legal minds across the country focusing on this, and figuring out how to pay these huge bills," Sam Quinones, the author of *Dreamland: The True Tale of America's Opiate Epidemic*, told me. "Everyone is groping for a legal theory that will work in court."

There is some significant evidence that pharmaceutical companies may have engaged in some activities that led to the opioid crisis. A *Los Angeles Times* investigation into Purdue Pharma, for instance, found that the drug maker, which marketed OxyContin as relieving pain for 12 hours, knew that the drug wore off before that time period. Since the drug didn't last as long as promised, some patients suffered withdrawal, which led them to become addicted. (Purdue responded that OxyContin had been approved by the FDA as a 12-hour drug, and said it was working to "address our nation's opioid epidemic.")

> **Yet using the "public nuisance" tactic against pharmaceutical companies has a similar flaw to the lawsuits brought by individuals.**

But the situation differs in significant ways from the tobacco example, and proving the pharmaceutical companies are responsible will be difficult. Individual plaintiffs who have sued pharmaceutical companies over how opioids have been marketed have rarely been successful, according to Richard Ausness, a professor at the University of Kentucky College of Law. Courts have made clear that they believe that individual victims are largely responsible for their addiction. People who die of overdoses are often using the pills not as they were prescribed, but are obtaining the pills on the black market. They are disregarding doctors' prescriptions and taking more than is safe. "It is difficult to persuade courts that FDA-approved prescription drugs are defective and that their warnings are inadequate," Ausness told me.

With the tobacco-industry lawsuits, customers were using the product as instructed and got sick. With opioids it's a different story: Customers are not using the pills as directed, and so it is harder to blame the pharmaceutical companies for the effects of that misuse, according to Lars Noah, a professor of law at the University of Florida. In addition, doctors, not consumers, were the ones targeted by the aggressive marketing campaigns undertaken by pharmaceutical companies, so it can be difficult to link consumer deaths with aggressive marketing.

State entities have been only a little more successful than individuals at suing pharmaceutical companies, according to Ausness. The most successful government lawsuits have taken a page from tobacco litigation, arguing that companies created financial costs for the state because of the widespread addiction. That tactic was what led to the 1998 settlement with the tobacco industry. The Ohio lawsuit, for instance, alleges that pharmaceutical companies created a "public nuisance" because they misrepresented their opioid drugs, downplaying their addictive nature. It seeks restitution for Ohio consumers and compensation for the state's Department of Medicaid, which paid for "excessive" opioid prescriptions. States are more sympathetic defendants than individual patients because they cannot be blamed for misusing pills, but still suffer financial consequences.

Yet using the "public nuisance" tactic against pharmaceutical companies has a similar flaw to the lawsuits brought by individuals. Pharmaceutical companies may be able to argue that they are not to blame because individuals misused the drug, and eventually used more than any doctor prescribed. The mere prescribing of opioids is not usually the problem, after all. Pharmaceutical companies are often able, in court, to shift the blame to doctors who prescribed the pills, absolving themselves of responsibility. "The overall effectiveness of civil litigation in this area is highly questionable," Ausness wrote, in a 2014 article about the role of litigation in fighting drug abuse. When the West Virginia attorney general sued Purdue Pharma in 2001 for creating a "public nuisance" because of its marketing and distribution of OxyContin, for example, the case settled for $10 million in 2004, a relatively small sum, which indicates that the state thought it was not likely to prevail in a trial, Ausness says.

It may be even more difficult to legally hold pharmaceutical companies accountable in 2017, according to Noah. Purdue, which was allegedly the most aggressive marketer of opioids, admitted wrongdoing and entered into a multi-million-dollar settlement with the federal government in 2007. (Three executives also pled guilty to criminal charges.) In the years since it has taken steps to reduce abuse, according to Noah of the University of Florida. Purdue changed its policies and made clearer warnings about how addictive the pills were, and also came out with a less-easily-abused version of Oxycontin, Noah said. That could make it difficult to allege that the company is still behaving in a way that creates a nuisance. "These strike me as an even longer shot than the handgun lawsuits," he said, referring to lawsuits filed against gun manufacturers after mass shootings such as Sandy Hook.

The companies say they work hard to deter abuse. They emphasize that some Americans who suffer from chronic pain depend on opioids to manage that pain.

"We share the attorney general's concerns about the opioid crisis and we are committed to working collaboratively to find solutions," Purdue Pharma said in a statement provided to the *Atlantic*. "We are an industry leader in abuse-deterrent technology."

Another company, Janssen Pharmaceuticals, said in response to the lawsuit that the company has acted "appropriately, responsibly, and in the best interests of patients" regarding opioid pain medications.

There are a lot of different parties that can be blamed for the opioid epidemic, Noah argues. Doctors were too loose with their prescribing practices. The scientific community published and depended on letters and papers that downplayed the risk of addiction from opioids. (Many doctors depended on a five-sentence letter from 1980 that said that the majority of a sample of hospital patients who had been prescribed opioids did not get addicted.) Pharmacies and distributors allegedly failed to report suspicious orders for controlled substances from patients or doctors. (One distributor, McKesson, entered into a $150 million settlement with the Justice Department in January over this issue.) The FDA approved new, more powerful opioids but did not demand further restrictions on how they were distributed. The DEA did not impose quotas on how many opioids were manufactured. "There are any number of actors who could have tried harder," Noah said.

What's more, the settlements from the tobacco industry were not particularly effective in preventing smoking. Very little of the money allocated actually went to tobacco prevention—states often used the money for unrelated expenditures. There's reason to believe that the windfall, if there is any, from the recent spate of opioid lawsuits may also not be helpful in stopping abuse. Such lawsuits take a long time to wind their way through the courts, and there may be no way to guarantee that states are using the money to address opioid addiction. Skeptics also say that the Ohio lawsuit is mostly political—DeWine is running for governor, and his Democratic opponents have made opioid abuse a central issue to their campaigns.

A better strategy than casting around for blame, then, may be to focus state efforts on how to curb the opioid epidemic before it gets any worse. They could adopt programs that monitor doctor's prescriptions of opioids, or try to prevent doctor-shopping, or collect unused prescription drugs. In the end, looking for someone to blame for the epidemic might be less useful than figuring out how to stop it.

Print Citations

CMS: Semuels, Alana. "Are Pharmaceutical Companies to Blame for the Opioid Epidemic?" In *The Reference Shelf: Prescription Drug Abuse*, edited by Betsy Maury, 191-194. Ipswich, MA: H.W. Wilson, 2017.

MLA: Semuels, Alana. "Are Pharmaceutical Companies to Blame for the Opioid Epidemic?" *The Reference Shelf: Prescription Drug Abuse*. Ed. Betsy Maury. Ipswich: H.W. Wilson, 2017. 191-194. Print.

APA: Semuels, A. (2017). Are pharmaceutical companies to blame for the opioid epidemic? In Betsy Maury (Ed.), *The reference shelf: Prescription drug abuse* (pp. 191-194). Ipswich, MA: H.W. Wilson. (Original work published 2017)

Ohio Sues Five Drugmakers, Saying They Fueled Opioid Crisis

By Jeanne Whalen
The Wall Street Journal, May 31, 2017

In one of the highest-profile cases to date against makers of prescription painkillers, Ohio filed suit against five drug companies, alleging they fueled the opioid addiction crisis by misrepresenting the addictive risks of their painkillers.

The complaint, filed in state court in Ross County on Wednesday, targets parent companies and various subsidiaries, including Purdue Pharma L.P.; Johnson & Johnson; Teva Pharmaceutical Industries Ltd.; Allergan PLC; and Endo International PLC's Endo Health Solutions unit.

Johnson & Johnson denied the allegations. The other companies either declined to comment or said officials were reviewing the allegations.

Ohio Attorney General Mike DeWine, a Republican who filed the lawsuit on behalf of the state, said at a news conference that the companies were dishonest with doctors and the public about their painkillers' risks.

"The evidence is going to show they knew what they were saying was not true and they did it to increase sales," he said.

In an interview, Mr. DeWine said opioid addiction has taken an extraordinary human and financial toll on Ohio, which has one of the highest opioid overdose death rates of any state. He said the addiction crisis has placed great financial burdens on the state, including the Medicaid program, which provides substance-abuse treatment, and foster-care programs, which are grappling with a big rise in children taken out of parental care because of addiction.

"You have so many people today who can't pass a drug test, who can't work in a factory, who can't be employed to drive a car or work around machinery or be store manager at McDonald's because they can't pass a drug test," Mr. DeWine said.

States and the federal government have previously pursued legal action against Purdue, alleging improper marketing of the painkiller OxyContin, and won settlements from the company. And some cities and counties have pursued lawsuits against broader groups of opioid painkiller makers.

Mr. DeWine said Ohio's lawsuit is among the most comprehensive taken by any state against a broad group of opioid painkiller makers. He said the only other similar lawsuit was filed by Mississippi in state court in December 2015, alleging similar wrongdoing against the same five companies. That suit is pending.

In an email, Mr. Moore said he sees "parallels" between the tobacco and opioid litigation, including the "misleading marketing."

One lawyer in private practice in Mississippi, John Davidson, is listed as outside counsel for the plaintiffs in both the Ohio and Mississippi cases.

Another lawyer listed as outside counsel for the state on the Ohio case, Mike Moore of Flowood, Miss., was Mississippi's attorney general in 1994 when the state filed the first state lawsuit against the tobacco industry, alleging companies misrepresented the health risks of their products. His suit touched off a flurry of litigation by states against the industry that ultimately concluded with a $206 billion settlement.

In an email, Mr. Moore said he sees "parallels" between the tobacco and opioid litigation, including the "misleading marketing."

In a statement about the Ohio case, Johnson & Johnson, parent of Janssen Pharmaceuticals, which sells Duragesic, said: "We firmly believe the allegations in this lawsuit are both legally and factually unfounded."

"Janssen has acted appropriately, responsibly and in the best interests of patients regarding our opioid pain medications, which are FDA-approved and carry FDA-mandated warnings about the known risks of the medications on every product label," said the company, referring to the U.S. Food and Drug Administration.

Teva said it is reviewing the complaint and didn't have a comment. Teva and its Cephalon Inc. unit sell the painkillers Actiq and Fentora.

Purdue said: "We share the attorney general's concerns about the opioid crisis and we are committed to working collaboratively to find solutions."

Allergan and Endo declined to comment. Allergan sells Kadian and Norco. Endo makes the painkiller Opana.

One of the biggest legal hits to a painkiller company came in 2007, when Purdue Frederick Co., an affiliate of Purdue Pharma, and three of its executives pleaded guilty in federal court to criminal charges of misleading the public about the addictive qualities of OxyContin. The company and executives agreed to pay the federal government and a group of states $634.5 million in fines.

That settlement grew out of a multistate investigation and a federal probe. In 2015, Kentucky reached a separate $24 million settlement with Purdue over its OxyContin marketing.

Elizabeth Burch, a law professor at the University of Georgia, said the Ohio suit is unsurprising, given that Purdue has paid settlements in the past.

"A lot of states are looking for money to subsidize substance-abuse programs. As they do that and as previous states reach settlements, there is blood in the water at this point," she said.

Ohio has been among the states hardest hit by opioid addiction, which has played a part in driving U.S. overdose deaths to all-time highs. Many people became addicted by taking powerful opioid painkillers and often progressed to heroin if they couldn't get access to pills. Public-health officials have long blamed aggressive company marketing and lax prescribing for sparking the crisis.

The Ohio case comes at a time when politicians are increasingly citing the addiction epidemic as a major policy priority.

President Donald Trump has pledged to address the opioid crisis and formed a task force earlier this year to study addiction, with New Jersey Gov. Chris Christie, a fellow Republican, as chairman. But critics have said the president's proposed budget for the fiscal year beginning Oct. 1 would slash funding for the Office of National Drug Control Policy and that the GOP's legislation to overhaul the Affordable Care Act envisions cuts to Medicaid, which pays for significant amounts of addiction treatment.

The Ohio complaint alleges the drug companies violated the Ohio Consumer Sales Practices Act through marketing programs that "falsely deny or trivialize the risks of opioids while overstating the benefits of using them for chronic pain." The state says the false marketing included medical journal advertising and sales representative statements.

It also alleges the companies engaged in misleading marketing by funding outside groups that have advocated for wider treatment of pain. These groups were "seemingly unbiased and independent patient and professional organizations" but disseminated information that played down the risks of opioids, the complaint alleges.

Ohio is seeking an injunction to stop the companies from their "misrepresentations" of the drugs' risks, and civil penalties to compensate the state for the costs tied to the addiction crisis.

Because the lawsuit was filed in state court, other states cannot join the suit as plaintiffs.

Some cities and counties have also sued opioid painkiller makers, alleging misleading marketing that fueled addiction.

West Virginia has sued drug distributors, alleging they improperly flooded the state with addictive painkillers. Earlier this year the distributors Cardinal Health Inc. and AmerisourceBergen agreed to pay West Virginia $36 million to settle the state's allegations.

Cardinal Health said it denied wrongdoing. In a statement, AmerisourceBergen said: "With this matter settled, we look forward to focusing our full attention on continuing to work diligently with regulatory agencies and our partners throughout the supply chain to combat diversion and support appropriate access to medications."

Print Citations

CMS: Whalen, Jeanne. "Ohio Sues Five Drugmakers, Saying They Fueled Opioid Crisis." In *The Reference Shelf: Prescription Drug Abuse,* edited by Betsy Maury, 195-198. Ipswich, MA: H.W. Wilson, 2017.

MLA: Whalen, Jeanne. "Ohio Sues Five Drugmakers, Saying They Fueled Opioid Crisis." *The Reference Shelf: Prescription Drug Abuse*. Ed. Betsy Maury. Ipswich: H.W. Wilson, 2017. 195-198. Print.

APA: Whalen, J. (2017). Ohio sues five drugmakers, saying they fueled opioid crisis. In Betsy Maury (Ed.), *The reference shelf: Prescription drug abuse* (pp. 195-198). Ipswich, MA: H.W. Wilson. (Original work published 2017)

Congress Probes West Virginia Opioid Shipments

By Eric Eyre

West Virginia Gazette–Mail, May 9, 2017

A congressional committee has started an investigation into prescription painkiller shipments to West Virginia.

The probe targets the nation's three largest wholesale drug distributors—McKesson, Cardinal Health and AmerisourceBergen.

The U.S. House Energy and Commerce Committee also is looking into whether the U.S. Drug Enforcement Administration shirked its responsibility to curtail the flow of highly addictive pain pills into West Virginia.

In letters sent Monday, the committee directed the companies and the DEA to turn over records that detail pain pill shipments. The letters cite reports by the *Charleston Gazette-Mail*, the *Washington Post*, CNN and MSNBC about prescription opioid sales and lax enforcement.

"These reports shine a light on a problem that many people have wondered about privately and publicly—how are opioids flooding into some of our communities and pharmacies?" said House Energy and Commerce Committee Chairman Greg Walden, R-Ore., and U.S. Rep. Frank Pallone, Jr., D-N.J., in a joint statement. "As we work to combat this epidemic head-on, it's critical we get answers to why such extremely high numbers of these powerful and addictive painkillers were distributed in small communities in West Virginia and if similar situations are happening elsewhere."

In December, the *Gazette-Mail* reported that drug wholesalers shipped 780 million hydrocodone and oxycodone pills to West Virginia pharmacies over six years. A small pharmacy in Kermit, a Southern West Virginia town with a population of 392, received nearly 9 million hydrocodone pills in just two years, DEA records show.

"If these reports are true, it would appear that the state of West Virginia may have received extraordinary amounts of opioids from distributors beyond what that population could safely use," according to the commitee's letter signed by Walden, Pallone, and U.S. Reps. David McKinley, R-W.Va., Tim Murphy, R-Pa., and Diana DeGette, D-Colo.

The committee members added that the reported "possible oversupply" of powerful painkillers suggests "such practices may have exacerbated the opioid problem

A small pharmacy in Kermit, a Southern West Virginia town with a population of 392, received nearly 9 million hydrocodone pills in just two years, DEA records show.

in the state" as many addicts have switched from prescription pain pills to street drugs like heroin and fentanyl.

West Virginia has the highest drug overdose death rate in the nation—and the deaths are rising. At last count, 864 people fatally overdosed on drugs in 2016—a record number.

"The opioid crisis in West Virginia has led to numerous deaths and social challenges for its residents," committee members said in the letter to distributors. "The state and federal government also have incurred costs of important social and addiction treatment services."

The House committee gave the drug wholesalers until June 8 to disclose the number of hydrocodone and oxycodone pills sold in West Virginia from 2005 to 2016. (The *Gazette-Mail* reported shipments from 2007 to 2012). The drug firms also must provide a list of their distribution warehouses.

The committee asked the wholesalers to answer numerous questions about their drug sales monitoring systems, policies and procedures, and whether they referred questionable orders for prescription painkillers to the DEA, West Virginia Board of Pharmacy or other authorities.

In the letters, committee members inquired about whether drug distributors could more easily identify suspicious drug orders placed by pharmacies if the DEA could share sales data with the companies. The wholesalers have complained for years that the DEA leaves them in the dark.

AmerisourceBergen spokesman Gabe Weissman said the DEA already has the sales data sought by the House committee.

"We look forward to responding to the letter from the committee and to continuing our work with regulators, enforcement agencies and other participants in the health care system to do our part in combating prescription drug abuse," Weissmsan said.

"AmerisourceBergen already provides daily reports about the quantity, type and receiving pharmacy of every single order of controlled substances we distribute directly to the Drug Enforcement Administration, and we maintain robust systems to stop suspicious orders and prevent diversion of prescription drugs."

Cardinal Health issued a similar statement.

"We look forward to working together with the committee and responding to their letter," said Ellen Barry, a Cardinal Health spokeswoman. The people of Cardinal Health care deeply about the devastation opioid abuse has caused American families and communities and are committed to helping solve this complex national public health crisis."

A McKesson spokeswoman declined comment Monday.

The committee also is investigating the DEA's decline in enforcement actions against drug wholesalers, following reports by the *Washington Post*.

"Considering that this reported decline in enforcement action occurred in the midst of the opioid epidemic—with the number of opioid prescriptions in the U.S. increasing from 112 million in 1992 to 249 million in 2015—it is imperative that the committee gather the facts about DEA's actions," House lawmakers wrote.

The committee directed the DEA to turn over all documents related to blocked or delayed enforcement against prescription drug distributors during the past six years.

A DEA spokeswoman would not comment on the investigation Monday.

In January, AmerisourceBergen and Cardinal Health agreed to pay the state a combined $36 million to settle a lawsuit filed by then-Attorney General Darrell Mc-Graw in 2012. The lawsuits alleged that the companies helped fuel West Virginia's drug problem by shipping an excessive number of pain pills to the state.

A similar lawsuit filed against McKesson by Attorney General Patrick Morrisey in January 2016 remains pending in Boone Circuit Court.

About a dozen West Virginia towns, cities and counties have filed lawsuits against the drug wholesalers—or announced their intentions to do so—since December.

Print Citations

CMS: Eyre, Eric. "Congress Probes West Virginia Opioid Shipments." In *The Reference Shelf: Prescription Drug Abuse*, edited by Betsy Maury, 199-201. Ipswich, MA: H.W. Wilson, 2017.

MLA: Eyre, Eric. "Congress Probes West Virginia Opioid Shipments." *The Reference Shelf: Prescription Drug Abuse*. Ed. Betsy Maury. Ipswich: H.W. Wilson, 2017. 199-201. Print.

APA: Eyre, E. (2017). Congress probes West Virginia opioid shipments. In Betsy Maury (Ed.), *The reference shelf: Prescription drug abuse* (pp. 199-201). Ipswich, MA: H.W. Wilson. (Original work published 2017)

States Require Opioid Prescribers to Check for "Doctor Shopping"

By Christine Vestal

PEW Charitable Trusts/Stateline, May 9, 2016

For more than a decade, doctors, dentists and nurse practitioners have liberally prescribed opioid painkillers despite mounting evidence that people were becoming addicted and overdosing on the powerful pain medications.

Now, in the face of a drug overdose epidemic that killed more than 28,000 people in 2014, a handful of states are insisting that health professionals do a little research before they write another prescription for highly addictive drugs like Percocet, Vicodin and OxyContin.

"We in the health care profession had a lot of years to police ourselves and clean this up, and we didn't do it," Kentucky physician Greg Jones, an anti-addiction specialist, said in an online training course he gives doctors in his state. "So the public got fed up with people dying from prescription drug abuse and they got together and they passed some laws and put some rules in place."

By tapping into a database of opioid painkillers and other federally controlled substances dispensed in the state, physicians can check patients' opioid medication history, as well as their use of other combinations of potentially harmful drugs, such as sedatives and muscle relaxants, to determine whether they are at risk of addiction or overdose death.

Prescribers also can determine whether patients are already receiving painkillers or other controlled substances from other sources, a practice known as doctor shopping. Patients with this type of history are at high risk for addiction and overdose and may be selling drugs illicitly.

In 2012, Kentucky became the first state to require doctors and other prescribers to search patients' prescription drug histories on an electronic database called a prescription drug

monitoring program (PDMP) before prescribing opioid painkillers, sedatives or other potentially harmful and addictive drugs.

Sixteen states have enacted similar laws, and experts, including the U.S. Centers for Disease Control and Prevention and the White House Office of National Drug Control Policy, are encouraging other states to do the same thing.

Maryland Gov. Larry Hogan, a Republican, signed a law in April that requires certain prescribers to use the state's monitoring system, and a similar bill is moving through the Legislature in California.

Prescribers can be required to check PDMP databases in 29 states, depending on conditions that vary from state to state, according to the National Alliance for Model State Drug Laws.

Although the American Medical Association supports physician use of drug tracking systems to identify potential addiction and drug diversion to the black market, state medical societies have argued against mandatory requirements they say interfere with the practice of medicine. Patients' privacy and legitimate pain needs, they say, could be jeopardized by requiring busy physicians to investigate potential patient abuse of pain medications.

Despite these objections from some in the medical profession, more states are imposing the requirements. "Comprehensive mandates are the single most effective thing states have done to curb opioid prescribing, and it seems to have an almost instantaneous effect," said John Eadie, who has evaluated state programs at Brandeis University's Prescription Drug Monitoring Program Center of Excellence in Massachusetts.

In states where physicians are required to use monitoring systems, overall opioid prescribing has plummeted, as have drug-related hospitalizations and overdose deaths, Eadie said. States also are seeing a rise in addiction treatment as more doctors refer patients to treatment after discovering they are taking painkillers from multiple sources and are likely addicted to them.

In Kentucky, hydrocodone (Vicodin) prescribing dropped 13 percent, oxycodone (Percocet) dropped 12 percent, oxymorphone (Opana) dropped 36 percent and tramadol (Ultram) dropped 12 percent between 2012 and 2013, the first year the law was implemented, according to an analysis by the University of Kentucky's College of Pharmacy.

Since the law was passed, overdose hospitalizations declined 26 percent, and prescription opioid deaths dropped 25 percent, the first reduction in nearly a decade, according to a March 2016 report by Shatterproof, a national advocacy organization that promotes prevention and treatment of drug addiction.

In another effort to stem overprescribing of opioid painkillers, which is widely blamed for the current epidemic, the CDC in March took the unprecedented step of issuing national opioid prescribing guidelines. Along with patient education, urine drug testing, and abuse-deterrent formulations of pain pills, the federal agency recommended prescribers check prescription databases before prescribing to reduce the risk of opioid overdose and addiction.

Vastly Underused

Prescription drug monitoring systems have existed in paper form since the 1930s, and every state except Missouri has some type of system. But the rules governing who has access, how quickly pharmacies must enter dispensing data, and which medications are included vary widely from state to state.

(The creation of a prescription drug monitoring system in Missouri has been blocked by a small group of legislators, led by state Sen. Rob Schaaf, a Republican and a doctor, who argue that allowing the government to keep prescription records violates patient privacy rights. In March, the opioid-plagued county of St. Louis adopted an ordinance to create a monitoring system, and advocates and some lawmakers continue to press for a statewide program.)

In general, state databases have been used effectively by law enforcement to track down so-called pill mills, where doctors indiscriminately prescribe opioid medications for cash. And a substantial number of pharmacists have consulted them before filling a prescription. But a relatively small percentage of medical professionals are signing on to the systems to detect patients who are at risk for addiction or overdose.

In most states, health care professionals who prescribe at least one controlled medication are encouraged to use PDMPs, but only on a voluntary basis. As a result, the typical state program in 2012 had only 35 percent of doctors signed up for access, according to the center at Brandeis. In 2014, 53 percent of doctors were signed up to one of the programs, according to a survey by Lainie Rutkow, an associate professor of public health at Johns Hopkins.

Most states require prescribers to obtain access to PDMPs and use them at their discretion when they suspect a patient is at high risk for addiction, drug diversion or overdose, according to the National Alliance for Model State Drug Laws.

The problem with that, said Van Ingram, Kentucky's director of drug control policy, is "people think doctors can just look at a patient and recognize this disease of addiction, and it's not that simple."

"People with addictions can fool their spouses, their children and their employers. They can definitely conceal the disease from their physician in a 15-minute visit."

A Diagnostic Tool

In Kentucky, doctors and some patients complained about the requirement when it was first adopted, Ingram said. But these days, he said, he mostly hears doctors saying, "Wow, I treated that patient for 20 years and had no idea he had a drug problem.

"If there's a tool out there that takes 15 seconds to use and can diagnose a disease, why wouldn't you want to use it? To me it's a no brainer," Ingram said.

Before Kentucky physicians were required to check the database, patients commonly visited multiple doctors to get prescriptions for opioid painkillers, the sedative Xanax, and the muscle relaxant Soma, according to the state's PDMP director, David Hopkins. "The cocktail," as it's known in Kentucky, produces a high that is similar to heroin and just as deadly. It has become much less prevalent since the law was enacted.

"We cracked down on that big time," Hopkins said. The number of people receiving the cocktail has dropped 30 percent since the law took effect and the number of doctor shoppers has dropped 52 percent, he said.

Kentucky is also trying to curtail dangerously high doses of prescribed painkillers by flagging the database when a patient is taking medications from multiple sources that add up to the equivalent of 100 milligrams or more of morphine per day. Last year, a calculator was added to the system so doctors wouldn't have to add up the morphine equivalents on their own.

> In Kentucky, doctors and some patients complained about the requirement when it was first adopted, Ingram said. But these days, he said, he mostly hears doctors saying, "Wow, I treated that patient for 20 years and had no idea he had a drug problem."

Hopkins said the state listened to doctors' complaints and added some common-sense exceptions after the initial rules came out. Prescribers are no longer required to check the database in emergencies or for patients in hospice, long-term care or cancer treatment. They can also skip the step if a patient was originally prescribed a pain medication by a fellow doctor in their practice and needs a refill or a different pain medicine.

Kentucky's prescriber rules, which were developed by the state Board of Medical Licensure, allow doctors to appoint a delegate to access the drug monitoring system and review patients' drug profiles. Doctors typically ask their assistants to run prescription drug histories on all the patients they will see the next day and add the information to their electronic medical records, said Michael Rodman, director of Kentucky's licensure board.

If a potential drug problem is detected, prescribers can query the database to determine how other physicians in the state are addressing the pain needs of similar patients and they can discuss an individual patient's drug history with another prescriber, something that was forbidden under previous state privacy laws.

Another part of Kentucky's 2012 opioid law requires prescribers to attend a certain number of free training sessions each year on addiction, pain management and use of the state's prescription monitoring system. (Jones conducts some of those training programs.)

To increase the effectiveness of drug monitoring programs, Kentucky and other states use reciprocal agreements to allow interstate sharing of drug dispensing information for pharmacists, law enforcement and physicians in nearby states. Kentucky has agreements with at least 20 other states. New Jersey Gov. Chris Christie, a Republican, announced in April that New York had joined his state in sharing PDMP information, along with Connecticut, Delaware, Minnesota, Rhode Island, South Carolina and Virginia.

As for what happens when a physician discovers a patient is doctor shopping, Rodman said, they often dismiss patients and no longer treat them.

But Jones, who heads the Kentucky Physicians Health Foundation, which supports doctors who suffer from substance use disorders, tells doctors not to do that to patients.

"Maybe you don't keep prescribing them 90 OxyContins with five refills," he said, "but don't throw them out. If you do, you're missing an important opportunity to save a life."

Print Citations

CMS: Vestal, Christine. "States Require Opioid Prescribers to Check for 'Doctor Shopping.'" In *The Reference Shelf: Prescription Drug Abuse*, edited by Betsy Maury, 202-206. Ipswich, MA: H.W. Wilson, 2017.

MLA: Vestal, Christine. "States Require Opioid Prescribers to Check for 'Doctor Shopping.'" *The Reference Shelf: Prescription Drug Abuse*. Ed. Betsy Maury. Ipswich: H.W. Wilson, 2017. 202-206. Print.

APA: Vestal, C. (2017). States require opioid prescribers to check for "doctor shopping." In Betsy Maury (Ed.), *The reference shelf: Prescription drug abuse* (pp. 202-206). Ipswich, MA: H.W. Wilson. (Original work published 2016)

Bibliography

"AAPM Facts and Figures on Pain." *AAPM*. American Academy of Pain Medicine. 2011. Web. 20 Aug 2017.

"A Brief History of Opioids: Pain, Opioids and Medicinal Use." *The Atlantic*. The Atlantic Monthly Group. 2017. Web. 17 Aug 2017.

"Abuse of Prescription (Rx) Drugs Affects Young Adults Most." *NIDA*. National Institute on Drug Abuse. Aug 2016. Web. 21 Aug 2017.

"Addiction in Women." *Harvard Health Publications*. Harvard Medical School. Jan 2010. Web. 22 Aug 2017.

"Adolescents and Young Adults." *NIDA*. National Institute on Drug Abuse. National Institute of Health. Aug 2016. Web. 20 Aug 2017.

Almendrala, Anna. "Needle Exchanges Are Vital, but There's Major Stigma around Them: Here's Why." *Huffpost*. Huffington Post. Mar 27 2015. Web. 25 Aug 2017.

"America's New Drug Policy Landscape." *Pew Research*. Pew Foundation. Apr 2 2014. Web. 24 Aug 2017.

Bachhuber, Marcus A., Saloner, Brendan, and Chinazo O. Cunningham, et al. "Medical Cannabis Laws and Opioid Analgestic Overdose Mortality in the United States, 1999-2010." *JAMA*. Journal of the American Medical Association. Oct 2014. Vol. 174, No. 10, 1668–73.

Ban, Thomas A. "Bromides." *INHN*. International Network for the History of Neurophychopharmacology. Feb 8 2017. Web. 17 Sep 2017.

Basca, Belinda. "The Elderly and Prescription Drug Misuse and Abuse." *Center for Applied Research Solutions*. California Department of Alcohol and Drug Programs. 2008. Pdf. 21 Aug 2017.

Bogdanowicz, Karolina M., et al. "Double Trouble: Psychiatric Comorbidity and Opioid Addiction—All-Cause and Cause-Specific Mortality." *Drug and Alcohol Dependence*. Mar 1 2015. Vol. 148, 85-92.

Broman, Clifford L., Miller, Paula K., and Emmanue Jackson. "Race-Ethnicity and Prescription Drug Misuse: Does Self-Esteem Matter?" *Journal of Child and Adolescent Behavior*. Sep 3 2015. Vol. 3, No. 239. Web. 21 Aug 2017.

"CDC Guidelines for Prescribing Opioids for Chronic Pain." *CDC*. Centers for Disease Control and Prevention. Mar 18 2016. Web. 25 Aug 2017.

"Chronic Pain: Symptoms, Diagnosis, & Treatment." *NIH*. NIH Medline Plus. Spring 2011. Web. 20 Aug 2017.

Cooper-White, Macrina. "Humans Have Been Getting High Since Prehistoric Times, Research Shows." *Huffpost*. Huffington Post. Feb 12 2015. Web. 25 Aug 2017.

Darke, Shane. "Pathways to Heroin Dependence: Time to Re-appraise Self-Medication." *Addiction*. Apr 2013. Vol. 108, No. 4, 659–67.

De Pinto, Jennifer, Backus, Fred, Khanna, Kabir, and Anthony Salvanto. "Marijuana Legalization Support at All-Time High." *CNS News*. Apr 20 2017. Web. 23 Aug 2017.

Dennis, Brady. "NIH: More Than 1 in 10 American Adults Experience Chronic Pain." *The Washington Post*. Nash Holdings. Aug 11, 2015.

"Drug Overdose Immunity and Good Samaritan Laws." *NCSL*. National Conference of State Legislatures. Jun 5 2017. Web. 25 Aug 2017.

Duenas, M., et al. "A Review of Chronic Pain Impact on Patients, Their Social Environment and the Health Care System." *Journal of Pain Research*. 2016. Vol. 9, 457–67.

Dwyer, Colin. "Ohio Sues 5 Major Drug Companies for 'Fueling Opioid Epidemic'." *NPR*. National Public Radio. May 31 2017. Web. 24 Aug 2017.

"Fact Sheet: Prescription Drug Abuse," *NCADD*. National Council on Alcoholism and Drug Dependence. 2012. Web. 17 Aug 2017.

"Facts & Statistics." *Anxiety and Depression Association of America*. 2017. Web. 20 Aug 2017.

"Generalized Anxiety Disorder (GAD)." *Anxiety and Depression Association of America*. 2017. Web. 20 Aug 2017.

Ghelardini, C., Mannelli, L., and E. Bianchi. "The Pharmacological Basis of Opioids." *Clinical Cases in Mineral and Bone Metabolism*. Sep-Dec 2015. Vol. 12, No. 3, 219–21.

Greenberg, Melanie. "Americans Just Broke a New Record for Stress and Anxiety." *Psychology Today*. Feb 19 2017. Web. 20 Aug 2017.

Greenfield, Shelly F., et al. "Substance Abuse in Women." *Psychiatric Clinical North American Journal*. Jun 2010. Vol. 33, No. 2, 339–55.

Hanson, G.R., Venturelli, P.J., and Annette E. Fleckenstein, eds. "CNS Depressants: Sedative-Hypnotics," in *Drugs and Society*. Burlington, MA: Jones & Bartless Learning, 2018.

Higham, Scott and Lenny Bernstein. "Drugmakers and Distributors Face Barrage of Lawsuits over Opioid Epidemic." *The Washington Post*. Nash Holdings. Jul 4 2016. Web. 24 Aug 2017.

Kelley, Maura. "An Anxiety Epidemic Is Sweeping the US." *Business Insider*. Business Insider, Inc. Jul 17 2012. Web. 26 Aug 2017.

Kelly, Brian C., et al. "Prescription Drug Misuse among Young Adults: Looking across Youth Cultures." *Drug Alcohol Review*. May 1 2014. Vol. 32, No. 3, 288–94. Web. 21 Aug 2017.

Lawson, Alex. "No Accident: Deadly Greed of Pharmaceutical Companies Drives the Heroin Epidemic." *Huffpost*. Huffington Post. Jan 20 2017. Web. 23 Aug 2017.

Luhrmann, T.M. "The Anxious Americans." *The New York Times*. The New York Times Co. Jul 18 2015. Web. 20 Aug 2017.

MacGillis, Alec. "The Wonder Drug." *Slate*. Slate Inc. Feb 9 2015. Web. 25 Aug 2017.

Macy, Beth. "Addicted to a Treatment for Addiction." *The New York Times*. The New York Times Co. May 28 2016. Web. 27 Aug 2017.

"Makers and Distributors of Opioid Painkillers Are under Scrutiny." *The Economist*. Economist. Apr 6 2017. Web. 22 Aug 2017.

Mandell, Brian F. "The Fifth Vital Sign: A complex Story of Politics and Patient Care." *Cleveland Journal of Medicine*. June 2016. Vol. 83, No. 6, 400–01.

McGraw, Daniel J. "How Big Pharma Gave America Its Heroin Problem." *PSMag*. Pacific Standard. Nov 30 2015. Web. 23 Aug 2017.

"Misuse of Prescription Drugs." *Drugabuse.gov*. National Institute on Drug Abuse (NIDA). 2016. Web. 22 Aug 2017.

Moghe, Sonia. "Opioid History: From 'Wonder Drug' to Abuse Epidemic." *CNN Health*. Oct 14 2016. Web. 17 Aug 2017.

Mole, Beth. "Early Study Suggests New Opioid Is Non-addictive, Works Only Where It Hurts." *Arstechnica*. Mar 4 2014. Web. 22 Aug 2017.

Mulvihill, Geoff, Whyte, Liz Essley, and Ben Wieder. "Drugmakers Fought State Opioid Limits Amid Crisis." *AP*. Associated Press. Sep 18 2016. Web. 25 Aug 2017.

"Painkiller Overdoses in Women." *The New York Times*. The New York Times Co. Jul 7 2013. Web. 22 Aug 2017.

Pappas, Stephanie. "Anxious Brains Are Inherited, Study Finds." *LiveScience*. Jul 8 2015. Web. 20 Aug 2017.

"Prescription Drug Abuse." *Drugabuse.gov*. National Institute on Drug Abuse (NIDA). Sep 22 2010. Web. 17 Aug 2017.

"Prescription Drug Misuse among Older Adults: Understanding the Problem." *SAMHSA*. Substance Abuse and Mental Health Services Administration. 2012. Web. 21 Aug 2017.

Preta, Adrian and Eduardo Dunayevich. "Stimulants." *Medscape*. WebMD, LLC. Dec 15 2015. Web. 26 Aug 2017.

Rabiner, David L., et al. "Motives and Perceived Consequences of Nonmedical ADHD Medication Use by College Students." *Journal of Attention Disorders*. Jul 29 2008. Web. 20 Aug 2017.

Rapaport, Lisa. "Another Look at the Surge in EpiPen Costs." *Reuters*. Reuters News Agency. Mar 27 2017. Web. 24 Aug 2017.

"Relieving Pain in America: A Blueprint for Transforming Prevention, Care, Education, and Research." *Institute of Medicine*. National Academies. 2011. Pdf. 20 Aug 2017.

Rettner, Rachael. "Prescription Drug Problem Sparks Debate over Solutions." *LiveScience*. Purch. Jun 21 2012. Web. 25 Aug 2017.

Salamon, Maureen. "Why Prescription Drug Addiction Is Growing among Teens." *LiveScience*. Feb 16 2012. Web. 21 Aug 2017.

Schwartz, Casey. "Generation Adderall." *The New York Times*. The New York Times Co. Oct 12 2016. Web. 25 Aug 2017.

"Screening, Brief Intervention, and Referral to Treatment (SBIRT)." *SAMHSA*. Substance Abuse and Mental Health Services Administration. 2016. Web. 25 Aug 2017.

Sifferlin, Alexandra. "Can Medical Marijuana Help End the Opioid Epidemic?" *Time*. Time Inc. Jul 28 2016. Web. 22 Aug 2017.

Smith, Brendan L. "Inappropriate Prescribing." *APA*. American Psychological Association. 2012. Vol. 43, No. 6, 36.

"Specific Populations and Prescription Drug Misuse and Abuse." *SAMHSA*. Substance Abuse and Mental Health Services Administration. Oct 27 2015. Web. 22 Aug 2017.

Szalavitz, Maia. "Opioid Addiction Is a Huge Problem, but Pain Prescriptions Are Not the Cause." *Scientific American*. Nature America, Inc. May 10 2016. Web. 23 Aug 2017.

Volkow, Nora D. and Thomas McLellan. "Opioid Abuse in Chronic Pain—Misconceptions and Mitigation Strategies." *NEJM*. New England Journal of Medicine. Mar 31 2016. Web. 22 Aug 2017.

Wesson, D.R. and D.E. Smith. "Prescription Drug Abuse. Patient, Physician, and Cultural Responsibilities." *Western Journal of Medicine*. May 1990. Vol. 152, No. 5, 613–16.

"What Is the Scope of Prescription Drug Misuse?" *Drugabuse.gov*. National Institute on Drug Abuse (NIDA). Aug 2016. Web. 17 Aug 2017.

"Women." *ADAA*. Anxiety and Depression Association of America. 2017. Web. 22 Aug 2017.

Whiting, Penny F., Wolff, Robert F., and Sohan Deshpande, et al. "Cannabinoids for Medical Use: A Systematic Review and Meta-analysis." *JAMA*. Journal of the American Medical Association. 2015. Vol. 313, No. 24, 2456–73.

Wight, Patty. "Intent on Reversing Its Opioid Epidemic, a State Limits Prescriptions." *NPR*. National Public Radio. Aug 23 2017. Web. 25 Aug 2017.

Websites

Centers for Disease Control and Prevention (CDC)

www.cdc.gov

The Centers for Disease Control and Prevention is a public health institute in the United States, part of the US Department of Health and Human Services. The CDC promotes information and creates guidelines for professionals addressing a variety of public health issues such as infectious diseases, food-borne illness, environmental hazards, and drug abuse and addiction. The CDC funds research into drug use and abuse and has created guidelines for physicians and hospitals about how to recognize and address abuse in patients.

National Institute on Drug Abuse (NIDA)

www.drugabuse.gov

The National Institute on Drug Abuse is a federal, public health, and research organization focused on drug abuse and addiction, and operating under the supervision of the National Institutes of Health and the US Department of Health and Human Services. The NIDA provides information on a wide variety of drug use and abuse issues and funds research on addiction treatment. One of several drug abuse branches within the federal government, NIDA concentrates primarily on funding and supporting research.

Substance Abuse and Mental Health Services Administration (SAMHSA)

www.samhsa.gov

The Substance Abuse and Mental Health Services Administration is a branch of the US Department of Health and Human Services specifically charged with monitoring and improving the quality of drug addiction and abuse treatment and rehabilitation services. Since the beginning of the opioid abuse crisis, SAMHSA provides information on how to identify and assist individuals suffering from potential opioid addiction.

American Psychological Association (APA)

www.apa.org

The American Psychological Association is the largest and oldest professional psychiatric organization in the United States and has a number of task forces focused on different aspects of psychiatric and psychological care and outreach. The APA considers drug abuse and addiction to be mental illnesses and provides data on the psychological factors motivating drug abuse and resulting from abuse and addiction. The APA also supports research into drug abuse and mental health.

National Council on Alcoholism and Drug Dependence (NCADD)

www.ncadd.org

The National Council on Alcoholism and Drug Dependence (NCADD) is an advocacy organization focused on combating alcoholism and drug addiction. The NCADD is composed of members from a variety of fields, including physicians and mental health professionals, scientific researchers, legislators, and welfare professionals, who advocate for the rights and humane treatment of individuals with alcohol and drug dependence and produce educational programs to promote the viewpoint that substance abuse is a mental health issue that should be addressed through treatment.

National Center on Addiction and Substance Abuse at Columbia University (CASAColumbia)

www.centeronaddiction.org

The National Center on Addiction and Substance Abuse is a multidisciplinary research organization focused on studies of drug and substance addiction. The organization funds research programs and provides articles by experts on a variety of addiction and recovery issues.

Narcotics Anonymous (NA)

www.na.org

Narcotics Anonymous is a social, advocacy, outreach organization for individuals suffering from drug abuse. Like Alcoholics Anonymous, NA focuses on a 12-step, "abstinence only" drug addiction recovery program and does not support the use of tapering drugs. The NA recovery program is largely based on the personal sponsorship model in combination with a vague pseudospiritual approach. Narcotics Anonymous also publishes a variety of short publications and information brochures aimed at helping addicts to turn to treatment options.

National Coalition Against Prescription Drug Abuse (NCAPDA)

www.ncapda.org

The National Coalition Against Prescription Drug Abuse (NCAPDA) is a nonprofit organization founded in 2010 and aimed at spreading information about the dangers of prescription drug abuse, focusing primarily on schools, colleges, and community organizations. The NCAPDA produces media and print reports and brochures about prescription drugs and treatment options for individuals who are abusing drugs.

Index